Arabic

for Everyda

SPOKEN ARABIC FOR ALL

"KNOWLEDGE IS POWER PAULA,

YOU SEEM TO HAVE A NATURAL

NACK FOR THIS TO ROLE OFF

YOUR TONGUE".

STUDY HARD .... APPLY YOURSELF

AND SEE WHAT GREAT THINGS HAPPEN

FROM HARD WORK.

Amanulla Vadakkangara was born in Vadakkangara in Malappuram district of Kerala, India. He completed a Masters degree in Arabic language and literature from the University of Calicut and a Masters degree in Library and Information Science from Annamalai University, Tamil Nadu.

He was inclined towards writing in his school days and published articles in dailies in Kerala. He taught Arabic and Islamic studies at Ansar English School in Perumpilavu for about five years and for over ten years he worked at the Ideal Indian School, Doha as a teacher, head of the department of the Arabic and Islamic Studies and Public Relation Officer of the school.

In Doha he has been a regular writer and columnist in Arabic and English dailies. He has been awarded the Lokseva award by the Government of India for his work on Alcoholism and the best Islamic Educationist award in 1998 for his articles published in Doha based English daily, Gulf Times. He won the Anti Narcotic Award 2005, Instituted by the Anti Narcotic Action Council of India. Among the author's published works are: Spoken Arabic Made Easy, Improve your Spoken Arabic, A literary history of the Arabs, Arabic Grammar Made Easy (2 parts), A Formula to Speak Arabic, CBSE Arabic Grammar, Arabic for the Beginners, Spoken Arabic Gurunathan, Spoken Arabic Tutor etc. Currently he is the Chief Executive Officer of Mediaplus W.L.L. an advertising and event management company in Qatar

AMANULLA VADAKKANGARA
P.B No.: 23143, Doha - Qatar
E-mail: ceo@mediaplus.com.qa

Arabic
for Everyday
SPOKEN ARABIC FOR ALL

AMANULLA VADAKKANGARA
Former Head of the Dept of
Arabic & Islamic Studies,
Ideal Indian School, Doha - Qatar

GOODWORD BOOKS

Dedicated to the fond memories
of my beloved father who left us
for his heavenly abode on 12th September 2010

First published 2011
Reprinted 2017

Goodword Books
A-21, Sector 4, NOIDA-201301, U.P., India
Tel. +9111-46010170, +9111-45651770, +91-8588822672
email: info@goodwordbooks.com
www.goodwordbooks.com

Goodword Books, Chennai
Mob. +91-9790853944, 9600105558

Printed in India

CONTENTS

PREFACE

Spoken Arabic has become one of the most demanded titles in most developed and underdeveloped countries for various reasons. The strategic importance of Arabian countries, economic booming in the Gulf and the emerging employment opportunities are some of the facts for the current resurgence in learning Arabic.

From its humble beginnings in the desert to its empire-sized nature of today, the Arabic language is a language of art and culture that has embellished our minds and eyes with it magnificent script. It is widely spoken today as native language to countless of nations, and as a consequence has acquired many dialectical forms. Divided into two distinct classes, the literary Arabic and spoken Arabic, this language is regarded as a daily essential to many for religious, social, economic and cultural activities and interactions.

Although English is increasingly used in business relationships even in the Arab world, in many situations Arabic is the key language, as you would expect. If you really want to learn the language, you should perhaps take concerted efforts depending recommended books on learning Arabic as well as personal interactions with those who know the language. What I have tried here is to introduce certain words, phrases and examples that might help you in building your own communication pattern. Arabs will be particularly impressed that you have at least made an effort to learn their language, and will score you some brownie points in a business situation. I have deliberately tried to spell the words to help you pronounce them correctly.

It is observed that Arabic is one of the most spoken languages in the world with over 220 million speakers worldwide. It is a Semitic language having a large number of speakers in Afghanistan, Algeria, Bahrain, Chad, Cyprus, Djibouti, Egypt, Eritrea, Iran, Iraq, Israel, Jordan, Kenya, Kuwait, Lebanon, Libya, Mali, Mauritania, Morocco, Niger, Oman, Palestinian West Bank & Gaza, Qatar, Saudi Arabia, Somalia, Sudan, Syria, Tajikistan, Tanzania, Tunisia, Turkey, UAE, Uzbekistan and Yemen. There are over 30 different varieties of colloquial Arabic which include:

- Egyptian - spoken by about 50 million people in Egypt and perhaps the most widely understood variety, thanks to the popularity of Egyptian-made films and TV shows
- Algerian - spoken by about 22 million people in Algeria
- Moroccan/Maghrebi - spoken in Morocco by about 19.5 million people
- Sudanese - spoken in Sudan by about 19 million people
- Saidi - spoken by about 19 million people in Egypt
- North Levantine - spoken in Lebanon and Syria by about 15 million people
- Mesopotamian - spoken by about 14 million people in Iraq, Iran and Syria
- Najdi - spoken in Saudi Arabia, Iraq, Jordan and Syria by about 10 million people

People learn Arabic for a variety of reasons: for work, for travel, for religious purposes, for marriage or friendship with an Arab, or simply as a hobby. In any case learning Arabic would be quite a rewarding experience to the learner, as the language is blessed with several unique advantages and peculiarities.

It is indubitable that since the Gulf countries give a multitude of openings to the skilled and unskilled, the number of people learning Arabic has tremendously increased over the years. This includes professionals and technicians of various communities. Due to the intensive nationalisation drive in almost all parts of the Gulf it has become essential to learn at least the basics of Arabic language for all those who are aspirants of finding a job in the region. The first thing to decide is whether you want to learn standard/classical Arabic or a colloquial dialect. Unless your interest is confined to one particular country, the safest option is to learn a version of the classical language known as Modern Standard Arabic. This is what is used in books, newspapers, radio and television news programmes, political speeches, etc. But here my focus is to introduce a mix of spoken and written Arabic aimed at facilitating a beginner to set his basics in Arabic Communication. In this way, I feel all those who are interested to learn spoken and written language can use it for various purposes.

Using standard Arabic in everyday conversation sounds a bit formal to Arab ears, but at least you can be sure of being understood by educated Arabs anywhere in the Middle East. It may be more difficult to understand what they say to you, unless they make the effort to speak more formally than usual. Having learnt some standard Arabic, however, it is relatively easy to adapt to a local dialect later. However, if you are confident to move with your limited resources of words, broken phrases and communication patterns, you will be able to face various situations and gradually mastering communication skills required for any occasions.

It is quite natural that these multitude prefer a working knowledge of the language rather than going to the details of its towering literary value and excellence. The demand to give a digestible but sustainable interactive course to the beginners of the language was found need of the hour. My fifteen years stay in Qatar has convinced me the importance of such a short course and I started to teach Arabic to the working people of various non-Arabic speaking communities in Qatar.

The more I interacted with people of various strata the more I was enlightened on the areas of great significance to the working people and I could conduct a number of batches of Spoken Arabic Course for the beginners in a short span of time. I was delighted to see that my short-term programme enabled the participants to strengthen the foundation of language learning and to communicate with the Arabic speaking people in a limited sense. Those who attended my course included diplomats of various countries, senior executives, managers, doctors, engineers and a good number of professionals. My students often asked me to recommend any books, which will ease their efforts in learning and serve as a source of reference. This made me think of compiling the course material in the form of a book, which will help thousands of people to improve their working knowledge in the language and help them understand the Arabic conversation in a simple way.

I discussed the matter with my friends and well wishers and I was overwhelmed with the support from all corners. I published half a dozen books focusing on different types of learners and the response to all these books was really encouraging. This is my seventh book on the subject.

I hope this book will help everyone with out any basic knowledge of the language to develop self-learning skills and communicate with others. However I feel it would be highly recommended to listen to the alphabet from those who know the language to get the actual pronunciation of words and phrases.

I need not state that perseverance and desire to learn the language should be there to attain the goal, Even though this book is meant for the beginners of the language, I hope there will be some lessons of common interest to the beginners as well as to the advanced level students.

The geopolitical importance of the Arab World is more evident today than ever before, because of its oil and gas wealth and its strategically important position between Eastern and Western hemispheres. The well paid posts in major oil and gas firms, in the Gulf states which give better hopes of perks and facilities require one to have a mastery over Arabic as well as English languages.

However this book will not be sufficient for those who opt for such posts, but definitely it will give them a clear insight to the language learning process and help them start learning in a simple way.

Greatness of a language is often measured by its capacity to incorporate words from other languages and vice versa. Arabic is a very successful language in this respect and studies show that there are about 1,000 main words of Arabic origin in the English language and many other words derived from Arabic. Arabic words can be found in every area of language use, ranging from the sciences to the arts, to foods and other areas of everyday life.

It is a proved fact that during the Middle Ages (The 8th to 13th centuries) the Arabic speaking people were the main bearers of the torch of knowledge and civilization. Arabic was the medium, through which science and philosophy of Greece and other ancient civilizations were recovered, Supplemented and transmitted in such a way as to make possible the European Renaissance in the full sense.

It should be underlined that in spoken language many grammatical points are dropped or ignored.

It is true that any language is best learnt in its natural environment. But it does not necessarily mean that no language can be learnt outside its native milieu. The absence of native milieu can be adequately, compensated by concerted efforts under guided directions to achieve tangible results.

I have attempted to make it simple and easy to the learners to understand and interact with native Arabs. If determined efforts are made, at the end of the course it is assumed that the student should be able to comprehend and to summarise the basic information (ideas, arguments, themes, issues) of almost any Arabic conversation, whether printed or spoken, and also to initiate and take part in simple and serious conversations with educated Arabs, to reproduce and appropriately modify patterns of simple spoken Arabic.

It is viewed that Arabic is one of the simplest languages of the world. If imparted properly, anybody blessed with a flair for language learning can master it without much difficulty.

While bringing out this book, I have to record my sincere thanks and profound sense of gratitude to my colleague Mr. Afsal Kilayil, Mediaplus, Qatar who typed the whole text with maximum accuracy and speed.

Thanks are due to my friend Mr. M.V. Joseph (Qatar Tribune) for his editorial assistance.

Sincere efforts have been made to ensure that this book is free from serious errors. However still I stake no claims that I have been hundred percent successful in achieving this end.

With these words let me present this humble work before learners. My request is to point out errors and mistakes, if any, and assure that suggestions and creative evaluations will be highly appreciated and looked into while modifying the book.

Amanulla Vadakkangara

LESSON ONE

ARABIC ALPHABET

Tutors have differences of opinion regarding teaching of spoken language. Some say it cannot be taught by books, others feel books can be supplementary. But I am of the opinion that books as well as direct lessons serve as prelude to the learning process and we cannot belittle the importance of any learning tools. Some people prefer systematic learning while others go for grabbing opportunities of practical experience as the foundation of their language learning. Whatever may be the arguments and suggestions, I genuinely feel that learning to read and write Arabic is the single most important thing you can do to speak fluent Arabic. Even if you are only interested in speaking Arabic you should still learn to read and write the language for obvious reasons.

In the Arab World everything is written in Arabic. Reading is an extremely important part of learning a language that helps you assimilate foreign words and structures much faster than simply relying on your hearing power even though listening to the natives and those who are fluent in language makes you more confident and thorough with spoken styles and phrases.

There are 28 letters in Arabic. Some of the sounds are unique to Arabic and difficult for foreigners to pronounce exactly, though you should be able to make yourself understood. From the 28 letters it is easy to make 84 sounds by using long and short vowels, still more sounds can be made. Here comes the advantage to all learners as mastering just a few letters enables them to produce so many sounds and form words.

As Arabic is read as it is written it will be easy to read and write simple words once you are thorough with the alphabet. At the very least, you will be able to recognize place names, destination signs on buses, and so on and this will work as a catalyst in your language learning Endeavour.

The Arabic script seems daunting at first, and some people try to avoid learning it by relying on transliterations of Arabic words.

This merely stores up problems later; it is much better to ignore transliterations and use the script from the start. But throughout this book, I have emphasized on reading the original script while giving transliteration as a support. I believe , if the learner makes some concerted efforts gradually he will be able to read the original Arabic script even without transliteration.

Don't try to learn the whole alphabet at once. If you learn three letters each day and practice for an hour every evening it will take less than two weeks.

Practice writing each letter in all its forms (initial, medial and final), pronouncing it aloud as you write.

After you have learned a few letters, practice writing them in groups of three, in the order they occur in the alphabet. Each time you write a group, drop the first letter from the beginning and add another to the end, working through the alphabet:

alif-ba-ta, ba-ta-tha, ta-tha-jim, tha-jim-ha, etc.

Do this once saying the names of the letters, and once pronouncing them as if they were a word: abata, batatha, tathaja, thajaha, etc.

Once you can do the whole series from memory, you are ready to start learning the language.

This drill can be tedious, but you won't regret it. Its advantage is that it teaches you the letters in all their forms, as well as those that cannot join to the following letter. It also implants in your brain the alphabetical order of the letters - very useful later when you want to use an Arabic dictionary.

So the first step is to familiarize with the Arabic alphabet, most of them are unique in many aspects. Once you are confident with reading and writing each letter in all its shapes and sounds, you can move to the words and try reading and writing them. Learners should note the shape of letter when it stands alone, when it comes as the first, middle or end letter of a word. This understanding will help to master joining practice also.

ARABIC ALPHABET

Thaa ث	Taa ت/ة	Baa ب	Alif ا
Daal د	Khaa خ	Ḥaa ح	Jeem ج
Seen س	Zaa ز	Raa ر	Zaal ذ
Thaa ط	Dhaad ض	Ṣaad ص	Sheen ش
Faa ف	Ghein غ	Ein ع	Dhaa ظ
Meem م	Laam ل	Kaaf ك	Qaaf ق
Yaa ي	Haa ه	Waow و	Noon ن

HOW TO MAKE VARIOUS SOUNDS

It is very easy to produce various sounds from the given alphabet. Just put (Fatah) on any letter then you will get a sound. If you put the symbol below the letter (Kasra) the sound will be e. If you put

Damma you will get u sound. Putting (sukoon) will give you a closing sound.

U اْ	U اُ	Ee اِ	Aa اَ
Bh بْ	Bu بُ	Be بِ	Ba بَ
Th تْ	Tu تُ	Ti تِ	Ta تَ
Th ثْ	Thu ثُ	Thi ثِ	Tha ثَ
Jh جْ	Ju جُ	Ji جِ	Ja جَ
Hh حْ	Hu حُ	Hi حِ	Ha حَ
Kh خْ	Khu خُ	Khi خِ	Kha خَ
Dh دْ	Du دُ	Di دِ	Da دَ
D ذْ	Du ذُ	Di ذَ	Da ذَ
Rh رْ	Ru رُ	Ri رِ	Ra رَ
Zh زْ	Zu زُ	Zi زِ	Za زَ
Sh سْ	Su سُ	Si سِ	Sa سَ
Shh شْ	Shu شُ	Shi شِ	Sha شَ

Swh صْ	Swu صُ	Swi صِ	Swa صَ
Dh ضْ	Dhu ضُ	Dhi ضِ	Dha ضَ
Th طْ	Thu طُ	Thi طِ	Tha طَ
Dh ظْ	Dhu ظُ	Dhi ظِ	Dha ظَ
Hh عْ	Hu عُ	Hi عِ	Ha عَ
Gh غْ	Ghu غُ	Ghi غِ	Gha غَ
Fh فْ	Fu فُ	Fi فِ	Fa فَ
Qh قْ	Qu قُ	Qi قِ	Qa قَ
Kh كْ	Ku كُ	Ke كِ	Kaa كَ
Lh لْ	Li لُ	Li لِ	La لَ
Mh مْ	Mu مُ	Mi مِ	Ma مَ
Nh نْ	Nu نُ	Ni نِ	Na نَ
Vh وْ	Vu وُ	Vi وِ	Va وَ
Hh هْ	Hu هُ	Hi هِ	Ha هِ
Yh يْ	Yu يُ	Yi يِ	Ya يَ

EXTENSION OF SOUNDS

We can extend all the a e u sounds. To extend a sound you need to add an alif to the letter. By adding ya to the letter you can extend e sound and va will help you to extend u sound. The examples will make things clearer.

Uoo اُو	U اُ	Ee اِي	E اِ	Aa آ	A اَ
Boo بُو	Bu بُ	Bee بِي	Bi بِ	Baa بَا	Ba بَ
Too تُو	To تُ	Tee تِي	Ti تِ	Taa تَا	Ta تَ
Thoo ثُو	Thu ثُ	Thee ثِي	Thi ثِ	Thaa ثَا	Tha ثَ
Joo جُو	Ju جُ	Jee جِي	Ji جِ	Jaa جَا	Ja جَ
Huu حُو	Hu حُ	Hee حِي	He حِي	Haa حَا	Ha حَ
Khoo خُو	Khu خُ	Khee خِي	Khi خِ	Khaa خَا	Kha خَ
Duu دُو	Du دُ	Dee دِي	Di دِ	Daa دَا	Da دَ
Duu ذُو	Du ذُ	Dee ذِي	De ذِ	Daa ذَا	Da ذَ
Roo رُو	Ru رُ	Ree رِي	Re رِ	Raa رَا	Ra رَ
Zoo زُو	Zo زُ	Zee زِي	Ze زِ	Zaa زَا	Za زَ
Suu سُو	Su سُ	See سِي	Se سِ	Saa سَا	Sa سَ
Shuu شُو	Shu شُ	Shee شِي	She شِ	Shaa شَا	Sha شَ

Swuu صُو Swu صُ Swee صِي Swe صِ Swaa صَا Swa صَ

Dhuu ضُو Dhu ضُ Dhee ضِي Dhe ضِ Dhaa ضَا Dha ضَ

Thuu طُو Thuw طُ Thwee طِي Thwe طِ Thaa طَا Tha طَ

Duu ظُو Du ظُ Dee ظِي De ظِ Daa ظَا Da ظَ

Huu عُو Hu عُ Hee عِي He عِ Haa عَا Ha عَ

Ghoo غُو Ghu غُ Ghee غِي Ghe غِ Ghaa غَا Gha غَ

Foo فُو Fu فُ Fee فِي Fe فِ Faa فَا Fa فَ

Qoo قُو Qu قُ Qee قِي Qe قِ Qaa قَا Qa قَ

Koo كُو Ku كُ Kee كِي Ke كِ Kaa كَا Ka كَ

Luu لُو Lu لُ Lee لِي Le لِ Laa لاَ La لَ

Moo مُو Mu مُ Mee مِي Me مِ Maa مَا Ma مَ

Nuu نُو Nu نُ Nee نِي Ne نِ Naa نَا Na نَ

Huu هُو Hu هُ Hee هِي He هِ Haa هَا Ha هَ

Vuw وُو Vu وُ Vee وِي Ve وِ Vaa وَا Va وَ

Yuu يُو Yu يُ Yee يِي Ye يِ Yaa يَا Ya يَ

NUNATION

Doubling of the symbol is called nunation. See how the letters are written and read with nunation.

Un اٌ	In اٍ	An اً
Bun بٌ	Bin بٍ	Ban بًا
Tun تٌ	Tin تٍ	Tan تًا
Thun ثٌ	Thin ثٍ	Than ثًا
Jun جٌ	Jin جٍ	Jan جًا
Khun خٌ	Khin خٍ	Khan خًا
Dun دٌ	Din دٍ	Dan دًا
Dun ذٌ	Din ذٍ	Dan ذًا

It will be difficult to find dettached letters in words. Mostly we find letters joined each other. So it is important to understand the shapes of each letter when it is written alone, when it comes as the first, middle or the last letter of a word.

Alone	Beginning	Middle	Last
ا	ا	ـا	ـا
ب	بـ	ـبـ	ـب
ت	تـ	ـتـ	ـت

ث	ثـ	ـثـ	ـث
ج	جـ	ـجـ	ـج
ح	حـ	ـحـ	ـح
خ	خـ	ـخـ	ـخ
د	د	ـد	ـد
ذ	ذ	ـذ	ـذ
ر	ر	ـر	ـر
ز	ز	ـز	ـز
س	سـ	ـسـ	ـس
ش	شـ	ـشـ	ـش
ص	صـ	ـصـ	ـص
ض	ضـ	ـضـ	ـض
ط	ط	ـط	ـط

ظ	ظـ	ـظـ	ـظ
ع	عـ	ـعـ	ـع
غ	غـ	ـغـ	ـغ
ف	فـ	ـفـ	ـف
ق	قـ	ـقـ	ـق
ك	كـ	ـكـ	ـك
ل	لـ	ـلـ	ـل
م	مـ	ـمـ	ـم
ن	نـ	ـنـ	ـن
و	و	ـو	ـو
ه	هـ	ـهـ	ـه
ي	يـ	ـيـ	ـي

LESSON TWO

READING AND WRITING PRACTICE

Father	*abu*	اب	ا ب
Brother	*akhu*	اخ	ا خ
Took	*akheda*	أخذ	أ خ ذ
Earth	*ard*	ارض	ا ر ض
Mother	*umm*	ام	ا م
Son	*ibn*	ابن	ا ب ن
Camel	*ibl*	ا بل	ا ب ل
In front of	*amam*	امام	ا م ا م
Leader	*imam*	امام	ا م ا م
Sister	*ukhth*	اخت	ا خ ت
Brothers	*ikhwa*	اخوة	ا خ و ة
Pot	*inae*	اناء	ا نا ء
Leadership	*imara*	امارة	ا م ا ر ة
Stool	*uskumla*	اسكملة	ا س ك م ل ة
Model	*uswa*	اسوة	ا س و ة
Professor	*ustad*	استاذ	ا س ت ا ذ
Stadium	*istad*	استاد	ا س ت ا د
Thousand	*alif*	الف	ا ل ف
Ordered	*amara*	امر	ا م ر

Order	*amr*	امر	امر
Create	*abdaa*	اَبدَعَ	اب دع
To Perfect	*atqana*	اتقَنَ	ا ت ق ن
Sometimes	*ahyan*	احيانا	ا ح ي ا ن ا
Respect	*ihtiram*	احترام	ا ح ت ر ا م
Statistics	*ihsae*	احصاء	ا ح ص ا ء
Performance	*adae*	اداء	ا د ا ء
Intention	*irada*	ارادة	ا ر ا د ة
Inheritance	*irth*	ارث	ا ر ث
Reception	*istiqbal*	استقبال	ا س ت ق ب ا ل
Participation	*ishtirak*	اشتراك	ا ش ت ر ا ك
Bought	*istare*	اشترى	ا ش ت ر ى
Lion	*asad*	اسد	ا س د
Beautiful	*aneeq*	انيق	ا ن ي ق
Security	*amn*	امن	ا م ن

LESSON THREE

VERBS

Verbs play an important role in any communication. Instead of going deep in to the grammatical and structural rules and regulations of verbs, I have opted for introducing a number of commonly used verbs, thinking it will enhance the language learning process.

Abolish	*batala*	*yubtil*	يبطل	بَطَلَ
Abuse	*hana*	*yuheen*	يهين	هان
Accept	*kabl*	*yaqbalu*	يقبل	قبل
Accompany	*rafaqa*	*yurafiq*	يرافق	رافق
Accustom	*htada*	*yaatad*	يعتاد	اعتاد
Spent/Act	*tassarafa*	*yatasarraf*	يتصرف	تصرف
Add	*adafa*	*yudeefu*	يضيف	اضاف
Admire	*ahjaba*	*yuejabu*	يعجب	اعجب
Succeed	*najaha*	*yanjahu*	ينجح	نجح
Lack	*iftaqara*	*yaftaqer ila*	يفتقر إلى	افتقر
Clap	*saffaqa*	*yusaffiq*	يصفق	صفق
Weaken	*adhafa*	*yudhefu*	يضعف	اضعف
Be aware	*adraka*	*yudrik*	يدرك	أدرك
Kill	*qatala*	*yaqtulu*	يقتل	قتل
Agree	*wafaqa*	*yuwafiq*	يوافق	وافق
Aid	*saada*	*yusaidu*	يساعد	ساعد
Meditate	*taammala*	*yatammal*	تأمل	يتأمّل
Blow	*nafakha*	*yanfakhu*	ينفخ	نفخ
Pant	*lahata*	*yalhath*	يلهث	لهث

Allow	*samaha*	*yasmahu*	يسمح	سمح
Answer	*jawaba*	*yujawab*	يجاوب	جاوب
Appear	*zahar*	*yazhar*	يظهر	ظهر
Approach	*iqtaraba*	*yaqarib*	يقترب	اقترب
Arrange	*rattaba*	*yurattib*	يرتب	رتب
Arrive	*wasala*	*yasilu*	يصل	وصل
Wake up	*istauqadh*	*yastaiqidh*	يستيقظ	استيقظ
Mix/Blend	*mazaja*	*yamzej*	يمزج	مزج
Participate	*sharaka*	*yusharik*	يشارك	شارك
Break	*kasara*	*yukasir*	يكسر	كسر
To inquire	*istalama*	*yastalem*	يستعلم	استعلم
Stop/Case	*awqafa*	*yuqif*	يوقف	اوقف
Make dirty	*awsaqa*	*yusiqu*	يوسخ	اوسخ
Invest	*astathmara*	*yastatmiru*	يستثمر	استثمر
Lead to	*ada*	*yuaddi ila*	يؤدي إلى	ادى
Make cold	*barrada*	*yubarrid*	يبرد	برد
Vomit	*taqayyaa*	*yataqayyaa*	يتقيأ	تقيأ
Finish	*anhaa*	*yunhee*	ينهي	انها
Whiten	*bayyada*	*yubayyed*	يبيض	بيض
Apologize	*ihtadar*	*yatadher*	يعتذر	اعتذر
Grow	*kabara*	*yakbor*	يكبر	كبر
Redden	*ahmara*	*yuhmiru*	يحمر	احمر
Fill	*malaha*	*yamlah*	يملأ	ملأ
Draw	*rasama*	*yarsom*	يرسم	رسم
Fly	*tara*	*yatheer*	يطير	طار

Sail	*abhara*	*yubhiru*	يبحر	ابحر
Exaggerate	*balaga*	*yubalig*	يبالغ	بالغ
Oblige to	*arghama*	*yurghimu alaa*	يرغم على	أرغم
Send	*arsala*	*yursil*	يرسل	ارسل
Light	*anara*	*yuneer*	ينير	انار
Fold	*tawa*	*yatwee*	يطوي	طوي
Wash	*gasala*	*yaghsil*	يغسل	غسل
Fall	*saqatha*	*yasquth*	يسقط	سقط
To load	*hammala*	*yuhammilu*	يحمل	حمل
Resemble	*sabaha*	*yusabeh*	يشابه	شابه
Catch	*iltaqata*	*yaltaqith*	يلتقط	التقط
Point	*ashara*	*yusheeru ila*	يشير إلى	اشار
to enter	*dakhala*	*yadkhul*	يدخل	دخل
Type	*tabaa*	*yatbaa*	يطبع	طبع
Cry	*bakaa*	*yabkee*	يبكي	بكى
Warn	*andher*	*yundher*	ينذر	انذر
Push	*dafaa*	*yadfau*	يدفع	دفع
Scream	*saaha*	*yaseehu*	يصيح	صاح
Yell	*sarakha*	*yasrikhu*	يصرخ	صرخ
Look	*nadara*	*yandur*	ينظر	نظر
Eat	*akala*	*yakul*	يأكل	أكل
Sweep	*kanasa*	*yaknos*	يكنس	كنس
Swim	*sabaha*	*yasbah*	يسبح	سبح
Tear	*mazaka*	*yumaziq*	يمزق	مزق
Tie	*rabata*	*yarbit*	يربط	ربط

Touch	*lamasa*	*yalmos*	يلمس	لمس
Study	*darasa*	*yadros*	يدرس	درس
Pass	*marra*	*yamurru*	يمرّ	مرّ
Stand	*waqafa*	*yaqef*	يقف	وقف
Give	*aahtha*	*yoaty*	يعطي	أعطى
Ask	*saala*	*yasal*	يسأل	سأل
Astonish	*adhasha*	*yudhish*	يدهش	أدهش
Attract	*ajdaba*	*yujdab*	يجذب	اجذب
Believe	*saddaqa*	*yusaddiqu*	يصدق	صدق
Belong	*khassa*	*yakhussu*	يخص	خص
Bless	*baraka*	*yubarik*	يبارك	بارك
Boil	*gala*	*yaglee*	يغلي	غلى
Clean	*naddafa*	*yunazzif*	ينظف	نظف
Borrow	*istaara*	*yastaeeru*	يستعير	استعار
Breathe	*tanaffasa*	*yatanfasu*	يتنفس	تنفس
Call	*nada*	*yunadee*	ينادي	نادي
Carry	*hamala*	*yahmilu*	يحمل	حمل
Change	*gayyara*	*yugayyir*	يغير	غير
Close	*qafala*	*yuqfilu*	يقفل	قفل
Close	*ahlaqa*	*yoghliq*	يغلق	أغلق
Collect	*jamae*	*yagmaa*	يجمع	جمع
Complain	*ishtakaa*	*yastakee*	يشتكي	اشتكي
Confess	*ihtarafa*	*yaatharif*	يعترف	اعترف
Consider	*ihtabara*	*yatabiru*	يعتبر	اعتبر
Contain	*ihtawaa*	*yahtawee*	يحتوي	احتوى

Copy	*nasakha*	*yansakhu*	ينسخ	نسخ
Count	*adda*	*yaoodd*	يعد	عد
Throw	*alqa*	*yolqee*	يلقي	القي
Meet	*laqiya*	*yalqa/iltaqa*	يلقى/التقى	لقي
Cry	*bakaa*	*yabkee*	يبكي	بكى
Dance	*raqasa*	*yarqusu*	يرقص	رقص
Decide	*qarrara*	*yuqarriru*	يقرر	قرر
Delay	*taakhara*	*yataakharu*	يتأخر	تأخر
Die	*mata*	*yamootu*	يموت	مات
Dislike	*kariha*	*yakrah*	يكره	كره
Dry	*anshafa*	*yonasshifu*	ينشف	أنشف
Obey	*ataa*	*yuteea*	يطيع	أطاع
Emigrate	*hajara*	*yohajjir*	يهاجر	هاجر
Employ	*waddafa*	*yowaddifu*	يوظف	وظف
Use	*istaemala*	*yastamilu*	يستعمل	استعمل
Explain	*sharaha*	*yausrahu*	يشرح	شرح
Fear	*khafa*	*yakhafu*	يخاف	خاف
Follow	*tabia*	*yatbahu*	يتبع	تبع
Hire	*istaejara*	*yastaajir*	يستأجر	استأجر
Inherit	*waratha*	*yarithu*	يرث	ورث
Insult	*ahana*	*yaheenu*	يهين	اهان
Invent	*ikhtara*	*yakhtaria*	يخترع	اخترع
Jump	*qafaza*	*yaqfazu*	يقفز	قفز
Trick	*ihtala*	*yahtalu*	يحتال	احتال
Laugh	*dahika*	*yadhaku*	يضحك	ضحك

Learn	*taallam*	*yatallamu*	يتعلم	تعلم
Lie	*kadaba*	*yakadibu*	يكذب	كذب
Live	*aasha*	*yaeeshu*	يعيش	عاش
Marry	*tazawwaja*	*yatazawwaj*	يتزوج	تزوج
Celebrate	*ihtafala*	*yahtafal*	يحتفل	احتفل
Accomplish	*atam*	*yutim*	يتمّ	أتم
Build	*banee*	*yabnee*	يبني	بنا
Think	*fakkar*	*yufakkir*	يفكر	فكر
Enjoy	*istamta*	*yastamtia*	يستمتع	استمتع
Cure	*shafaa*	*yashfee*	يشفي	شفى
Walk	*mashaa*	*yamshee*	يمشي	مشى
Punish	*addaba*	*yuadibu*	يعذّب	عذّب
Punish	*qasasa*	*yuqasi*	يقاصص	قاصص
Acquire	*aktasab*	*yaktasib*	يكتسب	اكتسب
Invade	*ghaza*	*yaghzou*	يغزو	غزى
Slow down	*abta*	*yubtia*	يبطئ	ابطأ
Drink	*sariba*	*yashrab*	يشرب	شرب
Answer/ Reply	*ajab*	*yujeeb*	يجيب	أجاب
Flight	*tasajar*	*yatasajar*	يتشاجر	تشاجر
Say	*qala*	*yaqoul*	يقول	قال
Write	*kataba*	*yaktubu*	يكتب	كتب
Put out	*athafa*	*yutfia*	يطفئ	أطفأ
Increase	*azdad*	*yazdad*	يزداد	ازداد
Memorize	*hafadah*	*yahfadh*	يحفظ	حفظ
Defend	*dafa*	*yudafia*	يدافع	دافع

Lose	*daha*	*yudeehu*	يضيع	ضاع
Offer/Give	*kadama*	*yukhaddim*	يقدّم	قدّم
Wait	*anthadara*	*yanthadir*	ينتظر	انتظر
Do	*fala*	*yafal*	يفعل	فعل
Bite	*gadda*	*yaguddu*	يغض	غضّ
Disappear	*aktafa*	*yuktafee*	يختفي	اختفى
Suffer	*hanee*	*yuhanee*	يعاني	عاني
Obtain	*hasala*	*yahsol ala*	يحصل على	حصل
Pick/Harvest	*katafa*	*yaktifu*	يقطف	قطف
Run	*rakada*	*yarkudu*	يركض	ركض
Died	*maata*	*yamutu*	يموت	مات
Come	*ataa*	*yahtee*	يأتي	اتي
Give as a present	*ahdee*	*yuhdee*	يهدي	أهدى
Catch	*amsaka*	*yumsik*	يمسك	امسك
Feel	*ahassa*	*yuhiss*	يحسّ	أحس
Keep/Preserve	*hafada*	*yuhafidu ala*	يحافظ على	حافظ
Escape	*haraba*	*yahrabu*	يهرب	هرب
Go	*karaja*	*yakhroj*	يخرج	خرج
Cover	*hataa*	*yughatee*	يغطّي	غطّى
See/View	*raa*	*yaraa*	يري	رأى
Sit	*galasa*	*yaglis*	يجلس	جلس
Know	*aalam*	*yahlam*	يعلم	علم
Can	*istithaa*	*yastateea*	يستطيع	استطاع
Dream	*halama*	*yahlam*	يحلم	حلم
Perform	*marasa*	*yumares*	يمارس	مارس

Smile	*abtasim*	*yabtasem*	يبتسم	ابتسم
Kick	*rakala*	*yarkul*	يركل	ركل
Broadcast	*idhah*	*yudeea*	يذيع	أذاع
Paint	*rasama*	*yarsum*	يرسم	رسم
Dress	*artadaa*	*yartadee*	يرتدي	ارتدى
Manage	*adar*	*yudeer*	يدير	أدار
Rotate	*daar*	*yadoor*	يدور	دار
Deliver	*wazza*	*yuwazzea*	يوزّع	وزّع
Watch	*shahid*	*yusahid*	يشاهد	شاهد
Divide	*aqsam*	*yaqsim*	يقسم	اقسم
Smoke	*dakhan*	*yudakhan*	يدخّن	دخّن
Scold	*yuanneb*	*yuanneb*	يؤنب	أنب
Pray	*salla*	*yusalyy*	يصلي	صلّى
levy	*gaba*	*yagboo*	يجبو	جبا
Swing	*tarjah*	*yataarjah*	يتأرجح	تأرجح
Snore	*sakhara*	*yaskhur*	يشخر	شخر
Cheat	*ghassa*	*yaghoshsh*	يغشّ	غشّ
Open	*fataha*	*yuftahu*	يفتح	فتح
Order	*amara*	*yaamuru*	يأمر	امر
Play	*laiba*	*yalab*	يلعب	لعب
Promise	*waada*	*yaidu*	يعد	وعد
Receive	*istalama*	*yastalim*	يستلم	استلم
Continue	*taabaha*	*yutabihu*	يتابع	تابع
Talk/Speak	*takallama*	*yatakallam*	يتكلم	تكلم
Smell	*shamma*	*yashumu*	يشم	شم

Taste	*tadawwaqa*	*yathawwaqu*	يتذوق	تذوق
Visit	*zara*	*yazooru*	يزور	زار
Work	*istagala*	*yastagilu*	يشتغل	اشتغل
Work	*hamala*	*yahmalu*	يعمل	عمل
Do	*fahala*	*yafhalu*	يفعل	فعل
Want	*arada*	*yureedu*	يريد	أراد
Turn	*dara*	*yudeer*	يدير	دار
To be able	*qadara*	*yaqdiru*	قدر	يقدر
Sing	*ghanni*	*yoghanni*	يغني	غنى
To play	*laiba*	*yalabu*	يلعب	لعب
To drive	*qada*	*yaqoodu*	يقو د	قاد
To deliver	*sallama*	*yusallimu*	يسلم	سلّم
To sell	*baa*	*yabee*	يبيع	با ع
To buy	*ishtara*	*yashtaree*	يشتري	اشترى
To advise	*nasaha*	*yansahu*	ينصح	نصح
To agree	*wafaqa*	*yuwafiqu*	يو افق	و افق
To help	*saada*	*yusaidu*	يساعد	ساعد
To arrive	*wasala*	*yasilu*	يصل	وصل
To cut	*qatae*	*yaqtahu*	يقطع	قطع
To see	*raa*	*yara*	يرى	رأي
To speak	*takallama*	*yatakallam*	يتكلم	تكلم
To sleep	*naama*	*yanama*	ينام	نام
To beat	*daraba*	*yadribu*	يضرب	ضرب
To leave	*taraka*	*yathruku*	يترك	ترك
To collect	*jamaa*	*yajmaa*	يجمع	جمع

To hear	*samia*	*yasmaa*	يسمع	سمع
To change	*baddala*	*yubaddil*	يبدل	بدل
To carry	*hamala*	*yahmil*	يحمل	حمل
To teach	*darrasa*	*yodarris*	يدرس	درس
To free	*faraqa*	*yufrug*	يفرغ	فرغ
To fear	*khafa*	*yakhafu*	يخاف	خاف
To forgive	*samaha*	*yusamihu*	يسامح	سامح
To grant	*manaha*	*yamnahu*	يمنح	منح
To know	*arafa*	*yaarifu*	يعرف	عرف
To invite	*daa*	*yadoo*	يدعو	دعا
To marry	*tazawwaj*	*yatazawwaju*	يتزوج	تزوج
To measure	*qasa*	*yaqeesu*	يقيس	قاس
To move	*taharraka*	*yataharraku*	يتحرك	تحرك
To transport	*naqala*	*yanqalu*	ينقل	نقل
To travel	*safara*	*yosafir*	يسافر	سافر

LESSON FOUR

SOME WORDS

Here are some words, which I feel will help you to form simple sentences without much difficulty. Learners have to practice making as many sentences as they can.

This (M)	*hada*	هذا
This (F)	*hadihi*	هذه
That (M)	*dalika*	ذلك
That (F)	*tilka*	تلك
He	*huwa*	هُوَ
She	*hiya*	هِيَ
You (M)	*inta*	انْتَ
You (F)	*inti*	انْتِ
I	*ana*	انا
We	*nehnu*	نحن
Yes	*namm, away, ee, balaa*	نعم/ايو/اي/بلى
No	*la, mafee, mush, mub, mu*	لا/مافي/مب/مش/م
Man	*rajol*	رجل
Woman	*mra'ah*	امرأة
High	*murtafi*	مرتفع
Low	*monkhafid*	منخفض
Close near	*qareeb*	قريب
Far	*baeed*	بعيد
Today	*alyawm*	اليوم
Tomorrow	*ams/albarihah*	البارحة/امس

Down	*that*	تحت
Up	*fawq*	فوق
Inside	*fiddakhil*	في الداخل
On the right	*alalyameen*	على اليمين
On the left	*alalyesar*	على اليسار
In between	*bayna*	بين
Beside	*bijenb*	بجنب
Short	*qaseer*	قصير
High	*rafeeh*	رفيع
Fat	*sameen*	سمين
Thin	*naheef*	نحيف
Low	*khafeed*	خفيض
Frightful	*mukheef*	مخيف
Amazing	*mudhish*	مدهش
Great	*azeem*	عظيم
Good/Pleasant	*tayyib*	طيب
Bad	*sayyia*	سيئ
Compact	*wajeez*	وجيز
Average	*motawassit*	متوسط
Complete/perfect/full	*kamil*	كامل
Incomplete	*naqis*	ناقص
Expensive	*qaali*	غالي
Cheap	*raxees*	رخيص
Difficult	*saab*	صعب
Easy	*sahl*	سهل

Clean	*nazeef*	نظيف
Dirty	*wasix*	وسخ
Strong	*qawiyy*	قوي
Weak	*daeef*	ضعيف
Broad	*wasih*	واسع
Narrow	*dayyiq*	ضيق
Beautiful	*jameel*	جميل
Ugly	*qabeeh*	قبيح
Big	*kabeer*	كبير
Small	*sageer*	صغير
New	*jadeed*	جديد
Old	*qadeem/ateeq*	قديم/عتيق
Long	*taweel*	طويل
Offers	*ard-urood*	عرض (ج) عُروض
Weekend offers	*uroodu nihayatil usbooh*	عروض نهاية الاسبوع
Season ending offers	*uroodu nihayatal fatra*	عروض نهاية الفترة
Giant Stores	*al makhazinul kubra*	المخازن الكبرى
Grand sale	*tanzeelat*	تنزيلات
Discount	*khasm*	خصم
Quantity	*kammiyya*	كمية
Quality	*jawda/nawiyya*	جودة/نوعية

SENTENCE FORMATION

Hope you are now in a position to form small sentences of your own. It will be interesting experience to frame words of your choice to make meaningful sentences. Needless to say this effort will definitely further motivate your desire to learn the language.

Once you learn these words, try to make your own sentences. Starting with simple nominal sentences you can go to verbal sentences and stronger and effective statements.

See various levels of sentences:

This is a house	*hada bayt*	هذا بيت
This is a teacher	*hada mudarris*	هذا مدرس
This is a boy	*hada walad*	هذا ولد
This is a clean house	*hada bayt nadeef*	هذا بيت نظيف
This is a new teacher	*hada mudarris jadeed*	هذا مدرس جديد
This is a smart boy	*hada walad shatir*	هذا ولد شاطر
His house is clean	baytuhu nadeef	بيته نظيف
His teacher is new	*mudarrisahoo jadeed*	مدرسه جديد
His son is smart	*waladu shatir*	ولده شاطر
The clean house is new	*al baytunnadeef jadeed*	البيت النظيف جديد
The new teacher is a scholar	*al mudarrisul jadeed aalim*	المدرس الجديد عالم
The smart boy is successful	*al waladu ssatiry najih*	الولد الشاطر ناجح
This is a company	*hadihi Sharika*	هذه شركة
This is a park	*hadihi hadeeqa*	هذه حديقة
This is a school	*hadihi Madrassa*	هذه مدرسة
This is a big company	*hadihi sharika kabeera*	هذه شركة كبيرة
This is a vast park	*hadihi hadeqa wasia*	هذه حديقة واسعة
This is a new teacher	*hadihi mudarrisa jadeeda*	هذه مدرسة جديدة
That is a man	*dalika rajul*	ذلك رجل
That is a carpenter	*dalika najjar*	ذلك نجار

That is a book	*dalika kitab*	ذلك كتاب
That is a good man	*dalika rajul tayyib*	ذلك رجل طيب
That is a expert carpenter	*dalika najjar mahir*	ذلك نجار ماهر
That is a useful book	*dalika kitab mufeed*	ذلك كتاب مفيد
That is a cow	*tilka baqara*	تلك بقرة
That is a school	*tilka madarassa*	تلك مدرسة
That is a bicycle	*tilka darraja*	تلك دراجة
That is a fat cow	*tilka baqara sameena*	تلك بقرة ثمينة
That is a small school	*tilka madrasa sageera*	تلك مدرسة صغيرة
That is an expensive bicycle	*tilka darraja galiya*	تلك دراجة غالية
The boy wrote the lesson	*katabal waladu addarasa*	كتب الولد الدرس
The teacher sat on the chair	*jalasal mudarris alal kuriy*	جلس المدرس على الكرسي
Father read the newspaper	*qaraal walidu aljareeda*	قرأ الوالد الجريدة
Mother cooks food	*tatbakhul ummu attaom*	تطبخ الأم الطعام
Child sleeps on the cot	*yanamul waladu alssareer*	ينام الولد على السرير
The student goes to school	*yadhabu ttalabu ilal madrasa*	يذهب الطالب إلى المدرسة

LESSON FIVE

WHAT IS YOUR NAME?

What is your name?	*shusmak?*	شــسـمـك؟
What is this?	*shoo haada?*	شــو هــذا؟
This is a boy	*haada valid*	هــذا ولد
What is this?	*shoo haadihi?*	شــو هــذه؟
This is a girl	*haadihi bint*	هــذه بـنت
What is this?	*shunu haada?*	شــن هــذا؟
This is a pen	*haada qalam*	هــذا قلم؟
What is this?	*shunu haadihi?*	شــن هــذه؟
This is a school	*haadihi madrasa*	هــذه مـدرسـة
What is this?	*esh haada?*	ايش هــذا؟
This is sugar	*haada sukkar*	هــذا سـكر
What is this?	*esh haadihi?*	ايش هــذه؟
This is an apple	*haadihi tuffaha*	هــذه تـفـاحـة؟
What is that?	*shunu daalika?*	شــن ذلـك؟
That is an orange	*daalika burtuqaal*	ذلـك بـرتـقال؟
What is that?	*shunu tilka?*	شــن تـلـك؟
That is a cow	*tilka baqara*	تـلـك بـقرة؟
What is the name of your father?	*shusmu abeeka?*	شـسـم أبـيـك؟
What is the name of your mother?	*shusmu ummika?*	شـسـمامـك؟
What is the name of your house?	*shusmu baitika?*	شـسـم بـيتـك؟
What is the name of your son?	*shusmu ibnika?*	شـسـم إبـنـك؟

What is the name of your daughter?	*shusmu ibnatika?*	شسم إبنتك؟
What is the name of your family?	*shusmu usratika?*	شسم اسرتك؟
What is the name of your car?	*shusmu sayyaaratika?*	شسم سيارتك؟
What is the name of your village?	*shusmu qaryatika?*	شسم قريتك؟
What is the name of your country?	*shusmu baladiaka?*	شسم بلدك؟
What is the name of your city?	*shusmu madeenatika?*	شسممدينتك؟
What is the name of your company?	*shusmu sharikatika?*	شسم شركتك؟
What is the name of your neighbour?	*shusmu sharikatika?*	شسم جارك؟
What is the name of your friend?	*shusmu zameelika?*	شسم زميلك؟
What is the name of your friend?	*shusmu zameelatika?*	شسم زميلتك؟
What is the name of your school?	*shusmu madrasatika?*	شسم مدرستك؟
What is the name of your college?	*shusmu kulliyatika?*	شسم كليتك؟
What is the name of your teacher?	*shusmu mudarrisika?*	شسم مدرسك؟
What is the name of your manager?	*shusmu mudeerika?*	شسم مديرك؟
What is the name of your supervisor?	*shusmu mushrifika?*	شسم مشرفك؟

What is the name of your partner?	*shusmu shareekika?*	شسم شريكك؟
What is his name?	*shusmuhoo?*	شسمه؟
What is her name?	*shusmuhaa?*	شسمها
What is the name of your husband?	*shusmu zawjika?*	شسم زوجك؟
What is the name of your wife?	*shusmu zawjatika?*	شسم زوجتك؟
What is the name of your brother?	*shusmu akheeka?*	شسم أخيك؟
What is the name of your sister?	*shusmu ukhtika?*	شسم اختك؟
What is the name of your servant?	*shusmu khaadimika?*	شسم خادمك؟
What is the name of your maid?	*shusmu khaadimatika?*	شسم خادمتك؟
What is the name of your doctor?	*shusmu twabeebika?*	شسم طبيبك؟
What is your sponsor's name?	*shusmu kafeelika?*	شسم كفيلك؟
What is the matter?	*shunu fee/ esh fee?*	شن فيه/ ايش فيه
What is the problem?	*shunu fee mushkila?*	شن فيه مشكلة؟
What you want?	*shunu tabgwi?*	شن تبغ؟
What do you want?	*shunu tureed/esh tureed?*	شن تريد؟/ ايش تريد؟
What do you do there?	*shusawwi hinaka?*	شسو هناك؟
What do you like to drink?	*tuhib tashrab esh?*	تحب تشرب ايش؟

What do you like to read?	*tuhib taqra esh?*	تحب تقرأ ايش؟
What do you like to study?	*tuhib tadrus esh?*	تحب تدرس ايش؟
What do you like to write?	*tuhib taktub esh?*	تحب تكتب ايش؟
What do you like to talk?	*tuhib tatakallam esh?*	تحب تتكلم ايش؟
What do you like to see?	*tuhib taraa esh?*	تحب ترى ايش؟
What do you like to cook?	*tuhib tatbakh esh?*	تحب تطبخ ايش؟
What do you like to wear?	*tuhib talbas esh?*	تحب تلبس ايش؟
What do you like to do?	*tuhib ta'amal esh?*	تحب تعمل ايش؟
What does he say?	*shunu yaqool/esh yaqool?*	شن يقول/ ايش يقول؟
What do you like to hear?	*tuhib tasma esh?*	تحب تسمع ايش؟
What does she say?	*shunu taqool/esh taqool?*	شن تقول/ ايش تقول؟
What do they call it in English?	*shusammoona haada bil injileezee?*	شسمون هذا بالإنجليزية؟
What do they call it in Arabic?	*shusammoona haada bil arabee?*	شسمون هذا بالعربي؟
What does it mean?	*shu ya'anee?*	شو يعني؟

Vocabulary:

A boy	*walad*	ولد	A girl	*bint*	بـنت
A pen	*qalam*	قلم	Sugar	*sukkar*	سـكر
An apple	*tuffaha*	تـفـاحـة	An orange	*burtuqaal*	بـرتـقال
A cow	*baqara*	بـقرة	Father	*ab*	أب
Mother	*umm*	ام	A house	*bayt*	بـيت
Son	*ibn*	إبـن	Daughter	*ibna*	إبـنة
Family	*usra*	اسـرة	Car	*sayyara*	سـيارة
Village	*qarya*	قريـة	Country	*balad*	بـلد
Town	*madeena*	مـدينـة	Company	*sharika*	شـركة
Neighbour	*jaar*	جـار	Friend (M)	*zameel*	زمـيل
Friend (F)	*zameela*	زمـيلة	School	*madrasa*	مـدرسـة
College	*kulliya*	كليـة	Teacher	*mudarris*	مـدرس
Manager	*mudeer*	مـدير	Supervisor	*mushrif*	مـشـرف
Partner	*shareek*	شـريـك	Husband	*zawj*	زوج
Wife	*zawja*	زوجـة	Brother	*akh*	أخ
Sister	*ukht*	اخـت	Servant	*khaadim*	خـادم
House maid	*khaadima*	خـادمـة	Doctor	*twabeeb*	طبـيب
Sponsor	*kafeel*	كـفـيل	Difficulty	*mushkila*	مـشـكلـة
Desire	*tabgi*	تـبـغ	Want	*tureed*	تـريد
Say	*yaqool*	يقول	Like	*tuhib*	تـحـب
Drink	*tashrab*	تـشـرب	Read	*taqra*	تـقرأ
Study	*tadrus*	تـدرس	write	*taktub*	تكـتب
Speak	*tatakallam*	تـتـكلم	cook	*tatbakh*	تطبـخ
Wear	*talbas*	تلبـس	do/work	*ta'amal*	تعـمل

LESSON SIX

WHERE ARE YOU FROM?

Where are you from?	*min wayn inta?*	مـن وين إنت؟
Where is he?	*wayn huwa?*	وين هـو؟
Where is she?	*wayn hiya?*	وين هي؟
Where is the manager	*wayn mudeer?*	وين مـدير؟
Where is he from?	*min wayn huwa?*	مـن وين هـو؟
Where is she from?	*min wayn hiya?*	مـن وين هي؟
Where is the Principal from?	*min wayn al mudeer?*	مـن وين المـدير؟
Where is the Engineer from?	*min wayn al muhandis?*	مـن وين المـهندس؟
Where is your house?	*wayn baituka?*	وين بيـتـك؟
Where is your car?	*wayn sayyaaratuka?*	وين سـيارتـك؟
Where is your magazine?	*wayn majallatuka?*	وين مـجـلـتـك؟
Where is your newspaper?	*wayn jareedatuka?*	وين جـريدتـك؟
Where is his office?	*wayn maktabuhoo?*	وين مـكـتـبـه؟
Where is her book?	*wayn kitaabuha?*	وين كـتابـها؟
Where do you go?	*wayn taruh?*	وين تـرح؟
Where do you work?	*wayn tashtagil?*	وين تـشـتـغـل؟
Where do you live?	*wayn taskun?*	وين تـسـكن؟
Where do you sit?	*wayn tajlis?*	وين تـجـلس؟
Where do you play?	*wayn tal'ab?*	وين تـلعـب؟

Where do you sleep?	*wayn tanaam?*	وين تنام؟
Where do you study?	*wayn tadrus?*	وين تدرس؟
Where do you cultivate?	*wayn tazra'a*	وين تزرع؟
Where is the room key?	*wayn miftaahul gurfa?*	وين مفتاح الغرفة؟
Where is the student's bag?	*wayn haqeebatu taalib?*	وين حقيبة الطالب؟
Where is the principal's chamber?	*wayn gurfatul mudeer?*	وين غرفة المدير؟
Where is Ahmed?	*wayn ahmed?*	وين أحمد؟
Where is Khadeeja?	*wayn khadeeja?*	وين خديجة؟
Where is the hostel?	*wayn al maskan?*	وين المسكن؟
Where is the mosque?	*wayn al masjid?*	وين المسجد؟
Where is the clinic?	*wayn al iyaada?*	وين العيادة؟
Where is the petrol station?	*wayn mahatwa albitrool?*	وين محطة البترول؟
Where is the driver?	*wayn assawwaq?*	وين السواق؟
Where is the hospital?	*wayn al mustashfaa?*	وين المستشفى؟
Where is the library?	*wayn al maktaba?*	وين المكتبة؟
Where is the graveyard?	*wayn al maqbara?*	وين المقبرة؟
Where is the park?	*wayn al hadeeqa?*	وين الحديقة؟
Where is the zoo?	*wayn hadeeqatul hayawaanat?*	وين حديقة الحيوانات؟
Where is the museum?	*wayn al mathaf?*	وين المتحف؟
Where is the sea?	*wayn al bahr?*	وين البحر؟

Where is the river?	*wayn annahr?*	وين النهر؟
Where is the swimming pool?	*wayn birkatussibaaha*	وين بـركـة السـبـاحـة؟
Where is the embassy?	*wayn assafaara?*	وين السـفـارة؟
Where is the ambassador?	*wayn assafeer?*	وين السـفـير؟
Where is the minister?	*wayn al wazeer?*	وين الوزير؟
Where is the accountant?	*wayn al muhasib?*	وين المـحـاسـب؟
Where is the club?	*wayn annaadee?*	وين النادي؟
Where is the ball?	*wayn al kura?*	وين الكـرة؟
Where is the playground?	*wayn al mal'ab?*	وين المـلعـب؟
Where is the nurse?	*wayn al mumarridha?*	وين المـمـرضـة؟
Where is the airport?	*wayn al matwaar?*	وين المـطار؟
Where is the book?	*wayn al kitaab?*	وين الكـتـاب؟
Where is the notebook?	*wayn addaftar?*	وين الدفـتـر؟
Where is the meeting?	*wayn al ijtimaa'u*	وين الإجـتـمـاع؟
Where is the competition?	*wayn al musaabaqa?*	وين المـسـابـقة؟
Where is the tournament?	*wayn al mubaarat?*	وين المـبـارات؟
Where is the examination?	*wayn al imtihaan?*	وين الإمـتـحـان؟
Where can I find a helper?	*wayn ajid musaa'id?*	وين أجـد مـسـاعـدا؟
Where can I find a teacher?	*wayn ajid mudarris?*	وين أجـد مـدرسـا؟
Where can I find a guard?	*wayn ajid haaris?*	وين أجـد حـارسـا؟
Where can I find a translator?	*wayn ajid mutarjim?*	وين أجـد مـتـرجـمـا؟

Where can I find an electrician?	*wayn ajid kahrubaa'iyan?*	وين أجد كهربائيا؟
Where can I find an artist?	*wayn ajid rassaam?*	وين أجد رساما؟
Where can I find a nurse?	*wayn ajid mumarridh*	وين أجد ممرضا؟
Where can I find a carpenter?	*wayn ajid najjaaran?*	وين أجد نجارا؟
Where can I find a driver?	*wayn ajid saa'iq?*	وين أجد سائقا؟
Where can I find an accountant?	*wayn ajid muhaasib?*	وين أجد محاسبا؟
Where can I find an air hostess?	*wayn ajid mudheefa?*	وين أجد مضيفة؟
Where can I find a contractor?	*wayn ajid muqaawil?*	وين أجد مقاولا؟
Where can I find a cook?	*wayn ajid twabbakh?*	وين أجد طباخا؟
Where can I find a lawyer?	*wayn ajid muhamee?*	وين أجد محاميا؟
Where can I find a porter?	*wayn ajid shayyaal?*	وين أجد شيالا؟
Where can I find an office boy?	*wayn ajid farraash?*	وين أجد فراشا؟
Where can I find a pharmacist?	*wayn ajid swaidalee?*	وين أجد صيدليا؟
Where can I find a tailor?	*wayn ajid khayyaatwan?*	وين أجد خياطا؟
Where can I find an agent?	*wayn ajid wakeel?*	وين أجد وكيلا؟

Where can I find a labourer?	*wayn ajid 'aamil?*	وين أجد عاملا؟
Where can I find a sponsor?	*wayn ajid kafeel?*	وين أجد كفيلا؟
Where can I find a partner?	*wayn ajid shareek?*	وين أجد شريكا؟
Where can I find a servant?	*wayn ajid kahaadim?*	وين أجد خادما؟
Where can I find a painter?	*wayn ajid swabbagwan?*	وين أجد صباغا؟
Where can I find a designer?	*wayn ajid muswammim?*	وين أجد مصمما؟
Where can I find an inspector?	*wayn ajid mufattish?*	وين أجد مفتشا؟
Where can I find a barber?	*wayn ajid hallaq?*	وين أجد حلاقا؟
Where can I find a farmer?	*wayn ajid muzaari'a?*	وين أجد مزارعا؟
Where can I find a clerk?	*wayn ajid kaatib?*	وين أجد كاتبا؟
Where can I find a manager?	*wayn ajid mudeer?*	وين أجد مديرا؟
Where can I find a player?	*wayn ajid laa'ib?*	وين أجد لاعبا؟
Where can I find a room?	*wayn ajid gurfa?*	وين أجد غرفة؟
Where can I find a house?	*wayn ajid bayt?*	وين أجد بيت؟
Where can I find a hospital?	*wayn ajid mustashfa?*	وين أجد مستشفى؟

Where can I find a hostel?	*wayn ajid maskan?*	وين أجـد مسكن؟
Where can I find Mr.Khalid?	*wayn ajid assayyid khalid?*	وين أجـد السيد خالد؟
Where can I find Mrs. Khadeeja?	*wayn ajid assayyida khadeeja?*	وين أجـد السيدة خديجة؟

Vocabulary:

He	*huwa*	هـو	She	*hiya*	هي
Magazine	*majalla*	مـجـلـة	Newspaper	*jareeda*	جـريدة
Office	*maktab*	مـكـتـب	Book	*kitaab*	كـتاب
You go	*taruh*	تـرح	You work	*tashtagil*	تـشـتـغـل
You live	*taskun*	تـسـكـن	You sit	*tajlis*	تـجـلس
You play	*tal'ab*	تـلعـب	You sleep	*tanaam*	تـنام
You cultivate	*tazra'u*	تـزرع	Key	*miftaah*	مـفـتـاح
Room	*gurfa*	غـرفـة	Hostel	*maskan*	مـسـكـن
Mosque	*masjid*	مـسـجـد	Clinic	*iyaada*	عـيادة
Station	*mahatwa*	مـحـطة	Driver	*sawwaaq*	سـواق
Hospital	*mustashfaa*	مستشفى	Library	*maktaba*	مـكـتـبـة
Graveyard	*maqbara*	مـقـبـرة	Park	*hadeeqa*	حـديـقة
Zoo	*hadeeqa al hayawanaat*	حديقة الحيوانات	Museum	*mathaf*	مـتـحـف
Sea	*bahr*	بـحـر	River	*nahr*	نهر
Swimming pool	*birkatus sibaha*	بركة السباحة	Embassy	*safaara*	سـفـارة

Ambassador	*safeer*	سفير	Minister	*wazeer*	وزير
Accountant	*muhaasib*	محاسب	Club	*naadee*	نادي
Ball	*kura*	كرة	Play ground	*mal'ab*	ملعب
Nurse (F)	*mumarridha*	ممرضة	Airport	*mataar*	مطار
Note book	*daftar*	دفتر	Mobile phone	*jawwaal*	جوال
Fridge	*thallaja*	ثلاجة	Restaurant	*mat'am*	مطعم
Hotel	*funduq*	فندق	Court	*mahkama*	محكمة
Bank	*bank*	بنك	Ship	*safeena*	سفينة
Shop	*mahal*	محل	Ambulance	*is'aaf*	إسعاف
Post office	*maktabul bareed*	مكتب البريد	Railway station	*mahatwa alqitaar*	محطة القطار
Market	*sooq*	سوق	harbour	*meenaa'u*	ميناء
Hero	*batwal*	بطل	sun	*shams*	شمس
Moon	*qamar*	قمر	star	*najm*	نجم
Meeting	*ijtimaa'u*	إجتماع	competition	*musaabaqa*	مسابقة
Tournament	*mubaaraat*	مبارات	examination	*imtihaan*	إمتحان
Helper	*musaa'id*	مساعد	teacher	*mudarris*	مدرس
Guard	*haaris*	حارس	electrician	*kahrubaa'ee*	كهربائي
Artist	*rassaam*	رسام	carpenter	*najjaar*	نجار
Air hostess	*mudheefa*	مضيفة	contractor	*muqaawil*	مقاول
Advocate	*muhaamee*	محامي	porter	*shayyaal*	شيال
Office boy	*farraash*	فراش	pharmacist	*swaydalee*	صيدلي
Tailor	*khayyaat*	خياط	agent	*wakeel*	وكيل

Labourer	*aamil*	عـامـل	sponsor	*kafeel*	كـفـيل
Painter	*swabbagh*	صـبـاغ	designer	*muswammim*	مـصـمـم
Inspector	*mufattish*	مـفـتـش	barber	*hallaaq*	حـلاق
Farmer	*muzaari'u*	مـزارع	clerk	*kaatib*	كاتـب
Player	*laa'ib*	لاعـب			

LESSON SEVEN

WHO ARE YOU?

Who are you?	*meen inta?*	مين إنت؟
I am a teacher	*ana mudarris*	أنا مدرس
Who is he?	*meen huwa?*	مين هو؟
He is an engineer	*huwa muhandis*	هو مهندس
Who are you?	*meen inta?*	مين إنت؟
I am a doctor	*ana twabeeb*	أنا طبيب
What is your father?	*meen abooka?*	مين أبوك؟
My father is an accountant	*abee muhasib*	أبي محاسب
What is your mother?	*meen ummuka?*	مين امك؟
My mother is a nurse	*ummee mumarridha*	امي ممرضة
What is your wife?	*meen zawjatuka?*	مين زوجتك؟
My wife is a supervisor	*zawjatee mushrifa*	زوجتي مشرفة
Who is your sponsor?	*meen kafeeluka?*	مينكفيلك؟
My sponsor is Acon Company	*kafeelee sharika acon*	كفيلي شركة أكون
Who is your neighbour?	*meen jaaruka?*	مين جارك؟
My neighbour is Mr. Hashim	*jaaree assayyid hashim*	جاري السيد هاشم
Who is your boss/ manager?	*meen mudeeruka?*	مين مديرك؟
My boss/manager is Mr. Abdul Shukoor	*mudeeree assayyid abdushukoor*	مديري السيد عبد الشكور
Who is your trainer?	*meen mudarribuka?*	مين مدربك؟
My trainer is Mr. George	*mudarribee assayyid george*	مدربي السيد جورج

Who is your teacher?	*meen mudarrisuka?*	مين مدرسك؟
My teacher is Dr. Abdullah	*mudarrisee addaktoor abdulla*	مدرسي الدكتور عبد الله.
Who is your friend?	*meen zameeluka?*	مين زميلك؟
My friend is Mr. Abdurrahman	*zameelee assayyid abdurahman*	زميلي السيد عبد الرحمن
Who is your partner?	*meen shareekuka?*	مين شريكك؟
My partner is Mr. Muhammed.	*shareekee assayyid muhammed*	شريكي السيد محمد
Who is going to Dubai today?	*meen yaruh dubai alyawm?*	مين يرح دبي اليوم؟
Who is coming from India today?	*min yajee minal hind alyawm?*	مين يجيئ من الهند اليوم؟
Who made a call?	*meen sawwee talafoon?*	مين سوي تلفون؟
Who closed the door?	*meen sakkaral baab?*	مين سكر الباب؟
Who opened the window?	*meen batwala shubbaak?*	مين بطل الشباك؟
Who got a prize?	*meen hassala jaa'iza?*	مين حصل جائزة؟
Who is absent today?	*meen gwa'ib alyawm?*	مين غائب اليوم؟
Who made a quarrel?	*meen sawwee jinjaal?*	مين سوي جنجال؟
Who registered first?	*meen sajjal awwal?*	مين سجل أولا؟
Who paid the money today?	*meen dafa'al fuloos alyawm?*	مين دفع الفلوس اليوم؟
Who is going to the manager?	*meen yaruh ilal mudeer?*	مين يرح إلى المدير؟
Who comes first?	*meen yajee awwal?*	مين يجيئ أولا؟
Who goes last?	*meen yaruh aakhir?*	مين يرح آخرا؟
Who cook food?	*meen yatwbakh attwa'aam?*	مين يطبخ الطعام؟

Who succeeded in the examination?	*meen najah fil imtihaan?*	مين نجح في الإمتحان؟
Who taught you English?	*meen allamakal injileezee?*	مين علمك الإنجليزي؟
Who spoke to me yesterday?	*meen kallamanee bil amsi?*	مين كلمني بالأمس؟
Who helped you in study?	*meen saa'adaka fiddiraasa?*	مين ساعدك في الدراسة؟
Who cleans the school?	*meen yunadhiful madrasa?*	مين ينظف المدرسة؟
Who is delivering the speech today?	*meen yulqee khutba alyawm?*	مين يلقي خطبة اليوم؟
Who is reading loudly?	*meen yaqra'u jahran?*	مين يقرأ جهرا؟
Who accepts repentance?	*meen yaqbaluttawba?*	مين يقبل التوبة؟
Who helped you in difficulty?	*meen saa'adaka fil mashaqqa?*	مين ساعدك في المشقة؟
Who plays with you?	*meen yal'ab ma'aka?*	مين يلعب معك؟
Whose book is this?	*kitaabu meen haada?*	كتاب مين هذا؟
Whose house is that?	*baitu meen daalika?*	بيت مين ذلك؟
Whose son has won?	*ibnu meen najaha?*	إبن مين نجح؟
Whose bag has been lost?	*haqeeba meen dhaa'at?*	حقيبة مين ضاعت؟
Whose car is this?	*sayyaaratu meen haadihee?*	سيارة مين هذه؟
Whose son is he?	*ibnu meen huwa?*	إبن مين هو؟
Whose daughter is she?	*ibnatu meen hiya?*	إبنة مين هي؟
Whose room is that?	*gwurfatu meen tilka?*	غرفة مين تلك؟
Whose chair is broken?	*kursee meen kassara?*	كرسي مين كسر؟
Who is on duty?	*dawaamu meen bukra?*	دوام مين بكرة؟
Whose opportunity has been lost?	*fursa meen dhaa'at?*	فرصة مين ضاعت؟

Whose pen is costly?	*qalamu meen gwaalee?*	قلم مين غالي؟
Whose car is cheap?	*sayyaaratu meen rakheeswa?*	سيارة مين رخيصة؟
Whose house is new?	*baitu meen jadeed?*	بيت مين جديد؟
Whose mobile phone is old?	*jawwaal meen qadeem?*	جوال مين قديم؟
Whose bag is heavy?	*haqeebatu meen thaqeela?*	حقيبة مين ثقيلة؟
Whose room is clean?	*gurfatu meen nadheefa?*	غرفة مين نظيفة؟
Whose son is tall?	*ibnu meen taweel?*	إبن مين طويل؟
Whose daughter is short?	*bintu meen qasweera?*	بنت مين قصيرة؟
Whose student is lazy?	*twaalib meen kaslaan?*	طالب مين كسلان؟
Whose student is smart?	*twaaliba meen shaatwira?*	طالبة مين شاطرة؟
Whose company is near?	*sharikatu meen qareeba?*	شركة مين قريبة؟
Whose school is far?	*madrasatu meen ba'eeda?*	مدرسة مين بعيدة؟
Whose son is big?	*ibnu meen kabeer?*	إبن مين كبير؟
Whose daughter is small?	*ibnatu meen sageera?*	إبنة مين صغيرة؟
Whose office is new?	*maktabu meen jadeed?*	مكتب مين جديد؟
Whose library is old?	*maktabu meen qadeema?*	مكتبة مين قديمة؟
Whose suitcase is light?	*shantwatu meen khafeefa?*	شنطة مين خفيفة؟
Who drives with you?	*ma'a meen tasooq?*	مع مين تسوق؟
Who sits with you?	*ma'a meen tajlis?*	مع مين تجلس؟
Who dances with you?	*ma'a meen tarqus?*	مع مين ترقص؟
Who sleeps with you?	*ma'a meen tanaam?*	مع مين تنام؟

Who walked with you?	*ma'a meen tamshee?*	مع مين تمشي؟
Who did you speak with?	*ma'a meen kallamt?*	مع مين كلمت؟
Who did you see?	*shufta meen?*	شفت مين؟
Who did you help?	*saa'adta meen?*	ساعدت مين؟
Who did you sponsor?	*kafalta meen?*	كفلت مين؟
Who did you teach?	*darrasta meen?*	درست مين؟
Who did you save?	*sallamta meen?*	سلمت مين؟
Who do you want?	*meen tabgi?*	مين تبغ؟
Who is with me?	*meen ma'ee?*	مين معي؟
Who is speaking?	*meen kallam?*	مين كلم؟
Who is at the door?	*meen indal baab?*	مين عند الباب؟
Who did you treat?	*aaalajta meen?*	عالجت مين؟
Who did you beat?	*dharabta meen?*	ضربت مين؟
Who did you overcome?	*gwalabta meen?*	غَلَبْتَ مينْ؟

Vocabulary:

You (M)	*anta*	أنْت	You (F)	*anti*	أنْت
Wife	*zawja*	زَوجَة	Supervisor	*mushrifa*	مُشْرفَة
Trainer	*mudarrib*	مُدَرِّب	Friend	*zameel*	زَميل
Coming	*yajee*	يَجيئ	Make	*sawwee*	سَوّي
Closed	*sakkar*	سَكَّر	Opened	*battala*	بَطَّلَ
Got	*hassala*	حَصَّل	Prize	*jaa'iza*	جَائزَة
Quarrel	*jinjaal*	جنْجَال	Registered	*sajjal*	سَجَّل
Paid	*dafa'a*	دَفَع	First	*awwal*	أوَّل
Last	*aakhir*	آخر	Cook	*yatbakh*	يَطْبَخ
Won/ succeeded	*najaha*	نَجَح	Taught	*allama*	عَلَّمَ

Spoke	*kallama*	كَلَّمَ	Helped	*saa'ada*	سَاعَدَ
Study	*diraasa*	دِرَاسَةَ	Clean	*ynnadhif*	يُنَظِّف
Deliver the speech	*yulqee khutba*	يلقي خطبة	Read	*yaqra'u*	يَقْرَأ
Loud	*jahr*	جَهْر	Accept	*yaqbal*	يَقْبَل
Difficulty	*mashaqqa*	مَشَقَّة	Lost	*dhaa'a*	ضَاعَ
Broken	*kassar*	كسَّر	Duty	*dawaam*	دوَام
Tomorrow	*bukra*	بُكْرة	Chance	*furswa*	فُرْصَة
Costly	*gaalee*	غَالي	Cheap	*rakhees*	رَخيص
New	*jadeed*	جَديد	Old	*qadeem*	قَديم
Bag	*haqeeba*	حَقيبَة	Mobile phone	*jawwaal*	جَوَّال
Heavy	*thaqeela*	ثَقيلَة	Clean	*nadheefa*	نَظيفَة
Tall	*taweel*	طَويل	Short	*qaseer*	قَصير
Student	*taalib*	طَالب	Lazy	*kaslaan*	كَسْلاَن
Smart	*shaatwira*	شَاطرَة	Near	*qareeba*	قَريبَة
Far	*ba'eeda*	بَعيدَة	Big	*kabeer*	كَبير
Small	*sageer*	صَغير	Light	*khafeefa*	خَفيفَة
Above/up	*fawqa*	فَوْق	Down	*tahta*	تَحْت
Traveller	*musaafir*	مُسَافر	Marriage	*ziwaaj*	زوَاج
Key	*miftaah*	مفْتَاح	Lost	*dhaa'a*	ضَاعَ
Child	*twifl*	طفْل	Slept	*naama*	نَامَ
Crying	*yabkee*	يَبْكي	Vacation	*ijaaza*	إجَازَة
Park	*hadeeqa*	حَديقَة	Work	*tashtagil*	تَشْتَغل

Drive	*tasooq*	تَـسُـوق	Dance	*tarqusu*	تَـرْقُص
Walk	*tamshee*	تَـمْـشـي	Talk	*kallama*	كَلَّمَ
Saw	*shufta*	شُـفْـت	Helped	*saa'ada*	سَـاعَـد
Sponsored	*kaffala*	كَـفَّـلَ	Taught	*darrasa*	دَرَّسَ
Saved	*sallama*	سَـلَّمَ	Treated	*aalaja*	عَـالَجَ
Beat	*dharaba*	ضَـرَبَ	Overcome	*galaba*	غَـلَبَ

LESSON EIGHT

HOW ARE YOU?

How are you?	*kaifa haalak?*	كَـيْفَ حَـالَكَ؟
How are you?	*shakhbarak?*	شـخـبارك؟
How are you?	*shlonak?*	شـلونك؟
How is he?	*kaifa huwa?*	كَـيْفَ هُـوَ؟
How is she?	*kaifa hiya?*	كَـيْفَ هيَ؟
How are you?	*kaifa inta?*	كَـيْفَ أنتَ؟
How are you?	*kaifaka?*	كَـيْفَـكَ؟
How is the business?	*kaifattijaara?*	كَـيْفَ التِّـجَـارَة؟
How is father?	*kaifa baaba?*	كَـيْفَ بَـابَـا؟
How is mother?	*kaifa maama?*	كَـيْفَ مَـامَـا؟
How are children?	*kaifal awlaad?*	كَـيْفَ الأوْلاد؟
How is the school?	*kaifal madrasa?*	كَـيْفَ الْمَـدْرَسَـة؟
How is the office?	*kaifal maktab?*	كَـيْفَ الْمَـكْـتَـب؟
How is the library?	*kaifal maktaba?*	كَـيْفَ الْمَـكْـتَـبَـة؟
How is the shop?	*kaifal mahal?*	كَـيْفَ الْمَـحَـل؟
How is the sponsor?	*kaifal kafeel?*	كَيْفَ الْكَـفـيل؟
How is the partner?	*kaifasshareek?*	كَيْفَ الشَّـريك؟
How is the wife?	*kaifazzawja?*	كَيْفَ الزَّوْجَـة؟
How is the husband?	*Kaifazzawj?*	كَيْفَ الزَّوْج؟
How is the driver?	*kaifassaa'iq?*	كَيْفَ السَّـائق؟

How is the servant?	*kaifal khaadim?*	كَيْفَ الْخَـادم؟
How is the housemaid?	*kaifal khaadima?*	كَيْفَ الْخَـادمَـة؟
How is the engineer?	*kaifal muhandis?*	كَيْفَ الْمُـهَنْدس؟
How is the contractor?	*kaifal muqaawil?*	كَيْفَ الْمُـقَاول؟
How is the guard?	*kaifal haaris?*	كَيْفَ الْحَـارس؟
How is the manager?	*kaifal mudeer?*	كَيْفَ الْمُـدير؟
How is the teacher?	*kaifal mudarris?*	كَيْفَ الْمُـدرِّس؟
How is the accountant?	*kaifal muhaasib?*	كَيْفَ الْمُحَاسـب؟
How is the inspector?	*kaifal mufattish?*	كَيْفَ الْمُـفَـتِّـش؟
How is the doctor?	*kaifattabeeb?*	كَيْفَ الطَّـبيب؟
How is the neighbour?	*kaifal jaar?*	كَيْفَ الْجَـار؟
How is the friend?	*kaifassadeeq?*	كَيْفَ الصَّـديق؟
How is the examination?	*kaifal imtihaan?*	كَيْفَ الإمْـتِـحَـان؟
How do you go to office?	*kaifa taruh maktab?*	كَيْفَ تَـرُحْ مَكْـتَـب؟
How do you go to school?	*kaifa taruh madrasa?*	كَيْفَ تَـرُحْ مَـدْرَسَـة؟
How do you go to mosque?	*kaifa taruh masjid?*	كَيْفَ تَـرُحْ مَـسْـجـد؟
How do you go to factory?	*kaifa taruh masna'u?*	كَيْفَ تَـرُحْ مَـصْـنَع؟
How do you go to the club?	*kaifa taruh annaadee?*	كَيْفَ تَـرُحْ الـنَّـادي؟
How do you go to the Cornish?	*kaifa taruh alkoorneesh?*	كَيْفَ تَـرُحْ الْكُورْنيش؟

How does he come from the school? | *kaifa yajee minal madrasa?* | كَيْفَ يَجِيءُ مِنَ الْمَدْرَسَةِ؟

How can I try? | *kaifa uhaawil?* | كَيْفَ أُحَاوِل؟

How can I forget? | *kaifa ansaa?* | كَيْفَ أَنْسٰى؟

How can I ignore? | *kaifa ahmal?* | كَيْفَ أَهْمَل؟

How can I remember? | *kaifa atadakkar?* | كَيْفَ أَتَذَكَّر؟

How can I write? | *kaifa aktub?* | كَيْفَ أَكْتُب؟

How can I read? | *kaifa aqra'u?* | كَيْفَ أَقْرَأ؟

How can I play? | *kaifa al'ab?* | كَيْفَ أَلْعَب؟

How can I walk? | *kaifa amshee?* | كَيْفَ أَمْشِي؟

How can I beat? | *kaifa adhrib?* | كَيْفَ أَضْرِب؟

How can I kill? | *kaifa aqtul?* | كَيْفَ أَقْتُل؟

How can I sit? | *kaifa ajlis?* | كَيْفَ أَجْلِس؟

How can I stand? | *kaifa aqoom?* | كَيْفَ أَقُوم؟

How can I stay here? | *kaifa askun hinee?* | كَيْفَ أَسْكُن هنِي؟

How can I live there? | *kaifa a'eeshu hinaaka?* | كَيْفَ أَعِيشُ هُنَاكَ؟

How did he pass the examination? | *kaifa najaha fil imtihaan?* | كَيْفَ نَجَحَ فِي الإمْتِحَان؟

How did he get the certificate? | *kaifa hassalas shahaada?* | كَيْفَ حَصَّلَ الشَّهَادَة؟

How is life? | *kaifal 'aish?* | كَيْفَ الْعَيش؟

How can I see? | *kaifa araa?* | كَيْفَ أَرٰى؟

How will you contact? | *kaifa tattasil?* | كَيْفَ تَتَّصِل؟

How can I connect this? | *kaifa rakkab haada?* | كَيْفَ رَكَّبَ هٰذَا؟

How can I record this?	*kaifa sajjal haada?*	كَيْفَ سَجِّل هٰذا؟
How can I study?	*kaifa adrus?*	كَيْفَ أَدْرُس؟
How can I teach?	*kaifa udarris?*	كَيْفَ أُدَرِّس؟
How can I memorise?	*kaifa ahfadh?*	كَيْفَ أحْفَظ؟
How can I help?	*kaifa usaa'id?*	كَيْفَ أُسَاعِد؟
How can I complete?	*kaifa ukammil?*	كَيْفَ أُكَمِّل؟

LESSON NINE

WHEN IS YOUR EXAMINATION?

When is your examination?	*mataa imtahaanuka?*	مَتَىٰ إمْتَحَانُكَ؟
When is his test?	*mataa ikhtibaaruhoo?*	مَتَىٰ إخْتِبَارُهُ؟
When does the shop close?	*mataa sakkaral mahal?*	مَتَىٰ سَكَّرَ الْمَحَل؟
When does the school open?	*mataa batalal madrasa?*	مَتَىٰ بَطَّلَ الْمَدْرَسَة؟
When is your marriage?	*mataa ziwaajuka?*	مَتَىٰ زِوَاجُكَ؟
When is your vacation?	*mataa ijaazatuka?*	مَتَىٰ إجَازَتُكَ؟
When is his duty?	*mataa dawaamuhoo?*	مَتَىٰ دَوَامُهُ؟
When can I see?	*mataa ashoofaka?*	مَتَىٰ أشُوفَكَ؟
When shall we go to Delhi?	*mataa naruh dalhee?*	مَتَىٰ نَرُحْ دِلْهِي؟
When will you make the arrangement?	*mataa sawwee tarteeb?*	مَتَىٰ سَوِّي تَرْتِيب؟
When will the manager come?	*mataa yajee almudeer?*	مَتَىٰ يَجِيءُ الْمُدِير؟
When shall we visit Ahmed?	*mataa nazoor Ahmed?*	مَتَىٰ نَزُور أحْمَد؟
When will you go to the zoo?	*mataa taruh ilaa hadeeqatil hayawaanaat?*	مَتَىٰ تَرُح إلَى حَدِيقَة الْحَيَوَانَات؟
When will you buy a car?	*mataa tashtaree sayyaara?*	مَتَىٰ تَشْتَرِي سَيَّارَة؟
When will you give me a party?	*mataa tu'utinee waleema?*	مَتَىٰ تُعْطِنِي وَلِيمَة؟

When will you go to India?	*mataa taruh al hind?*	مَتَى تَرُحْ الْهِنْد؟
When is her interview?	*mataa muqaabalatuhaa?*	مَتَى مُقَابَلَتُهَا؟
When did you get the money?	*mataa hasswaltal fuloos?*	مَتَى حَصَّلْتَ الْفُلُوس؟
When did you see her?	*mataa shuftahaa?*	مَتَى شُفْتَهَا؟
When did you join this company?	*mataa iltahaqta bihaadihi sharika?*	مَتَى الْتَحَقْتَ بِهَذِه الشَّرِكَة؟
When did you contact him?	*mataa ittasalta bihee?*	مَتَى اتَّصَلْتَ بِه؟
When did you sell your car?	*mataa bi'uta sayyaarataka?*	مَتَى بِعْتَ سَيَّارَتَكَ؟
When shall we play football?	*mataa nal'abu kura?*	مَتَى نَلْعَبُ كُرَة؟
When shall we walk together?	*mataa namshee ma'an?*	مَتَى نَمْشِى مَعًا؟
When shall I come to you?	*mataa ajee ilaika?*	مَتَى أجِئ إلَيْكَ؟
When is the take off?	*matal iqlaa'u?*	مَتَى الإقْلاَع؟
When is the landing?	*mataa al hubootw?*	مَتَى الْهُبُوط؟
When is the programme?	*matal barnaamaj?*	مَتَى الْبَرْنَامَج؟
When is the meeting?	*mataal ijtimaa'u?*	مَتَى الإجْتِمَاع؟
When was he appointed?	*mataa uyyina?*	مَتَى عُيِّنَ؟
When did you send him?	*mataa arsaltahoo?*	مَتَى أرْسَلْتَهُ؟
When did you speak to him?	*mataa kallamtahoo?*	مَتَى كَلَّمْتَهُ؟
When did you entrust him?	*mataa sallamtahoo?*	مَتَى سَلَّمْتَهُ؟

When did you help her?	*mataa saa'adtahaa?*	مَـتٰـى سَـاعَـدْتَـهَا؟
When did you travel with him?	*mataa saafarta ma'ahu?*	مَـتٰـى سَـافَـرْتَ مَـعَـهُ؟
When will you pay the fee?	*mataa tadfa'urrusoom?*	مَـتٰـى تَـدْفَـعُ الرُّسُـوم؟
When will you drive your new car?	*mataa tasooq sayyaaratakal jadeeda?*	مَـتٰـى تَـسُـوق سَـيَّارَتَـكَ الْجَـدِيـدَة؟
When shall we have dinner together?	*mataa nata'assha ma'an?*	مَـتٰـى نَـتَـعَـشّٰـى مَـعًـا؟
When did you get the salary?	*mataa hassaltal ma'aash?*	مَـتٰـى حَـصَّـلْتَ الْمَـعَـاش؟
When did you pay the penalty?	*mataa dafa'utal gwaraama?*	مَـتٰـى دَفَـعْـتَ الْغَـرَامَـة؟
When did she come?	*mataa ja'at?*	مَـتٰـى جائت؟
When did he quarell?	*mataa sawwee jinjal*	مَـتٰـى سوِّي جنجال؟
When did you marry he	*mataa tazawwajtaha?*	مَـتٰـى تزوجـتها؟
When did you drop hin	*mataa wadda'etahu?*	مَـتٰـى ودَّعـته؟
When do you ride a bicycle?	*mataa tarkabu ddarraja?*	مَـتٰـى تركب الدرَّاجـة؟

LESSON TEN

WHY ARE YOU LATE?

Why are you late?	*leysh inta muta'akhir?*	لَيْشْ أنْتَ مُتَأخِّر؟
Why is he angry today?	*leysh huwa za'ulaan alyawm?*	لَيْشْ هُوَ زَعْلاَن الْيَوْم؟
Why is he absent today?	*leysh huwa ga'ib alyawm?*	لَيْشْ هُوَ غَائِب الْيَوْم؟
Why are you busy now?	*leysh inti mashgoola alheen?*	لَيْشْ أنْت مَشْغُولَة الْحين؟
Why are you happy?	*leysh inta farhaan?*	لَيْشْ أنْتَ فَرْحَان؟
Why did he go early?	*leysh ruh mubakkir?*	لَيْشْ رُحْ مُبَكِّرًا؟
Why didn't you come yesterday?	*leysh lam tajee ams?*	لَيْشْ لَمْ تَجِئ أمْس؟
Why did you close the door?	*leysh sakkaral baab?*	لَيْشْ سَكَّرَ الْبَاب؟
Why are you tired today?	*leysh inta ta'ubaan alyawm?*	لَيْشْ أنْتَ تَعْبَان الْيَوْم؟
Why didn't you attend the meeting?	*leysh lam tahdhuril hafla?*	لَيْشْ لَمْ تَحْضُرِ الْحَفْلَة؟
Why did he go late?	*leysh ruh muta'akhir?*	لَيْشْ رُحْ مُتَأخِّرًا؟
Why did you finish fast?	*leysh khallaswta sur'a?*	لَيْشْ خَلَّصْتَ سُرْعَة؟
Why are you free today?	*leysh inta fadhee alyawm?*	لَيْشْ أنْتَ فَاضِي الْيَوْم؟

Why did you close the shop today?	*leysh sakkaral mahal alyawm*	لَيْشْ سَكَّرَ الْمَحَل الْيَوْمْ؟
Why did you terminate him from the job?	*leysh fannashtahoo mina shugal?*	لَيْشْ فَنَّشْتَهُ مِنَ الشُّغَلْ؟
Why did you resign from the school?	*leysh istaqalta minal madrasa?*	مِنَ الْمَدْرَسَةِ؟ لَيْشْ إسْتَقَلْتَ
Why did you visit her day before yesterday?	*leysh zurtahaa awwal amsi?*	لَيْشْ زُرْتَهَا أوَّلْ أمْسِ؟
Why are you going to Dubai today?	*leysh ruh Dubai alyawm?*	لَيْشْ رُحْ دُبَي الْيَوْمْ؟
Why is she going today?	*leysh hiya raa'iha alyawm?*	لَيْشْ هِيَ رَائِحَة الْيَوْمْ؟
Why is the banana costly today?	*leysh almawzu gaalee alyawm?*	لَيْشْ الْمَوْزُ غَالِي الْيَوْمْ؟
Why is he not available today?	*leysh huwa gair mawjood alyawm?*	لَيْشْ هُوَ غَيْرْ مَوْجُودْ الْيَوْمْ؟
Why did you switch off the telephone?	*leysh sakkarta ttalafoon?*	لَيْشْ سَكَّرْتَ التَّلَفُون؟
Why did you speak to him about the company?	*leysh kallamtahoo 'anisharika?*	لَيْشْ كَلَّمْتَهُ عَنِ الشَّرِكَة؟
Why did you trouble him?	*leysh az'ajtahoo?*	لَيْشْ أزْعَجْتَهُ؟
Why did you quarrel with him?	*leysh sawwaita jinjaal ma'ahoo?*	لَيْشْ سَوَّيْتَ جِنْجَال مَعَهُ؟
Why did you marry again?	*leysh zawwajta marra thaania?*	لَيْشْ زَوَّجْتَ مَرَّة ثَانِيَة؟

Why did you leave your friend?	*leysh tarakta swadeeqaka?*	لَيْشْ تَرَكْتَ صَدِيقَكَ؟
Why did you promise him?	*leysh wa'adttahoo?*	لَيْشْ وَعَدْتَّهُ؟
Why did you break your promise?	*leysh akhlafta wa'adaka?*	لَيْشْ أَخْلَفْتَ وَعْدَكَ؟
Why do you love her?	*leysh tuhibbuhaa?*	لَيْشْ تُحِبُّهَا؟
Why do you hate him?	*leysh takrahuhoo?*	لَيْشْ تَكْرَهُهُ؟
Why do you help him always?	*leysh tusaa'idu daa'iman?*	لَيْشْ تُسَاعِدُهُ دَائِمًا؟
Why did he come first?	*leysh yajee awwal?*	لَيْشْ يَجِيئ أَوَّلاً؟
Why did you like this?	*leysh sawwaita kadaa?*	لَيْشْ سَوَّيْتَ كَذَا؟
Why do you live here?	*leysh taskun hinee?*	لَيْشْ تَسكن هني؟
Why are you playing now?	*leysh tal'ab al-heen?*	لَيْشْ تلعب الحين؟
Why do you sleep early?	*leysh tanam mubakkir?*	لَيْشْ تنام مُبكرا؟

LESSON ELEVEN

HOW MANY BROTHERS HAVE YOU GOT?

How many brothers have you got?	*kam akhan laka?*	كَمْ أخًا لَكَ؟
How many sisters have you got?	*kam ukhtan laka?*	كَمْ أُخْتًا لَكَ؟
How many pens have you got?	*kam qalaman indaka?*	كَمْ قَلَمًا عِنْدَكَ؟
How many books has he got?	*kam kitaaban indahoo?*	كَمْ كِتَابًا عِنْدَهُ؟
How many bags has she got?	*kam haqeebatan indahaa?*	كَمْ حَقِيبَةً عِنْدَهَا؟
How many pages are there in the book?	*kam swafhatan fil kitaab?*	كَمْ صَفْحَةً فِي الْكِتَابِ؟
Howmany magazines are there in the library?	*kam majalla fil maktaba?*	كَمْ مَجَلَّة فِي الْمَكْتَبَةِ؟
Howmany newspapers are there in your house?	*kam jareeda fee baytika?*	كَمْ جَرِيدَة فِي بَيْتِكَ؟
Howmany pages did you write today?	*kam swafha katabta alyawm?*	كَمْ صَفْحَة كَتَبْتَ الْيَوْم؟
Howmany children has she got?	*kam ibnan lahaa?*	كَمْ إبْنًا لَهَا؟
How many children are there in the ground?	*kam waladan fil mal'ab?*	كَمْ وَلَدًا فِي الْمَلْعَبِ؟
How many teachers are there in the school?	*kam mudarrisan fil madrasa?*	كَمْ مُدَرِّسًا فِي الْمَدْرَسَةِ؟

<table>
<tr><td>Howmany workers are there in your company?</td><td>kam ‘aamilan fee sharikatika?</td><td>كَمْ عَامِلاً فِي شَرِكَتِكَ؟</td></tr>
<tr><td>Howmany doctors are there in the hospital?</td><td>kam twabeeban fil mustashfaa?</td><td>كَمْ طَبِيبًا فِي الْمُسْتَشْفَى؟</td></tr>
<tr><td>How many pilots are there in the flight?</td><td>kam twayyaaran fittaa’ira?</td><td>كَمْ طَيَّارًا فِي الطَّائِرَةِ؟</td></tr>
<tr><td>How many doors are there for the room?</td><td>kam baababn lil gurfa?</td><td>كَمْ بَابًا لِلْغُرْفَةِ؟</td></tr>
<tr><td>How many times do you eat a day?</td><td>kam marra ta’ukulu fil yawm?</td><td>كَمْ مَرَّةً تَأْكُلُ فِي الْيَوْمِ؟</td></tr>
<tr><td>How many days you want?</td><td>kam yawm tabgwi?</td><td>كَمْ يَوْمْ تَبْغِ؟</td></tr>
<tr><td>How many riyals have you got?</td><td>kam riyaalan indaka?</td><td>كَمْ رِيالاً عِنْدَكَ؟</td></tr>
<tr><td>How many accountants are there in your company?</td><td>kam muhaasiban fee sharikatika?</td><td>كَمْ مُحَاسِبًا فِي شَرِكَتِكَ؟</td></tr>
<tr><td>How many engineers are there in your office?</td><td>kam muhandisan fee maktabika?</td><td>كَمْ مُهَنْدِسًا فِي مَكْتَبِكَ؟</td></tr>
<tr><td>How many cars are there in your house?</td><td>kam sayyaara fee baytika?</td><td>كَمْ سَيَّارَةً فِي بَيْتِكَ؟</td></tr>
<tr><td>How many newspapers do you read everyday?</td><td>kam jareeda taqra’u kulla yawm?</td><td>كَمْ جَرِيدَةً تَقْرَأُ كُلَّ يَوْمٍ؟</td></tr>
<tr><td>How many hours do you work daily?</td><td>kam saa’a ta’umal yawmiyyan?</td><td>كَمْ سَاعَةً تَعْمَلُ يَوْمِيًّا؟</td></tr>
</table>

How many hours do you sleep daily?	*kam saa'a tanaamu yawmiyyan?*	كَمْ سَاعَةً تَنَامُ يَوْمِيًّا؟
How many hours do you play?	*kam saa'a tal'ab?*	كَمْ سَاعَةً تَلْعَبُ؟
How many hours do you relax?	*kam saa'a tartaahu?*	كَمْ سَاعَةً تَرْتَاحُ؟
How many hours do you travel?	*kam saa'a tusaafiru?*	كَمْ سَاعَةً تُسَافِرُ؟
How many partners are there in your company?	*kam shareekan fee sharikatika?*	كَمْ شَرِيكًا فِي شَرِكَتِكَ؟
How old are you?	*kam umruka?*	كَمْ عُمْرُكَ؟
How many days are there in a week?	*kam yawman fil usboo'u?*	كَمْ يَوْمًا فِي الأُسْبُوعِ؟
How many months are there in a year?	*kam shahran fissana?*	كَمْ شَهْرًا فِي السَّنَةِ؟
How many cows are there in the field?	*kam baqaratan fil haql?*	كَمْ بَقَرَةً فِي الْحَقْلِ؟
How many days did you work here?	*kam yawman 'amilta hinee?*	كَمْ يَوْمًا عَمِلْتَ هِنِي؟
How many houses did you buy?	*kam baytan ishtarayta?*	كَمْ بَيْتًا إِشْتَرَيْتَ؟
How many hours did you wait for him?	*kam saa'a intadhartahoo?*	كَمْ سَاعَةً إِنْتَظَرْتَهُ؟
How many plants did you plant in the garden?	*kam nabaatan garasta fil hadeeqa?*	كَمْ نَبَاتًا غَرَسْتَ فِي الْحَدِيقَةِ؟

LESSON TWELVE

HOW MUCH IS THIS BOOK?

How much is this book?	*kam haadal kitaab?*	كَمْ هٰـذَا الْكِـتَـاب؟
How much is this pen?	*kam haadal qalam?*	كَمْ هٰـذَا الْقَلَم؟
How much is this watch?	*kam haadihi ssaa'a?*	كَمْ هٰـذِهِ السَّـاعَـة؟
How much is the rent?	*kam al eejaar?*	كَمْ الإِيجَـار؟
How much is the penalty?	*kam al garaama?*	كَمْ الْغَـرَامَـة؟
How much is this car?	*bikam haadihis-sayyaara?*	بِـكَمْ هٰـذِهِ السَّـيَّارَة؟
How much is this house?	*bikam haadihil bayt?*	بِـكَمْ هٰـذَا الْبَـيْت؟
How much is this bag?	*bikam haadihil haqeeba?*	بِكَمْ هٰذِهِ الْحَقِيبَـة؟
How much do you spend everyday?	*kam tunfiq kulla yawm?*	كَمْ تُـنْفـِقْ كُلَّ يَـوْم؟
How much do you promise, but you don't fulfil your promise?	*kam ta'id walaa tafee?*	كَمْ تَـعِـدْ وَلاَ تَـفِـي؟
How much did you get?	*kam hasswalta?*	كَمْ حَـصَّـلْتَ؟
How much do you love her?	*kam tuhibbuha?*	كَمْ تُـحِـبُّـهَا؟
How much will you get?	*kam tanaal?*	كَمْ تَـنَال؟
How much will you give?	*kam tu'utwee?*	كَمْ تُـعْـطِي؟
How long will you stay here?	*kam tabqaa hinee?*	كَمْ تَـبْـقَى هِـنِي؟

How much will you suffer?	*kam tu'aanee?*	كَمْ تُعَانِي؟
How much will you see?	*kam taraa?*	كَمْ تَرىٰ؟
How much will you forget?	*kam tansaa?*	كَمْ تَنْسىٰ؟
How much will you memorise?	*kam tahfadh?*	كَمْ تَحْفَظْ؟
How much do you desire?	*kam targab?*	كَمْ تَرْغَبْ؟
How much will you carry?	*kam tahmil?*	كَمْ تَحْمِلْ؟
How much do you care?	*kam tar'aa?*	كَمْ تَرْعىٰ؟
How much is this?	*kam haada?*	كَمْ هٰذَا؟
What is the last price?	*aakhir kam?*	آخِرْ كَمْ؟
What is the discount?	*khasm kam?*	خَصْمْ كَمْ؟
What time is the meeting?	*saa'a kam al ijtimaa'u?*	سَاعَة كَمْ الإجْتِمَاعْ؟
What time is the dinner?	*saa'a kam al 'asha'u?*	سَاعَة كَمْ الْعَشَآء؟
What time is the interview?	*saa'a kam al muqaabala?*	سَاعَة كَمْ الْمُقَابَلَة؟
What time is the flight?	*saa'a kam attaa'ira?*	سَاعَة كَمْ الطَّائِرَة؟
What time is the reception?	*saa'a kam al istiqbaal?*	سَاعَة كَمْ الإسْتِقْبَال؟
What time is the farewell?	*saa'a kam al widaa'u?*	سَاعَة كَمْ الْوِدَاع
What time is the exhibition?	*saa'a kam al ma'uradh?*	سَاعَة كَمْ الْمَعْرِض؟
What time is the appointment?	*saa'a kam al maw'id?*	سَاعَة كَمْ الْمَوْعِد؟

What time is the discussion?	*saa'a kam al munaaqasha?*	سَاعَة كَمْ الْمُنَاقَشَة؟
What time do you go office?	*saa'a kam taruh maktab?*	سَاعَة كَمْ تَرُحْ مَكْتَب؟
What time do you return?	*saa'a kam tarji'u?*	سَاعَة كَمْ تَرْجِع؟
What time does the office close?	*saa'a kam sakkaral maktab?*	سَاعَة كَمْ سَكَّر الْمَكْتَب؟
What time does he finish job?	*saa'a kam khallasa shugwal?*	سَاعَة كَمْ خَلَّصَ الشُّغْل؟
What time will he come?	*saa'a kam yajee?*	سَاعَة كَمْ يَجِيء؟
What time did he speak?	*saa'a kam kallama?*	سَاعَة كَمْ كَلَّمَ؟
What time did you contact him?	*saa'a kam ittasalta bihee?*	سَاعَة كَمْ اتَّصَلْتَ بِه؟
What time did you visit her?	*saa'a kam zurtahaa?*	سَاعَة كَمْ زُرْتَهَا؟
What time will the doctor come?	*saa'a kam yajee attabeeb?*	سَاعَة كَمْ يَجِيئ الطَّبِيب؟
What time will the manager come?	*saa'a kam yajee almudeer?*	سَاعَة كَمْ يَجِيئ الْمُدِير؟
What time does he get up?	*saa'a kam yaqoom?*	سَاعَة كَمْ يَقُوم؟
What time does he sleep?	*saa'a kam yanaam?*	سَاعَة كَمْ يَنَام؟
What time does he eat?	*saa'a kam ya'ukul?*	سَاعَة كَمْ يَأْكُل؟
What time does he play?	*saa'a kam yal'ab?*	سَاعَة كَمْ يَلْعَب؟
What time will you come to me?	*saa'a kam tajee ilayya?*	سَاعَة كَمْ تَجِيئ إِلَيَّ؟
What time will you pay the amount?	*saa'a kam tadfa'ul mablagwu?*	سَاعَة كَمْ تَدْفَعُ الْمَبْلَغ؟

What time does the shop close?	*saa'a kam sakkaral mahal?*	سَاعَة كَمْ سَكَّرَ الْمَحَل؟
What time will you go to the ground?	*saa'a kam taruh ilal maydaan?*	سَاعَة كَمْ تَرُحْ إلَى الْمَيدَان؟
What time is the cultural programme?	*saa'a kam al barnamajuth-thaqaafee?*	سَاعَة كَمْ الْبَرْنَامَجُ الثَّقَافِي؟
What time is the tournament?	*saa'a kam al mubaaraat?*	سَاعَة كَمْ الْمُبَارَات؟
What time is the competition?	*saa'a kam al musaabaqa?*	سَاعَة كَمْ الْمُسَابَقَة؟
What time do you go to school?	*saa'a kam taruh madrasa?*	سَاعَة كَمْ تَرُحْ مَدْرَسَة؟
What time do you go to cornish?	*saa'a kam taruh koorneesh?*	سَاعَة كَمْ تَرُحْ كُورْنِيش؟
What time do you go to the club?	*saa'a kam taruh ila nnaadee?*	سَاعَة كَمْ تَرُحْ إلَى النَّادِي؟
What time do you go to the restaurant?	*saa'a kam taruh ilal mat'am?*	سَاعَة كَمْ تَرُحْ إلَى الْمَطْعَم؟
What time do you take bath?	*saa'a kam taghtasil?*	سَاعَة كَمْ تَغْتَسِل؟
What time will you contact her?	*saa'a kam tattaswil biha?*	سَاعَة كَمْ تَتَّصِلْ بِهَا؟
What time is the train?	*saa'a kam al qitaar?*	سَاعَة كَمْ الْقِطَار؟
What time is the bus?	*saa'a kam al baas?*	سَاعَة كَمْ الْبَاص؟
What time shall we reach India?	*saa'a kam nasil al hind?*	سَاعَة كَمْ نَصِلْ الْهِنْد؟

LESSON THIRTEEN
MAY I HELP YOU?

May I help you?	*mumkin usaa'iduka?*	مُـمْـكِنْ أُسَـاعِـدُكَ؟
Can you try for me?	*mumkin tuhaawil lee?*	مُـمْـكِنْ تُـحَـاوِلْ لِى؟
Can you try for me once more?	*mumkin tuhaawil lee marra thaaniya*	مُـمْـكِنْ تُـحَـاوِلْ لِي مَـرَّة ثَانِيَـة؟
Can you drop me home?	*mumkin khallinee bayt?*	مُـمْـكِنْ خَـلِّنِى بَـيْت؟
Can you drop me at the school?	*mumkin kallinee almadrasa?*	مُـمْـكِنْ خَـلِّنِي الْـمَـدْرَسَـة؟
Can you drop him at the airport?	*mumkin khallihil mataar?*	مُـمْـكِنْ خَـلِّه الْـمَـطَار؟
Can you come to me tomorrow?	*mumkin ta'tinee bukra?*	مُـمْـكِنْ تَـأْتِـنِي بُـكْرَة؟
Can you make the arrangement?	*mumkin sawwee tarteeb?*	مُـمْـكِنْ سَـوِّي تَـرْتِـيب؟
Can you talk to him?	*mumkin tukallimuhoo?*	مُـمْـكِنْ تُـكَـلِّـمُـه؟
Can you finish it today?	*mumkin khallisil yawm?*	مُـمْـكِنْ خَـلِّص الْـيَـوْم؟
Can I come with you?	*mumkin ajee ma'aka?*	مُـمْـكِنْ أجِـى مَـعَـكَ؟
Can I speak to the manager?	*mumkin ukallimal mudeer?*	مُـمْـكِنْ أُكَـلِّمَ الْـمُـدِيـر؟
Can I go with her?	*mumkin aruh ma'ahaa?*	مُـمْـكِنْ أرُح مَـعَـهَا؟
Can we visit him today?	*mumkin nazooruhul yawm?*	مُـمْـكِنْ نَـزُورُهُ الْـيَـوْم؟
Can you give me 100 Dollars?	*mumkin tu'utinee mi'a doolar?*	مُـمْـكِنْ تُـعْـطِـينى مـائَـة دُولاَر؟

Can we play football today?	*mumkin nal'ab kura alyawm?*	مُمْكِنْ نَلْعَبْ كُرَةَ الْيَوْمْ؟
Can we go together?	*mumkin naruh ma'an?*	مُمْكِنْ نَرُحْ مَعًا؟
Can I stay with you?	*mumkin askun ma'aka?*	مُمْكِنْ اسْكُنْ مَعَكَ؟
Can I go now?	*mumkin aruh alheen?*	مُمْكِنْ أرُحْ الْحِينْ؟
Can I see you today?	*mumkin ashoofakal yawm?*	مُمْكِنْ أشُفَكَ الْيَوْمْ؟
Can you replace this?	*mumkin baddal haada?*	مُمْكِنْ بَدِّلْ هٰذَا؟
Can you ask her?	*mumkin tas'alhaa?*	مُمْكِنْ تَسْأَلْهَا؟
Can you help him?	*mumkin tusaa'idhu?*	مُمْكِنْ تُسَاعِدْهُ؟
Can you give me special discount?	*mumkin tu'utwinee khasm khas?*	مُمْكِنْ تُعْطِنِي خَصْمْ خَاصّْ؟
Can you send it now?	*mumkin tursil haada alheen?*	مُمْكِنْ تُرْسِل هٰذَا الْحِينْ؟
Can you see me after some time?	*mumkin taraanee ba'ada shuway?*	مُمْكِنْ تَرَانِي بَعْدَ شُوَيْ؟
Can you come afterwards?	*mumkin tajee ba'adayn?*	مُمْكِنْ تَجِئْ بَعْدَيْنْ؟
Can you call after some time?	*mumkin tattasil ba'ada shuway?*	مُمْكِنْ تَتَّصِلْ بَعْدَ شُوَيْ؟
Can you write to him now?	*mumkin taktub lahoo alheen?*	مُمْكِنْ تَكْتُبْ لَهُ الْحِينْ؟
Can you send him now?	*mumkin tursilhu alheen?*	مُمْكِنْ تُرْسِلْهُ الْحِينْ؟
Can you drive?	*mumkin tasooq?*	مُمْكِنْ تَسُوقْ؟

He might come	*mumkin yajee*	مُـمْـكِنْ يَجِـيء
He might go	*mumkin yaruh*	مُـمْـكِنْ يَرُوحْ
He might get	*mumkin hassal*	مُـمْـكِنْ حَـصَّـلْ
He might win	*mumkin yanjah*	مُـمْـكِنْ يَنْجَـحْ
He might agree	*mumkin yuwaafiq*	مُـمْـكِنْ يُوافِـق
He might give up	*mumkin yatruk*	مُـمْـكِنْ يَـتْـرُكْ
He might protect	*mumkin yahfadh*	مُـمْـكِنْ يَحْـفَـظْ
He might escape	*mumkin yaslam*	مُـمْـكِنْ يَسْلَمْ
He might finish	*mumkin khallas*	مُـمْـكِنْ خَـلَّصْ
He might get angry	*mumkin yagwdhab*	مُـمْـكِنْ يَغْـضَـبْ
He might travel	*mumkin yusaafir*	مُـمْـكِنْ يُسَـافِـرْ
He might come back now	*mumkiŋ yarji'u al heen*	مُـمْـكِنْ يَرْجِـعُ الْحِـين
The manager might come today	*mumkin yajee almudeeru alyawm*	مُـمْـكِنْ يَجِـيء الْمُـدِيرُ الْيَـوْمْ
We might get the salary today	*mumkin nahsil alma'aash alyawm*	مُـمْـكِنْ نَـحْـصِـلْ الْمَـعَـاشْ الْيَـوْمْ
He might give you a prize	*mumkin yu'uteeka jaa'iza*	مُـمْـكِنْ يُعْـطِـيكَ جَـائِـزَة
He might go first	*mumkin yaruh awwalan*	مُـمْـكِنْ يَرُوحْ أَوَّلاً
He might speak to you today	*mumkin yukallimaka alyawm*	مُـمْـكِنْ يُكَلِّـمَـكَ الْيَـوْم
He might give up this project	*mumkin yatruk haada almashroo'u*	مُـمْـكِنْ يَـتْـرُكْ هٰـذَا الْمَـشْـرُوع

LESSON FOURTEEN

PLEASE CLOSE THE DOOR

Please close the door	*sakkaral baab min fadhlika*	سَكَّرَ الْبَاب مِنْ فَضْلِكَ
Please give me this	*min fadhlika a'utinee haada*	مِنْ فَضْلِكَ أَعْطِنِى هٰذَا
Please make it fast	*min fadhlika sawwee sur'a*	مِنْ فَضْلِكَ سَوِّي سُرْعَةَ
Please send him to the manager	*min fadhlika arsilhu ilal mudeer*	مِنْ فَضْلِكَ أرسِلْه إِلَى الْمُدِيرَ
Please repeat the words	*min fadhlika karriril kalaam*	مِنْ فَضْلِكَ كَرِّرِ الْكَلاَمِ
Please teach him good manners	*min fadhlika allimhul aadaab*	مِنْ فَضْلِكَ عَلِّمْهُ الآدَابَ
Please speak to him today	*min fadhlika kallimhul yawm*	مِنْ فَضْلِكَ كَلِّمْهُ الْيَومْ
Please do not raise your voice	*min fadhlika laa tarfa'u sawtaka*	مِنْ فَضْلِكَ لاَ تَرْفَعْ صَوْتَكَ
Please keep your promise	*min fadhlika ihfadh wa'udaka*	مِنْ فَضْلِكَ احْفَظ وَعْدَك
Please give me a chance	*min fadhlika a'utwinee furswa*	مِنْ فَضْلِكَ أَعْطِني فُرْصَةَ
Please feed the poor	*min fadhlika at'imil fuqaraa'u*	مِنْ فَضْلِكَ أَطْعِمِ الْفُقَرآء

Please give me one more chance.	*min fadhlika a'utwinee furswa ukhraa*	مِنْ فَضْلِكَ أَعْطِنِي فُرْصَةً أُخْرَى
Please drop him at the airport	*min fadhlika khallihee fil matwar*	مِنْ فَضْلِكَ خَلِّهِ فِي الْمَطَار
Please switch off the AC	*min fadhlika bannadil kandeeshan*	مِنْ فَضْلِكَ بَنِّدْ الْكَنْدِيشَن
Please switch on the AC	*min fadhlika shagilil kandeeshan*	مِنْ فَضْلِكَ شَغِّلِ الْكَنْدِيشَن
Please reserve a room for him in a nice hotel	*min fadhlika ahjiz lahu gwurfa fee funduq zain*	مِنْ فَضْلِكَ أَحْجِزْ لَهُ غُرْفَة فِي فُنْدُق زَيْن
Please reserve a ticket for him	*min fadhlika ahjiz lahu tadkira*	مِنْ فَضْلِكَ أَحْجِزْ لَهُ تَذْكِرَة
Please drop the children at the school	*min fadhlika waddi'il awlaad fil madrasa*	مِنْ فَضْلِكَ وَدِّعِ الأَوْلاَد فِي الْمَدْرَسَة
Please respect the elders	*min fadhlika ihtarim alkibaar*	مِنْ فَضْلِكَ إِحْتَرِم الْكِبَار
Please leave me today	*min fadhlika khallinee alyawm*	مِنْ فَضْلِكَ خَلِّنِي الْيَوْم

LESSON FIFTEEN

WHICH DAY YOU PREFER?

Which?	*ayyu?*	أيُّ؟
Which day do you prefer?	*ayyu yawm tufadhil?*	أيَّ يَوْم تُفَضِّلْ؟
Which day is this?	*ayyu yawm haada?*	أيَّ يَوْم هٰذَا؟
Which country is this?	*ayyu baladin haada?*	أيَّ بَلَد هٰذَا؟
Which company is this?	*ayyu sharikatin haadihee?*	أيَّ شَرِكَة هٰذِه؟
Which book do you want?	*ayyu kitaab tabgi?*	أيُّ كِتَابً تَبْغِ؟
Which market do you go to?	*ayyu sooq taruh?*	أيَّ سُوق تَرُحْ؟
Which one do you buy?	*ayyu waahid tashtaree?*	أيَّ وَاحِد تَشْتَرِي؟
Which magazine do you read?	*ayyu majalla taqra'u?*	أيَّ مَجَلَّة تَقْرَأَ؟
Which city do you like?	*ayyu madeena tuhibb?*	أيَّ مَدِينَة تُحِبُّ؟
Which profession do you select?	*ayyu mihna takhtaar?*	أيَّ مِهْنَة تَخْتَار؟
Which nationality does he want?	*ayyu jinsiyya yabgi?*	أيَّ جِنْسِيَّة يَبْغِ؟
Which newspaper do you read everyday?	*ayyu jareeda taqra'u kulla yawm?*	أيَّ جَرِيدَة تَقْرَأ كُلَّ يَوْم؟
Which one does she want?	*ayyu wahid tabgi?*	أيَّ وَاحِد تَبْغِ؟
Which one is better?	*ayyuhumaa ahsan?*	أيُّهُمَا أحْسَن؟
Which village do you live in?	*fee ayyi qarya taskun?*	فِي أيِّ قَرْيَة تَسْكُن؟

In which college do you study?	*fee ayyi kulliya tadrus?*	فِي أيِّ كُلِّيَّة تَدْرُس؟
In which company do you work?	*fee ayyi sharika tashtagil?*	فِي أيِّ شَرِكَة تَشْتَغِل؟
In which room do you sleep?	*fee ayyi gurfa tanaam?*	فِي أيِّ غُرْفَة تَنَام؟
In which school do you teach?	*fee ayyi madrasa tudarris?*	فِي أيِّ مَدْرَسَة تُدَرِّس؟
Which area do you live in?	*fee ayyi mintaqa taskun?*	فِي أيِّ مِنْطَقَة تَسْكُنْ؟
Which book are you reading now?	*ayyi kitaab taqra'u alheen?*	أيَّ كِتَاب تَقْرَأ اَلْحِينْ؟
In which car had she gone?	*fee ayyi sayyaara raahat?*	فِي أيِّ سَيَّارَة رَاحَتْ؟
Which hospital do you go to?	*ayya mustashfaa taruh?*	أيَّ مُسْتَشْفَى تَرُحْ؟
Which language do you like?	*ayyu luga tuhibb?*	أيَّ لُغَة تُحِبُّ؟
Which colour did you select?	*ayya lawn takhtaar?*	أيَّ لَوْن تَخْتَار؟
Which chapter do you memorise?	*ayya soora tahfadh?*	أيَّ سُورَة تَحْفَظ؟
Which lesson are you studying now?	*ayya dars tadrus alheen?*	أيَّ دَرس تَدْرُسُ الْحِين؟
In which bank do you have account?	*fee ayyi bank indaka hisaab?*	فِي أيِّ بَنْك عِنْدَكَ حِسَاب؟
Which flight do you travel in?	*fee ayyi taa'ira tusaafir?*	فِي أيِّ طائِرَة تُسَافِرُ؟
Which country do you go to?	*ila ayya baladin taruh?*	إِلَى أيَّ بَلَدٍ تَرُح؟

You will get anything you want	*hassalta ayya shay tabgwi?*	حَصَّلْتَ أيَّ شَيْئ تَبْغِ
Which team has won?	*ayyalfareeqayn najaha?*	أيَّ الْفَرِيقَيْن نَجَحَ؟
Which chair has been broken?	*ayya kursee kassar?*	أيَّ كُرْسَي كَسَّر؟
Which building has collapsed?	*ayya mabna inhadam?*	أيَّ مَبْنٰى إنْهَدَم؟

LESSON SIXTEEN

IF YOU DON'T MIND, CLOSE THE DOOR

If you don't mind, close the door	*law samahta sakkiril baab*	لَوْ سَمَحْت سَكِّر الْبَابَ
If you don't mind, come here	*law samahta ta'aal hinee?*	لَوْ سَمَحْت تَعَالْ . هني
If you don't mind, drop her at home	*law samahta waddi'uhal bayt*	لَوْ سَمَحْت وَدِّعْهَا الْبَيْت
If you don't mind, leave me today	*law samahta khallinee alyawm*	لَوْ سَمَحْت خَلِّني الْيَوْم
If you don't mind, pay the fee today	*law samahta idfa'irrusoom alyawm*	لَوْ سَمَحْت إدْفَع الرُّسُومَ الْيَوْمْ
If you don't mind, come tomorrow	*law samahta ta'aal bukra*	لَوْ سَمَحْت تَعَالْ بُكْرَة
If you don't mind, make it fast	*law samahta sawwee sur'ah*	لَوْ سَمَحْت سَوِّي سُرْعَة
If you don't mind, speak to him today	*law samahta kallimhul yawm*	لَوْ سَمَحْت كَلِّمْهُ الْيَوم
If you don't mind, give your car to him for one day	*law samahta a'utihee sayyaarataka liyawm*	لَوْ سَمَحْت أعْطه سَيَّارَتَكَ لِيَوْم
If you don't mind, give me a copy	*law samahta a'utwinee nuskha*	لَوْ سَمَحْت أعْطني نُسْخَة
If you don't mind, take her to a doctor	*law samahta khudhaa ilaa twabeeb*	لَوْ سَمَحْت خُذْهَا إلى طَبِيب

LESSON SEVENTEEN

SOME USEFUL EXPRESSIONS

How are you? *kaifal hal / kaifa halak / kaifak / shlonak / shakhbarak*

كَيْفَ الْحَال/ كَيْفَ حَالَكْ/ كَيْفَكْ/ شْلُونَكْ/ شَخْبَارَكْ؟

Good, Well, Fine, Perfect, All right, Praise be to Allah

bikhair/ thayyib/ zayn/ kuwayyis/ tamam/ mathboot/ alhamdu lillah

بِخَيْرْ/ طَيِّبْ/ زَيْنْ/ كُوَيْس/ تَمَام/ مَثْبُوت/ اَلْحَمْدُ لله

Peace be upon you	*assalamu Alaikum*	اَلسَّلاَمُ عَلَيْكُم
Peace and mercy of Allah be upon you too	*wa alaikumussalam wa rahmatullah*	وَعَلَيْكُمُ السَّلاَم وَرَحْمَةُ الله
Good morning	*sabahal khair*	صَبَاحَ الْخَيْر
Good morning (rep.)	*sabahannoor*	صَبَاحَ النُّور
Good evening	*masa'al khair*	مَسَآءَ الْخَيْر
Good evening	*masa'annoor*	مَسَآءَ النُّور
Never mind	*ma laysh*	مَا لَيْش
No problem	*ma fee mushkil*	مَا فِي مُشْكِل
Tired	*ta'eban*	تَعْبَان
Active / Smart	*shatir / nasheet*	شَاطِر/ نَشِيط
Industrious/Hard working	*mujtahid*	مُجْتَهِد
If you dont mind	*law samaht*	لَوْ سَمَحْت
Please	*min fadlik*	مِنْ فَضْلك
Excuse me	*afwan / samihnee*	عَفْواً/ سَامِحْنِي
(Hello) Welcome	*marhaba*	مَرْحَبًا
(Hello) Welcome (rep.)	*marhabatayn*	مَرْحَبَتَين
Welcome	*ahlan*	اَهْلاً

Welcome (rep.)	*ahlan wa sahlan*	اَهْـلاً وَسَـهْلاً
I will see you tomorrow	*ashoofak bukra*	اَشُـوفَـك بُـكْرَةً
I will see you later	*ashoofak ba'adyn*	اَشُـوفَـك بَـعْـدَيْن
May Allah save you	*allah yusallimak*	اَلله يُسَـلِّـمَـك
May Allah save you	*allah khalleek*	اَلله خَـلِّـيـك
May Allah protect you	*allah yahfadka*	اَلله يَحْـفَـظُـك
May Allah be pleased with you	*allah yarda alaika*	اَلله يَرْضَـى عَـلَيْـك
May Allah cure you	*allah yashfeek/ shafakallah*	اَلله يَشْـفِـيـك/ شَـفَـاكَ الله
May Allah give you good reward	*jazakallah khair*	جَـزَاكَ الله خَـيْراً
May Allah bless you	*barakallah feek*	بَارَكَ الله فِـيـك
May Allah give you relief	*allah yu'eteekal afiya*	اَلله يُعْـطِـيـكَ الْعَـافِـيَة
May Allah accept	*taqabbalallah*	تَـقَبَّـلَ الله
May Allah be merciful to your parents	*allah yarham walidayk*	اَلله يِرحَـم وَالِدَيْـك
God willing	*insha allah*	انْ شَـاءَ الله
Call afterwards	*ittasil ba'edayn*	اَتَّـصَـل بَـعْـدَيْن
Call after some time	*ittasil ba'eda shuway*	اتَّـصَـل بَـعْـدَ شُـوَي
Wait a little	*intadir shuway*	انْـتَـظِر شُـوَي
Thank you for calling	*shukran alattisalik*	شُـكْرًا عَلَى اتِّـصَـالك
This number is temporarily out of service	*hadarraqmu mawqoof muwaqqatan*	هٰـذَا الرَّقَـمُ مَـوْقُوف مُؤَقَّـتًـا
His line is busy	*khattuhu mashgool*	خَـطُّهُ مَـشْـغُـول

Please come	*faddal / tafaddal*	فَضَّل / تَفَضَّل
Come here	*ta'al hinee*	تَعَال هني
Come tomorrow	*ta'al bukra*	تَعَال بُكْرَة
Come afterwards	*ta'al ba'edayn*	تَعَال بَعْدَيْن
Please take your seat	*istarih*	اسْتَرِح
Go	*ruh*	رُحْ
Go up	*ruh fouq*	رُحْ فَوْق
Go down	*ruh taht*	رُحْ تَحْت
Go to the airport	*ruh matar*	رُحْ مَطَار
Go afterwards	*ruh ba'edayn*	رُحْ بَعْدَين
Go tomorrow	*ruh bukra*	رُحْ بُكْرَة
Go to the passport office	*ruh jawazat*	رُحْ جَوَازَات
Go to the hospital	*ruh mustashfa*	رُحْ مُسْتَشْفَى
Congratulations	*mabrook*	مَبْرُوك
Thousand congratulations	*alf mabrook*	الف مبروك
Be fast / Quick	*ya allah sur'a*	يَا اَلله سُرْعَة
Get lost	*ya allah barra*	يَا اَلله بَرًّا
Do you know Arabic?	*inta araf arabi?*	انْتَ عَرَف عَرَبِي؟
I know little	*araf shuway shuway*	عَرَف شُوَي شُوَي
Do you understand Arabic?	*tafhamu arabi*	تَفْهَم عَرَبي
Yes, I know/Yes, I understand	*iy araf /iy afhamu*	أيّ عَرَف/ أيّ أفْهَم
Wish you all the best	*atamanna laka kullal khair*	أتَمَنّى لَكَ كُلَّ الْخَيْر
Wish you good health and well being	*atamanna laka ssihha wal afiya*	أتَمَنّى لَكَ الصِّحَّة وَالْعَافِيَة

I don't know	*ana ma araf*	أَنَا مَا عَرَف
Can I help you	*mumkin usa'edak?*	مُمْكِن أُسَاعِدك؟
As you wish/As you like it	*ala kaifak*	عَلَى كَيْفَك
Of course	*tab'an*	طَبْعًا
Let me see it	*khallinee shuf / da'enee ara*	خَلِّنِي شُف/ دَعنِي أرى
Please wait	*yurja al intidar*	يُرْجَى الإنْتِظَار
No entry	*mamnu'u ddukhool*	مَمْنُوع الدُّخُول
No parking	*mamnu'ul wuqoof*	مَمْنُوع الْوُقُوف
No overtaking	*mamnu'u ttajawuz*	مَمْنُوع التَّجَاوَز
No smoking	*mamnu'u ttadkheen*	مَمْنُوع التَّدْخِين
No touching	*mamnu'u llams*	مَمْنُوع اللَّمْس
No sitting	*mamnu'ul juloos*	مَمْنُوع الْجُلُوس
No exit	*mamnu'ul khurooj*	مَمْنُوع الْخُرُوج
No talking	*mamnu'ul kalam*	مَمْنُوع الْكَلَام
No eating	*mamnu'ul akl*	مَمْنُوع الأكْل
No spitting	*mamnu'ul basaq*	مَمْنُوع الْبَصَق
Can you try for me?	*mumkin tuhawil lee?*	مُمْكِنْ تُحَاوِل لي؟
Can you help me?	*mumkin tusa'ednee*	مُمْكِنْ تُسَاعِدْنِي؟
Happy new year	*kulla aam wa antum bi khair*	كُلَّ عَام وأَنْتُم بِخَيْر
Happy new year (rep.)	*kulla sana tayyib*	كُلَّ سَنَة طَيِّب
Eid greetings	*eidukum mubarak / eid mubarak*	عِيدكُمْ مُبَارَكْ/ عَيدْ مُبَارَكْ
This is not nice	*hada mub zayn*	هَذَا مُب زَيْن
He is an expert	*huwa khabeer*	هُوَ خَبِير

We are going to the park	*naruh ilal hadeeqa*	نَرُحْ إِلَى الْحَـدِيقَة
Give me a tea/ Bring tea	*a'utinee shay / jub shay*	أَعْـطني شَـاي/ جـب شَـاي
I don't have time	*maa 'indee waqt*	مَـا عِـنْدي وَقْت
My wife is a teacher	*zawjatee mudarrisa*	زَوْجَـتِـي مُـدَرِّسَـة
His son is a doctor	*ibnuhu twabeeb*	إبـنُهُ طَـبِـيب
Her father is an engineer	*abooha muhandis*	أَبُـوهَـا مُـهَنْدس
His office is near	*maktabuhu qareeb*	مَـكْـتَـبُـهُ قَرِيب
Our car is new	*sayyaaratuna jadeeda*	سَـيَّارَتُـنَا جَـدِيدَة
The manager is coming	*almudeeru yaji / almudeeru jaa'in*	الْمُـدِيرُ يَجِيئ/ الْمُـدِيرُ جَـاء
We have a party today	*'indanaa hafla alyawm*	عِـنْدَنَا حَـفْـلَة الْيَوْم
They have a party tomorrow	*'indahum hafla bukra*	عِـنْدَهُـمْ حَـفْـلَة بُـكْرَة
He is smart	*huwa shaatir*	هُوَ شَـاطِر
Sorry, I am not free	*aasif ana mush fadhee*	آسِـفْ، أَنَا مُـشْ فَـاضِـي
Sorry I am busy	*aasif ana mashghool*	آسِـفْ، أَنَا مَـشْـغُـول
I request your approval	*arjoo muwafaqatukum*	أَرْجُـو مُـوَافَـقَـتُـكُم
Take a tablet three times a day	*khud habba thalaatha marrat fil yawm*	خُـذْ حَـبَّـة ثَلاَثَ مَـرَّات فِي الْيَوْم
After food or before food	*ba'udal akli aw qablahu*	بَـعْـدَ الأَكْل أَوْ قَبْـلَهُ
I am busy throughout	*ana mashgool alattool*	أَنَا مَـشْـغُـول عَـلَى الطُّولُ
Let us go there	*khalli naruh hunaka*	خَـلِّ نَرُحْ هُـنَاكُ

Please drop me at the Airport	*min fadhlika khallini almataar*	مِنْ فَضْلِكَ خَلِّنِي المَطَار
Please give me time	*min fadhlika a'utinee waqt*	مِنْ فَضْلِكَ أَعْطِنِي وَقْتُ
Please write a letter to him today	*min fadhlika uktub lahu khitab alyawm*	مِنْ فَضْلِكَ أُكْتُبْ لَهُ خِطَاب الْيَوْم
Please take rest for a while	*min fadhlika istarih shuwai*	مِنْ فَضْلِكَ اسْتَرِحْ شُوَي
Please give me the invoice / bill	*min fadhlika a'tinee alfaatoora*	مِنْ فَضْلِكَ أَعْطِنِي الْفَاتُورَة
Please go after an hour	*min fadhlika ruh ba'ada saa'a*	مِنْ فَضْلِكَ رُحْ بَعْدَ سَاعَة
Please speak to the manager	*min fadhlika kallimil mudeer*	مِنْ فَضْلِكَ كَلِّم الْمُدِير
Please reduce your sound	*min fadhlika ikhfidh swatak*	مِنْ فَضْلِكَ إِخْفِضْ صَوْتَك
Please take this from here	*min fadhlika khud haada min hinee*	مِنْ فَضْلِكَ خُذْ هٰذَا مِنْ هِنِي
If you don't mind, check the invoice	*min fadhlika fattishil faatoora*	مِنْ فَضْلِكَ فَتِّش الْفَاتُورَة
If you don't mind, repeat the words	*min fadhlika karriril kalaam*	مِنْ فَضْلِكَ كَرِّر الْكَلَام
If you don't mind, think again	*min fadhlika fakkir marra ukhra*	مِنْ فَضْلِكَ فَكِّر مَرَّة أُخْرٰى
If you don't mind, make arrangement	*min fadhlika sawwee tarteeb*	مِنْ فَضْلِكَ سَوِّي تَرْتِيب
If you don't mind, find out a housemaid for him	*min fadhlika awjid lahu khaadima*	مِنْ فَضْلِكَ أَوْجِدْ لَه خَادِمَة

I am in a hurry	*ana musta'ujil*	أنَا مُسْتَعْجِل
I am sick / I am tired	*ana mareedh / ana ta'ubaan*	أنَا مَريض/ أنَا تَعْبَان
He is very busy	*huwa mashgool wajid*	هُوَ مَشْغُول وَاجد
This is wonderful	*hada jameel*	هذا جميل
I will be right back	*sa arjiu halan*	سأرجع حالاً
I lost my way	*Adaetu tareeqee*	اضعت طريقي
You are kind	*Inta lateef*	انت لطيف
I have to go now	*Yajibu an adhhabal heen*	يجب أن أذهب الحين

LESSON EIGHTEEN
TRANSLATION PRACTICE

Do you go to school everyday? — *hal tadhabu ilal madrasati kulla yawm* — هَلْ تَذْهَبُ إِلَى الْمَدْرَسَةَ كُلَّ يَومْ؟

This boy has passed the exam — *qad najaha haadal waladu fil imtihaan* — قَدْ نَجَحَ هٰذَا الْوَلَدُ فِى الإِمْتِحَان

You are an intelligent boy? — *anta waladun dakiyyun* — أَنْتَ وَلَدٌ ذَكِىٌّ؟

She is a smart girl — *hiya bintun shatwiratun* — هِىَ بِنْتٌ شَاطِرَةٌ

How did you reach the school? — *kayfa wasaltal madrasa?* — كَيْفَ وَصَلْتَ الْمَدْرَسَةَ؟

My friend has returned from India — *qad raja'a swadeeqee minal hind?* — قَدْ رَجَعَ صَدِيقِي مِنَ الْهِنْدْ

These birds are very small — *haadihittuyooru sageera jiddan* — هٰذه الطُّيُورُ صَغَيرَة جِداًّ

The train was very fast — *kaanal qitaaru saree'an jiddan* — كَانَ الْقِطَارُ سَرِيعًا جِداًّ

I am angry today — *ana za'ulaan alyawm* — أَنَا زَعْلاَنْ الْيَوْمْ

He is tired now — *huwa ta'baan alheen* — هُوَ تَعْبَانْ الْحِينْ

I love my country very much — *uhibbu baladee jiddan* — أُحِبُّ بَلَدِي جِداًّ

Have you got a text book, note book and a pen? — *hal indaka kitaabun waqalamun wakurraasa?* — هَلْ عِنْدَكَ كِتَابٌ وَقَلَمٌ وَكُرَّاسَةٌ؟

Don't play (M. Plural) in the class — *laa tal'aboo fil fasl* — لاَ تَلْعَبُوا فِي الْفَصْلْ

He wants to travel to Delhi	*yureedu an yusaafira ilaa dalhee*	يُرِيدُ أَنْ يُسَافِرَ إِلَى دَلْهِي
My friend told me	*qaala lee sadeeqee*	قَالَ لِي صَدِيقِي
Do you like to read this book?	*hal tuhibbu an taqra'u haadal kitaab*	هَلْ تُحِبُّ أَنْ تَقْرَأَ هٰذَا الْكِتَابَ؟
Our school is in New Delhi	*madrasatuna fee dalhee aljadeed*	مَدْرَسَتُنَا فِي دَلْهِي الْجَدِيدْ
His examination starts tomorrow	*yabda'u imtihaanuhu gadan*	يَبْدَأُ إِمْتِحَانُهُ غَداً
A book is a very good friend	*al kitaab swadeequn jayyid jiddan*	الْكِتَاب صَدِيق جَيِّد جِداًّ
Railway station is near to his house	*mahattwa alqitaar qareeb min baytihee*	مَحَطَّةُ الْقِطَار قَرِيب مِنْ بَيْتِه
Howmany books has your friend got?	*kam kitaaban inda swadeeqika?*	كَمْ كِتَابًا عِنْدَ صَدِيقِكَ؟
What profession will you opt after the exam?	*ayyu mihna takhtaaru ba'adal imtihaan*	أَيُّ مِهْنَةَ تَخْتَارُ بَعْدَ الإِمْتِحَانْ؟
A lazy student will never succeed	*lan yanjaha ttaalib alkaslaan*	لَنْ يَنْجَحَ الطَّالِب الْكَسْلاَن
Where is your shop in the city?	*ayna dukaanukum fil madeena?*	أَيْنَ دُكَانُكُمْ فِي الْمَدِينَةَ؟
My brother and sister have read two books	*qara'a akhee wa ukhtee kitaabayn*	قَرَأَ أخى وَأُخْتِي كِتَابَيْن
Knowledge is better than wealth	*al ilm khayr minatharwa*	الْعِلْم خَيْر مِنَ الثَّرْوَة

Unity is strength	*al ittihaad quwwa*	الإتِّحَاد قُوَّة
Prevention is better than cure	*al wiqaayat khayr minal mu'aajala*	الْوِقَايَة خَيْر مِنَ الْمُعَالَجَة
Time is money	*al waqtu maalun*	الْوَقْتُ مَال
One who digs a ditch falls in it	*man hafara hufra yaqa'u feehaa*	مَنْ حَفَرَ حُفْرَة يَقَعُ فِيهَا
I met her in the library today	*laqeetuha fil maktaba alyawm*	لَقِيتُهَا فِي الْمَكْتَبَة الْيَوْم
One who sows will rea	*man zara'a haswada*	مَنْ زَرَعَ حَصَدَ
Strike the iron when it is hot	*idhribil hadeed haamiyan*	إضْرب الْحَدِيد حَامِياً
As you sow, so shall you reap	*kamaa tazra'u tahswudu*	كَمَا تَزْرَعُ تَحْصُدُ
A friend in need is a friend indeed	*assadeequ 'inda dhayyiq*	الصَّدِيقُ عِنْدَ الضَّيِّق
If speech is silver, silence is gold	*idaa kaana alkalaam min fidha fassukoot min dahab*	إذَا كَانَ الْكَلاَم مِن فِضَّة فَالسُّكُوتُ مِن ذهب
Little knowledge is dangerous	*al 'ilmul qaleel khatarun*	الْعِلْمُ الْقَلِيل خَطَرٌ
Opportunities do not wait	*al furasu laa tantadhiru*	الْفُرَص لاَ تَنْتَظِر
Laziness is the reason to poverty	*al kaslu miftaahul faqr*	الْكَسْل مِفْتَاحُ الفَقْر
Necessity is the mother of inventions	*al haaja ummul ikhtiraa'u*	الْحَاجَة أُمُّ الإخْتِرَاع
All that glitters is not gold	*laysa kullamaa yalma'u dahab*	لَيْسَ كُلَّمَا يَلْمَعُ ذَهَب

Too many cooks spoil the soup	*kathura attabbakheen tafsadu attabkha*	كَثْرَةُ الطَّبَّاخين تَفْسَدُ الطَّبْخَة
Empty vessel makes much noise	*al inaa'ul faari'u yarinnu katheeran*	الانَاءُ الْفَارِغُ يَرَنُّ كَثيراً
Actions speak more than words	*al a'umaal ablagu minal aqwaal*	الأَعْمَال أَبْلغُ مِن الأَقْوَال
Send this draft by speed post	*irsil haadihil hawaala 'abral bareed al'aajil*	ارْسِل هٰذه الْحَوَالَة عَبْرَ الْبَرِيَدِ الْعَاجِل
Saving is better than spending	*al iddikhaaru khayr minal infaaq*	الإدخَارُ خَير مِنَ الإنْفَاق
Banking sector is very strong in our country	*qitaa'ul masaarif qawiyyun jiddan fee baladina*	قِطَاعُ الْمَصَارِف قَوِي جِداً فِيَ بَلَدِنَا
Euro is the most popular currency in the world	*yooroo 'umla waasi'a attarweej fil 'aam*	يُورُو عُمْلَة وَاسِعَة التَّرويج فِيَ الْعَالَم
Yes, I have an international licence	*na'am indee rukhsa dooliya*	نَعَمْ عِنْدى رُخْصَة دُولِيَة
Have you visited Cairo?	*hal zurta al qaahira?*	هَلْ زُرْتَ الْقَاهِرَة؟
What can I do for you?	*ayyu khidma?*	أيُّ خِدْمَة؟
Can I help you?	*mumkin usaa'iduka?*	مُمْكِن أُسَاعِدُكَ؟
I would like to cash this cheque	*ureedu sarfa haada asheek*	أُرِيدُ صَرْفَ هٰذَا الشِّيك
Have you got an account in the bank?	*hal laka hisaab fil bank?*	هَلْ لَكَ حِسَاب فِي البَنْك؟

Are you an employee of this bank?	*hal inta muwadhaf fee haadal bank?*	هَلْ أَنْتَ مُوَظَّف فِي هٰذَا البَنْك؟
I want to buy a piece of cloth	*ureedu shiraa'a qit'a qamaash*	أُرِيدُ شِرَاءَ قِطْعَة قَمَاش
Did your sister go with you?	*hal dahabat ukhtuka ma'ak?*	هَلْ ذَهَبَتْ أُخْتُكَ مَعَك؟
I was in the market	*kuntu fissooq*	كُنْتُ فِي السُّوق
What did you buy from the market?	*maada ishtarayta minassooq?*	مَاذَا اشْتَرَيْتَ مِنَ السُّوق؟
What do you want to buy?	*maada tureedu 'an tashtaree?*	مَاذَا تُرِيدُ أَن تَشْتَرِي؟
Try	*hawil*	حَاوِلْ
Try again	*hawil marra thaniya*	حَاوِلْ مَرَّة ثَانِيَة
Try once more	*hawil marra ukhra*	حَاوِلْ مَرَّة أُخْرَى
Try later	*hawil ba'edayn*	حَاوِلْ بَعْدَيْنْ
Try after some time	*hawil ba'uda shuway*	حَاوِلْ بَعْدَ شُوَيْ
I will try	*uhawil*	أُحَاوِلْ
Can you try for me again?	*mumkin tuhawil lee marra thaniya*	مُمْكِنْ تُحَاوِلْ لِي مَرَّة ثَانِيَة
How can I try?	*kayf uhawil?*	كَيْفَ أُحَاوِلْ؟
Never mind	*ma leysh*	مَا لَيْشْ
Not difficult (No problem)	*ma fee mushkila*	مَا فِي مُشْكِلَة
Don't speak	*ma fee kalaam*	مَا فِي كَلَامْ
Keep quiet	*uskut*	أُسْكُتْ

Who will you go with?	*ma'a meen taruh?*	مَعَ مينْ تَرُحْ؟
I am going with my father	*aruh ma'a baaba*	أرُحْ مَعَ بَابَا
I am going with my mother	*aruh ma'a mama*	أُرُحْ مَعَ مَامَا
I am going with my husband	*aruh ma'a zawj*	أرُحْ مَعَ زَوْج
I am going with my friend	*aruh ma'a rafeeq*	أرُحْ مَعَ رَفيقْ
Who is with you?	*meen ma'ak?*	مينْ مَعَكْ؟
You should keep right	*ilzam yameen*	إلْزَمْ يَمينْ
You should keep left	*ilzam yasar*	إلْزَمْ يَسَارْ
You should keep the law	*ilzam alqanoon*	إلْزَمْ الْقَانُون
After one week	*ba'uda usboo'e*	بَعْدَ أُسْبُوع
Check after 3 days	*muraja'a ba'uda thalatha ayyam?*	مُرَاجَعَة بَعْدَ ثَلاَثَة أيَّامى
Renewal of Residence permit	*tajdeedul iqama*	تَجْديدُ الإقَامَة
Congratulations	*Mabrook*	مَبْرُوكْ
1000 congratulations	*alf mabrook*	ألْف مَبْرُوكْ
May God bless you	*baarakallaah feek*	بَارَكَ الله فيك
Contract	*Aqd*	عَقْد
License / Permission	*Rukhsa*	رُخْصَة
What is today's exchange rate?	*sa'iritahweela kam alyawm?*	سَعر التَّحْويلَة كَمْ الْيَوْم؟
Exit	*Khurooj*	خُرُوجْ
Entry	*dukhool*	دُخُولْ

Passport	*jawaaz*	جَـوَازْ
Change of sponsorship	*naql kafaala*	نَقْلْ كَفَـالَةَ
Release	*tanaazil*	تَـنَازِلْ
Visa	*ta'esheera*	تَأشْـيرَةَ
Visit visa	*ta'esheera ziyaara*	تَأشْـيرَةَ زِيَارَةَ
Residence visa	*ta'esheera iqaama*	تَأشْـيرَةَ إقَامَـة
Tourist visa	*ta'esheera siyaaha*	تَأشْـيرَةَ سِـيَاحَـة
Transit visa	*ta'esheera muroor*	تَأشْـيرَةَ مُـرُورْ
Work visa	*ta'esheera 'amal*	تَأشْـيرَةَ عَـمَـلْ
Business visa	*ta'esheera rijaal a'umaal*	تَأشْـيرَةَ رِجَـال أعْـمَـال
Application	*Talab*	طَلَب
Commercial registration (CR)	*sijil attijaari*	سِـجِـلْ التِّـجَـاري
Reservation	*hajz*	حَـجْـزْ
Police	*Shurta*	شُـرْطَة
Traffic police	*shurtal muroor*	شُـرْطَة الْمُـرُور
Please	*Arjook*	أرْجُـوك
(Request) Please give me time	*arjook an tu'utinee waqt*	أرْجُـوك أنْ تُعْـطِيني وَقْت
Perhaps / Possible / May be	*Mumkin*	مُـمْـكِنْ
Telephone	*haatif*	هَـاتـفْ
Possible, for you to give me your telephone no home/office	*mumkin tu'utinee raqm hatif / bayt am maktab*	ممكن تعطيني رقم هاتف/بيت أم مكتب
If you don't mind,	*law smaht*	لَوْ سَـمَـحْـت أعْـطني كُل

give me all	*a'utwinee kul*	
Have you got a mobile?	*'indaka jawwaal?*	عـنْدَكَ جَـوَّالْ؟
What is the number?	*raqm kam?*	رَقَمْ كمْ؟
Have you got a car?	*'indaka sayyara?*	عـنْدَكَ سَـيَّارَةْ؟
Have you got a servant?	*'indaka khaadim?*	عـنْدَكَ خَـادمْ؟
Have you got a maid?	*'indaka khaadima?*	عـنْدَكَ خَـادمَـة؟
Have you got a house?	*'indaka bayt?*	عـنْدَكَ بَـيْتْ؟
Come	*ta'aal*	تَـعَـالْ
Come after a little while	*ta'aal ba'uda shuway*	تَـعَـالْ بَـعْـدَ شُـوَي
Come after one hour	*ta'aal ba'uda saa'a*	تَـعَـالْ بَـعْـدَ سَـاعَـة
Where is the file?	*wayn al malaf?*	وَيْنْ الْمَـلَفْ؟
Present	*mawjood*	مَـوْجُـودْ
Let me see	*khallinee shuf*	خَـلِّني شُـفْ
Leave it on the table	*kallee 'ala ttaawila*	خَـلِّي عَـلَى الطَّاولَة
Secretary	*amen*	أمـينْ
Leave it with the secretary	*khallee ma'alameen*	خَـلِّي مَـعَ الأمـينْ
See how?	*shuf kayf?*	شُـفْ كَيْفَ؟
You must help	*lazim musa'ida*	لاَزِمْ مُـسَـاعَـدَة
Make	*sawwee*	سَـوِّي
What are you doing there?	*shoo sawwee hinaak?*	شُـو سَـوِّي هـنَاك؟
Make a copy	*sawwee nuskha*	سَـوِّي نُـسْـخَـة
Hurry up	*ya allaah sur'a*	يَا ألله سُـرْعَـة

LESSON NINETEEN

DO YOU SPEAK ARABIC?

Do you speak Arabic?	*hal tatakallamu arabee?*	هَلْ تَتَكَلَّمُ عَرَبِي؟
Do you speak English?	*hal tatakallamu injileezee?*	هَلْ تَتَكَلَّمُ إِنْجِلِيزِي؟
Does any one here speak Arabic?	*hal yoojad ahad yatakallamu arabee?*	هَلْ يُوجَد أَحَد يَتَكَلَّمُ عَرَبِي؟
Does any one here speak English?	*hal yoojad ahad yatakallamu injileezee?*	هَلْ يُوجَدَ أَحَدٌ يَتَكَلَّمُ إِنْجلِيزي؟
Are you busy?	*hal inta mashgool?*	هَلْ أَنْتَ مَشْغُول؟
Is he coming?	*hal huwa jaa'in?*	هَلْ هُوَ جَاء؟
Is he smart?	*hal huwa shaatwir?*	هَلْ هُوَ شَاطِر؟
Is he experienced?	*hal huwa mutajarrib?*	هَلْ هُوَ مُتَجَرِّب؟
Is this new?	*hal haada jadeed?*	هَلْ هٰذَا جَدِيد؟
Is that old?	*hal daalika qadeem?*	هَلْ ذٰلِكَ قَدِيمَ؟
Is the room furnished?	*halil gurfa mafroosha?*	هَلِ الْغُرْفَةُ مَفْرُوشَة؟
Is this your school?	*hal haadihee madrasatuka?*	هَلْ هٰذِه مَدْرَسَتُكِ؟
Is that your office?	*hal daalika maktabuka?*	هَلْ ذٰلِكَ مَكْتَبُكَ؟
Is this his factory?	*hal haada masna'uhu?*	هَلْ هٰذَا مَصْنَعُهُ؟
Did Muhammed come to you?	*hal ataaka muhammed?*	هَلْ أَتٰيكَ مُحَمَّد؟

Did you pass the examination?	*hal najahta fil imtihaan?*	هَـلْ نَجَـحْـتَ فِي الإمْـتِـحَـانِ؟
Did you get the accommodation?	*hal wajadtassakan?*	هَـلْ وَجَـدْتَ السَّـكَـنَ؟
Is he busy?	*hal huwa mashgool?*	هَـلْ هُـوَ مَـشْـغُـول؟
Is he free?	*hal huwa faadhee?*	هَـلْ هُـوَ فَـاضِـي؟
Have you got an appointment?	*hal laka maw'id?*	هَـلْ لَكَ مَـوْعِـدَ؟
Have you got guests today?	*hal 'indaka dhuyoof alyawm?*	هَـلْ لَكَ ضُـيُوف الْيَـوْم؟
Your passport please	*jawaazu safarika min fadhlika?*	جَـوَازُ سَـفَـرِكَ مِـنْ فَـضْـلِـكَ
Here is my passport	*hal huwa jawaazu safaree*	هَـا هُـوَ جَـوَازُ سَـفَـرِي
I will be staying here for two weeks	*sa'abqaa huna usboo'ayn*	سَـأبْـقٰى هُـنَا أُسْـبُـوعَـيْن
I will be staying here for a few days	*sa'abqaa huna ba'udhal ayyaam*	سَـأبْـقٰى هُـنَا بَـعْـضَ الأيَّام
I will be staying here for one month	*sa'abqaa hunaa shahran*	سَـأبْـقٰى هُـنَا شَـهْرًا
I don't know yet	*laa a'urifu ba'ada*	لاَ أعْـرِفُ بَـعْـد
I'am here on holiday	*ana huna fee ijaaza*	أنَا هُـنَاَ فِي إجَـازَة
I'am here on business	*ana huna litijaara*	أنَا هُـنَا لِـتِـجَـارَة
I'am here on tourism	*ana huna fee siyaha*	أنَا هُـنَا فِي سِـيَاحَـة
I'am here for work	*ana huna lishugl*	أنَا هُـنَا لِـشُـغْـلِ
I'am here on duty	*ana huna fiddawaam*	أنَا هُـنَا فِي الـدَّوَام
Do you have	*hal 'indaka shay'un lil*	هَـلْ عِـنْدَكَ شَـيْءٌ

anything to declare?	*i'ulaani 'anhu?*	للإعْلاَن عَنْهُ؟
Where is the entry visa?	*wayn ta'usheeratud dukhool*	وَيْنْ تَأْشِيرَةُ الدُّخُولَ؟
Please open this bag	*min fadhlika iftah haadihil haqeeba*	مِنْ فَضْلِكَ إفْتَحْ هٰذه الْحَقِيبَة
Have you got any other luggage?	*hal 'indaka haqaa'ib ukhraa?*	هَلْ عِنْدَكَ حَقَائِب أُخْرٰى؟
It is for my personal use	*haada li'isti'umaali asshakhsee*	هٰذَا لإسْتِعْمَال الشَّخْصي
Passport control	*muraaqabatu jawaazu ssafar*	مُرَاقَبَةُ جَوَازُ السَّفَر
Customs	*aljamrak*	الجَمْرَك
Porter	*shayyaal*	شَيَّال
Please take this to the car	*min fadhlika khud haada ila ssayyaara*	مِنْ فَضْلِكَ خُذْ هٰذَا إلَى اَلسَّيَّارَة
Please take this bag to the hotel	*min fadhlika khud haadihil haqeeba ilal funduq*	مِنْ فَضْلِكَ خُذْ هٰذه الْحَقِيبَة إلَى الفُنْدُق
One piece is missing	*naaqis qit'a waahida*	نَاقِص قِطْعَة وَاحِدَة
Where are the luggage trolleys?	*wayn 'arabatul haqaa'ib*	وَيْنْ عَرَبَةُ الْحَقَائِب؟
Where is the currency exchange office?	*wayn maktabu ttahweel*	وَيْنْ مَكْتَبُ التَّحْوِيل؟
Can you exchange for me traveller's cheque?	*mumkin tuhawwil lee shikaat siyaahiya*	مُمْكِنْ تُحَوِّلْ لي شِيكَات سِيَاحِيَة
What is the exchange rate today?	*maa si'uru ttahweel alyawm?*	مَا سِعْرُ التَّحْوِيل اليَوْم؟

Where is the booking /reservation office?	*wayn maktabul hajz?*	وَيْنْ مَكْتَبُ الحَجْزِ؟
Where is the car rental office?	*wayn maktabu ta'ujeer assayyaaraat?*	وَيْنْ مَكْتَب تَأْجِير السَّيَّارَات؟
Where is the duty free shop?	*wayn assooqul hurra?*	وَيْنْ السُّوقُ الْحُرَّة؟
Where can I get a taxi?	*wayn ajidu taaksee?*	وَيْنْ أجِدُ تَاكْسِي؟
Where can I hire a car?	*wayn asta'ujiru sayyaara?*	وَيْنْ أَسْتَأجِرُ سَيَّارَة؟
Do you have a hotel guide?	*hal 'indaka daleelul fanaadiq?*	هَلْ عِنْدَكَ دَلِيلُ الفَنَادق؟
Can you book a room for me in a hotel?	*mumkin tahjiz lee gurfa fee funduq*	مُمْكِنْ تَحْجِزْ لِي غُرْفَةَ فِي فُنْدُق
A hotel near to the airport	*funduq qareeb min al mataar*	فُنْدُقْ قَرِيب مِنَ الْمَطَار
A single room	*gurfa lishakhs*	غُرْفَة لِشَخْص
A double room	*gurfa lishakhsayn*	غُرْفَة لِشَخْصَين
Is the room expensive?	*halil gurfa gaaliya?*	هَلْ الغُرْفَة غَالِيَة؟
Not very expensive	*laysat gaaliya katheera*	لَيسَتْ غَالِيَة كَثِيرَة
I want a taxi	*ureedu taaksee*	أُرِيدُ تَاكْسِي
Can you get me a taxi?	*mumkin tajid lee taaksee?*	مُمْكِنْ تَجِدْ لِي تَاكْسِي؟
I would like to hire a small car	*ureedu ta'ujeera sayyaara sageera*	أُرِيدُ تَأجِيرَ سَيَّارَة صَغِيرَة
I would like to hire a big car	*ureedu ta'ujeera sayyaara kabeera*	أُرِيدُ تَأجِيرَ سَيَّارَة كَبِيرَة
I would like to hire a car with driver	*ureedu ta'ujeera sayyaara bisaa'iq*	أُرِيدُ تَأجِيرَ سَيَّارَة بِسَائق

I would like to hire a car for a week	*ureedu ta'ujeera sayyaara li usboo'u*	أُرِيـدُ تَأْجِيرَ سَيَّارَة لأسْبُـوع
I would like to hire a car for a month	*ureedu ta'ujeera sayyaara li shahr*	أُرِيـدُ تَأْجِيرَ سَـيَّارَة لِشَـهْر
Is there special rate for long term?	*hal toojad as'aar khaassa limudda taweela?*	هَـلْ تُوجَـد أَسْـعَارْ خَـاصَّـة لِمُـدَّة طَوِيلَة؟
Is there special rate for the weekends?	*hal toojad as'aar khaasswa linihaayatil usboo'u?*	هَـلْ تُوجَـدْ أَسْـعَارْ خَـاصَّـة لِنِـهَايَـة الأَسْبُـوع؟
What is the charge per day?	*kam alhisaab fil yawm?*	كَـمِ الْحِسَـابُ فِي الْيَوم؟
What is the charge per week?	*kam alhisaab fil usboo'u?*	كَـمِ الْحِسَـابُ فِي الأَسْبُـوع؟
What is the charge per month?	*kam alhisaab fi shahr?*	كَـم الْحِسَـابُ فِي الشَّـهْر؟
With driver or without driver?	*bisaa'iq aw bidoona saa'iq?*	بِسَـائِقْ أَوْ بِـدُونَ سَـائِق؟
How do I pay?	*kayfa adfa'u?*	كَـيْفَ أَدْفَـعُ؟
I have a credit card	*'indee kart masrafee*	عِـنْدِى كَارْتْ مَـصْـرَفِى
Have you got a credit card?	*hal 'indaka kaart masrafee?*	هَـلْ عِـنْدَكَ كَارْتْ مَـصْـرَفِي
All payment in advance	*addaf'u kullun muqaddaman*	الدَّفْـعُ كُلٌّ مُـقَدَّمًـا
I want full insurance	*ureedu ta'umeen shaamil*	أُرِيـدُ تَـأْمِـين شَـامِـل
Have you got a driving licence?	*hal 'indaka rukhsa qiyaada?*	هَـلْ عِـنْدَكَ رُخْـصَـة قِيَادَة؟
Here is my driving licence	*haadihee rukhsa qiyaadatee*	هٰـذِه رُخْـصَـة قِيَادَتِي

Take me to a doctor	*khudnee ilaa tabeeb*	خُـذْنى إِلَى طَبِـيب
Take me to the clinic	*khudbnee ilal 'iyaada*	خُـذْنَي إِلَى الْعِـيَادَةَ
Take me to the emergency	*khudnee ila ttawaaree*	خُـذْنِي إِلَى الطَّوَارِئ
Take me to the embassy	*khudnee ila ssafaara*	خُـذْنِي إِلَى السَّـفَـارَةَ
Take me to the cornish	*khudnee ilaa koorneesh*	خُـذْنِي إِلَى كُورْنِيشْ
Take me to the airport	*khudnee ilal mataar*	خُـذْنِي إِلَى الْمَطَار
Take me to the harbour	*khudnee ilal meenaa'u*	خُـذْنِي إِلَى الْمِـينَاء
Take me to the principal	*khudnee ilal mudeer*	خُـذْنِي إِلَى الْمُـدِير
A day	*yawm*	يَوْم
Today	*al yawm*	الْيَوْم
Day	*nahaar*	نَهَار
Morning	*subh*	صُبْـح
Noon	*dhuhr*	ظُهْر
Evening	*masaa'u*	مَـسَـاء
Night	*layl/layla*	لَيْل/ لَيْـلَـة
Now	*al aan*	الآن
Afterwards	*ba'dayn*	بَـعْـدَيْن
Sunday	*yawmul ahad*	يَوْمُ الأحَـد
Monday	*yawmul ithnayn*	يَوْمُ الإثْـنَيْـن
Tuesday	*yawmul thalaatha*	يَوْمُ الثَّلاثَاء
Wednesday	*yawmul arbi'aa*	يَوْمُ الأرْبِـعَاء
Thursday	*yawmul khamees*	يَوْمُ الْخَـمِـيس
Friday	*yawmul jumu'a*	يَوْمُ الْجُـمُـعَـة

Saturday	*yawmussabt*	يَوْمُ السَّبْت
Tomorrow	*bukra/ghad*	بُكْرَة/ غَد
day after tomorrow	*ba'uda bukra*	بَعْدَ بُكْرَة
yesterday	*amsi*	أَمْس
day before	*yesterday*	أَوَّل أَمْس
after one week	*ba'uda usboo'u*	بَعْدَ أُسْبُوع
last week	*al usboo'ul maadhee*	الأسْبُوعُ الْمَاضِي
next week	*al usboo'il qaadim*	الأسْبُوعُ الْقَادِم
last month	*ashahrul maadhee*	الشَّهْرُ الْمَاضِي
next month	*ashahrul qaadim*	الشَّهْرُ الْقَادِم
last year	*assna almaadhiya*	السَّنَةُ الْمَاضِيَة
next year	*assanatul qaadima*	السَّنَةُ الْقَادِمَة
yearly	*sanawe*	سنوي
monthly	*shahry*	شهري
daily	*yaume*	يومي
mid-day	*montasafi nnhar*	منتصف النهار
mid-night	*montasafi llayl*	منتصف الليل
Afternoon	*baad azzohr*	بعد الظهر
Sunrise	*shorooqi sshams*	شروق الشمس
Sunset	*goroobi sshams*	غروب الشمس
Four seasons	*alfusool alarbaha*	الفصول الاربعة
Season	*fasl*	فصل
Winter	*aashitaa*	الشتاء
Autumn	*alxareer*	الخريف
Spring	*arrabeeh*	الربيع
Summer	*assayf*	الصيف

The Weather	altaqas	الطقس
The sun	*asshams*	الشمس
The moon	*al qamar*	القمر
The air	*alhawaa*	الهواء
The snow	*athalaj*	الثلج
The clouds	*alguyoom*	الغيوم
Hot weather	*taqs harr*	طقس حار
Rainy weather	*taqs momtir*	طقس ممطر
Cold weather	*taqs barid*	طقس بارد
How is the weather today?	*kayfa halottaqs alyawm?*	كيف حال الطقس اليوم
Sunny day	*yawmon moshmis*	يوم مشمس
Cold day	*yawm barid*	يوم بارد
Windy day	*yawm aasif*	يوم عاصف

Colours الألوان

White	*abyadh*	أبْيَض
Black	*aswad*	أسود
Red	*ahmar*	أحمر
Green	*akhdhar*	أخضر
Blue	*azraq*	أزرق
Yellow	*asfar*	أصفر
Grey	*ramaadee*	رمادي
Orange	*burtuqaalee*	برتقالي
Violet	*banafsajee*	بنفسجي
Silver	*fiddhi*	فضّي

Gold	*dahabee*	ذهبي
Pink	*zahree*	زهري
Brown	*boniyy*	بنيّ
Light red	*asmar*	أسمر
Dark blue	*azraq qamiq*	أزرق غامق
Sky-blue	*azraq samawee*	أزرق سماوي
Cyan	*samawee*	سماوي
Oil green	*zaytyi*	زيتي

LESSON TWENTY

WHAT IS THE TIME NOW?

What is the time now?	*kamissaal aan*	كم الساعة الآن؟
It is nine o'clock	*innahaa saa ttasiah*	إنها الساعة التاسعة
It is five past eight	*athaaminah wa khasu daqaiq*	الثامنة وخمس دقائق
It is quarter past six	*assadisa warrubu*	السادسة والربع
It is twenty past three	*athalitha wa thulth*	الثالثة والثلث
It is ten to ten	*al ashira illa ashara daqaiq*	العاشرة إلا عشر دقائق
It is quarter to two	*assaatah athaniya illa ruboo*	الساعة الثانية إلا ربع
It is twenty to seven o'clock	*assaath ssabia illa thulth*	الساعة السابعة إلا ثلث
It is five o'clock	*assath alkhamisa tamam*	الساعة الخامسة تمام
Hour	*saah*	ساعة
Minute	*daqeeqah*	دقيقة
Second	*thaniyah*	ثانية
Moment	*lahzah*	لحظة
Half an hour	*nisf saah*	نصف ساعة
Quarter	*roba saah*	ربع ساعة
Twenty minutes	*thulth saaha*	ثلث ساعة
Time	*al waqt*	الوقت
One hour	*saa'ah*	ساعة
Half an hour	*nisfu saa'a*	نصف ساعة

1 'o clock	*assaa'atul waahida*	**الساعة الواحدة**
2 'o clock	*assaa'atu thaaniya*	**الساعة الثانية**
3 'o clock	*assaa'atu thaalitha*	**الساعة الثالثة**
4 'o clock	*assaa'aturraabi'a*	**الساعةالرابعة**
5 'o clock	*assaa'atul khaamisa*	**الساعة الخامسة**
6 'o clock	*assaa'atussaadisa*	**الساعة السادسة**
7 'o clock	*assaa'atussaabi'a*	**الساعة السابعة**
8 'o clock	*assaa'atuthaamina*	**الساعة الثامنة**
9 ' o clock	*assaa'atuttaasi'a*	**الساعة التاسعة**
10 'o clock	*assa'atul aashira*	**الساعة العاشرة**
11 'o clock	*assaa'atul haadee 'ashara*	**الساعة الحادي عشر**
12 'o clock	*assaa'atuthaaniya ashara*	السَّاعَةُ الثَّانيَة عَشَرَة
a quarter past five (5:15)	*assaa'atul khaamisa warrubu'u*	السَّاعَةُ الْخَامسَة وَالرُّبع
twenty minutes to 4 'o clock (3:40)	*assaa'aturraabi'a illa thuluth*	السَّاعَةُ الرَّابعَة إلاَّ ثُلُث
a quarter to 7 'o clock (6:45)	*assaa'atussaabi'a illaa rubu'u*	السَّاعَةُ السَّابعَة إلاَّ رُبْع
ten past eight (8:10)	*assaa'atu thaamina wa ashara daqaa'iq*	السَّاعَةُ الثَّامنَة وَعَشَر دقَائق
it is twenty past three (3:20)	*assaa'atuthaalitha wathuluth*	السَّاعَةُ الثَّالثَة وَالثُّلُث

Measurements المقايس

Milimeter	*milimitr*	**مليمتر**
Centimeter	*centimitr*	**سنتيمتر**

Square meter	*mitr morabba*	متر مربع
Cubic meter	*mitr mokaab*	متر مكبع
Gram	*gram*	غرام
Inch	*insh*	إنش
Foot	*qadam*	قدم
Yard	*yard*	يارد
Mile	*meel*	ميل
Hectare	*hiktar*	هكتار
Ton	*ton*	طن

LESSON TWENTY ONE

DATE AND NUMBER

Numbers العدد

0	Zero	*swifr*	صفر	٠
1	one	*wahid*	واحد	١
2	Two	*ithnaani*	إثنان	٢
3	three	*thalaatha*	ثلاثة	٣
4	four	*arba'a*	أربعة	٤
5	Five	*khamsa*	خمسة	٥
6	six	*sitta*	ستّة	٦
7	Seven	*sab'a*	سبعة	٧
8	eight	*thamaaniya*	ثمانية	٨
9	Nine	*tis'a*	تسعة	٩
10	Ten	*'ashara*	عشرة	١٠
11	Eleven	*ahada ashara*	أحد عشر	١١
12	Twelve	*ithnaa ashara*	إثنا عشر	١٢
13	Thirteen	*thalaatha ashara*	ثلاثة عشر	١٣
14	Fourteen	*arba'ata ashara*	أربعة عشر	١٤
15	Fifteen	*Khamsata ashara*	خمسة عشر	١٥
16	Sixteen	*sitta ashara*	ستّة عشر	١٦
17	Seventeen	*sab'a ashara*	سبعةَ عشر	١٧
18	Eighteen	*thamaaniya ashara*	ثمانية عشر	١٨
19	Nineteen	*this'a ashara*	تسعة عشر	١٩
20	Twenty	*ishroon*	عشرون	٢٠

21	Twenty one	*waahid wa ishroon*	واحد وعشرون	٢١
22	Twenty two	*ithnaani wa ishroon*	إثنان وعشرون	٢٢
23	twenty three	*thalaatha wa ishroon*	ثلاثة وعشرون	٢٣
24	Twenty four	*arba'a wa ishroon*	أربعة وعشرون	٢٤
25	Twenty five	*khamsa wa ishroon*	خمسة وعشرون	٢٥
26	Twenty six	*sitta wa ishroon*	ستّة وعشرون	٢٦
27	twenty seven	*sab'a wa ishroon*	سبعة وعشرون	٢٧
28	Twenty eight	*thamaaniya wa ishroon*	ثمانية وعشرون	٢٨
29	Twenty nine	*tis'a wa ishroon*	تسعة وعشرون	٢٩
30	thirty	*thalaathoon*	ثلاثون	٣٠
40	Forty	*arba'oon*	أربعون	٤٠
50	Fifty	*khamsoon*	خمسون	٥٠
60	Sixty	*sittoon*	ستّون	٦٠
70	seventy	*sab'oon*	سبعون	٧٠
80	Eighty	*thamaanoon*	ثمانون	٨٠
90	Ninety	*tis'oon*	تسعون	٩٠
100	One hundred	*mi'a*	مائة	١٠٠
1000	One Thousand	*alf*	ألْف	١٠٠٠
10,00,000	One million	*milyoon*	مليون	١٠٠٠٠٠٠

½	Half	*niswf*	نصف	٢/١
¼	Quarter	*rubu'u*	ربع	٤/١
⅓	One third	*thuluth*	ثلث	٣/١
%	precent	*fil mi'a*	في المائة	٪
Whole		*kull*		كُلّ
Part		*juzu'u*		جزُءْ
Full		*Kaamil*		كاملْ

How to count Male (Nouns)

One boy	*waladun waahid*	ولد واحد
Two boys	*waladaani ithnaani*	ولدان إثنان
Three boys	*thalaatha awlaadin*	ثلاثةُ أولاد
Four boys	*arba'a awlaadin*	أربعةُ أولاد
Five boys	*khamsa awlaadin*	خسمة أولاد
Six boys	*sitta awlaadin*	ستَّةُ أوْلاد
Seven boys	*sab'a awlaadin*	سبعةُ أولادً
Eight boys	*thamaaniya awlaadin*	ثمانيةُ أولادً
Nine boys	*tis'a awlaadin*	تسعةُ أولاد
Ten boys	*ashara awlaadin*	عشرةُ أولاد
Eleven boys	*ahada 'ashara waladan*	أحد عشر ولداً
Thirteen boys	*thalaatha 'ashara waladan*	ثلاثة عشر ولداً
Fourteen boys	*arba'a 'ashara waladan*	أربعة عشر ولداً
Fifteen boys	*khamsa 'ashara waladan*	خمسة عشر ولداً
Sixteen boys	*sitta 'ashara waladan*	ستّة عشر ولداً
Seventeen boys	*sab'a 'ashara waladan*	سبعة عشر ولداً
Eighteen boys	*thamaaniya 'ashara waladan*	ثمانية عشر ولداً

Nineteen boys	*tis'a 'ashara waladan*	تسعة عشرَ ولداً
Twenty boys	*ishroona waladan*	عشرون ولداً
Twenty one boys	*waahid wa ishroona waladan*	واحد وعشرون ولداً
Twenty two boys	*ithnaani wa ishroona waladan*	إثنان وعشرون ولداً
Twenty three boys	*thalaatha wa ishroona waladan*	ثلاثة وعشرون ولداً
Twenty four boys	*arba'a wa ishroona waladan*	أربعة وعشرون ولداً
Twenty five boys	*khamsa wa ishroona waladan*	خمسة وعشرون ولداً
Twenty six boys	*sitta wa ishroona waladan*	ستّة وعشرون ولداً
Twenty seven boys	*sb'a wa ishroona waladan*	سبعة وعشرون ولِداً
Twenty eight boys	*thamaaniya wa ishroona waladan*	ثمانية وعشرون ولداً
Twenty nine boys	*tis'a wa ishroona waladan*	تسعة وعشرون ولداً
Thirt boys	*thlaathoona waladan*	ثلاثون ولداً
Forty boys	*arba'oona waladan*	أربعونَ ولداً
Fifty boys	*khamsoona waladan*	خمسون ولداً
Sixty boys	*sittoona waladan*	ستّون ولداً
Seventy boys	*sab'oona waladan*	سبعون ولداً
Eighty boys	*thamaanoona waladan*	ثمانون ولداً
Ninety boys	*tis'oona waladan*	تسعون ولداً
One thousand boys	*alf waladin*	ألف ولدٍ

Female (Nouns)

One girl	*bintun waahid*	بنتٌ واحدة
Two girls	*Bintani ithnatani*	بنتان اثنتان
Three girls	*thalaathu banaatin*	ثلاث بنات
Four girls	*arba'u banaatin*	أربع بنات
Five girls	*khamsu banaatin*	خمس بنات
Six girls	*sittu banaatin*	ست بنات
Seven girls	*sab'u banaatin*	سبع بنات
Eight girls	*thamaanu banaatin*	ثمان بنات
Nine girls	*tis'u banaatin*	تسع بنات
Ten girls	*ashru banaatin*	عشرُ بنات
Eleven girls	*ihdaa 'ashara bintan*	إحْدٰى عَشَرَةَ بِنْتًا
Twelve girls	*ithanathaa 'ashara bintan*	إثْنَتَا عَشَرَةَ بنْتًا
Thirteen girls	*thalaatha 'ashara bintan*	ثَلاَثَ عَشَرَةَ بنْتًا
Fourteen girls	*arba'a 'ashara bintan*	أرْبَعَ عَشَرَةَ بنْتًا
Fifteen girls	*khamsa 'ashara bintan*	خَمْسَ عَشَرَةَ بنْتًا
Sixteen girls	*sitta 'ashara bintan*	ستَّ عَشَرَةَ بنْتًا
Seventeen girls	*sab'a 'ashara bintan*	سَبْعَ عَشَرَةَ بنْتًا
Eighteen girls	*thamaaniya 'ashara bintan*	ثَمانيَ عَشَرَةَ بنْتًا
Nineteen girls	*tis'a 'ashara bintan*	تسْعَ عَشَرَةَ بنْتًا
Twenty girls	*'ishroona bintan*	عشْرُونَ بنْتًا
Twenty one girls	*waahida wa 'ishroona bintan*	وَاحدَةَ وَعشْرُونَ بنْتًا
Twenty two girls	*ithnathaani wa 'ishroona bintan*	إثْنَتَان وَعشْرُونَ بنْتًا

Twenty three girls	*thalaathun wa 'ishroona bintan*	ثَلاَثٌ وَعِشْرُونَ بِنْتًا
Twenty four girls	*arba'un wa 'ishroona bintan*	أَرْبَعٌ وَعِشْرُونَ بِنْتًا
Twenty five girls	*khamsun wa 'ishroona bintan*	خَمْسٌ وَعِشْرُونَ بِنْتًا
Twenty six girls	*sittun wa 'ishroona bintan*	سِتٌّ وَعِشْرُونَ بِنْتًا
Twenty seven girls	*sab'un wa 'ishroona bintan*	سَبْعٌ وَعِشْرُونَ بِنْتًا
Twenty eight girls	*thamaanun wa 'ishroona bintan*	ثَمَانٌ وَعِشْرُونَ بِنْتًا
Twenty nine girls	*tis'un wa 'ishroona bintan*	تِسْعٌ وَعِشْرُونَ بِنْتًا
Thirty girls	*thalaathoona bintan*	ثَلاَثُونَ بِنْتًا
Forty girls	*arba'oona bintan*	أَرْبَعُونَ بِنْتًا
Fifty girls	*khamsoona bintan*	خَمْسُونَ بِنْتًا
Sixty girls	*sittoona bintan*	سِتُّونَ بِنْتًا
Seventy girls	*sab'oona bintan*	سَبْعُونَ بِنْتًا
Eighty girls	*thamaanoona bintan*	ثَمَانُونَ بِنْتًا
Ninety girls	*tis'oona bintan*	تِسْعُونَ بِنْتًا
One hundred girls	*mi'a bintin*	مِائَةُ بِنْتٍ
One thousand girls	*alfu bintin*	أَلْفُ بِنْتٍ

LESSON TWENTY TWO

MISCELLANY

Parts of the body أعضاء الجسم

Head	*ra'es*	رَأسْ
Hair	*sha'r*	شَعْر
Forehead	*jabeen*	جَبِينْ
Ear	*udun*	أُذْنْ
Nose	*anf*	أنْفْ
Face	*wajh*	وَجْهْ
Eye	*'ayin*	عَيْنْ
Cheek	*khadd*	خَدْ
Mouth	*fam*	فَمْ
Tongue	*lisaan*	لِسَانْ
Lip	*shafat*	شَفَةْ
Tooth	*sinn*	سِنْ
Chest	*swadr*	صَدْرْ
Heart	*qalb*	قَلْبْ
Stomach	*batwan*	بَطَنْ
Thigh	*fakhd*	فَخْذْ
knee	*rukba*	رُكْبَةْ
foot	*qadam*	قَدَمْ
hand	*yad*	يَدْ
leg	*rijl*	رِجْلْ
nail	*dhufr*	ظُفْرْ

back	*dhahr*	ظَهْرْ
finger	*isba'u*	إصْبَعْ
beard	*lihya*	لحْيَةْ
skin	*jild*	جلد
shoulder	*katif*	كتف
neck	*onoq*	عنق
waist	*khasr*	خصر
hip	*warik*	ورك
blood	*dam*	دم
chin	*thaqn*	ذقن
mustache	*shawarib*	شوارب
artery	*shriyan*	شريان
bone	*azm*	عظم
Brain	*dimag*	دماغ
lungs	*riatan*	رئتان
intestines	*amaa*	أمعاء
liver	*kabid*	كبد
kidney	*kilyah*	كلية
flesh	*lahm*	لحم
heel	*kaab*	كعب
Eyebrow	*hajib*	حاجب
Eyelid	*jafn*	جفن
Wrist	*mihsam*	معصم
Small intestine	*amaae daqeeqa*	امعاء دقيقة
Large intestine	*amaee galeeda*	امعاء غليظة

Respiratory system	*al jihazultanaffusee*	الجهاز التنفسي
Digestive system	*al jihazul hadme*	الجهاز الهضمي
Cardiac system	*jihazul qalb*	جهاز القلب
Nervous system	*al jihazul asabee*	الجهاز العصبي
Muscular system	*al jihazul adalee*	الجهاز العضلي
Reproductive system	*al jihazul thanasulee*	الجهاز التناسلي
Urinary system	*jihazul bawl*	جهاز البول
Cell	*khaliyya*	خلية
Saliva	*luab*	لعاب
Wound	*jurh*	جرح
Bleeding	*nazeef*	نزيف
Navel	*surra*	سرّة
Tear	*dame*	دمع
Sweet	*araq*	عرق
Womb	*rahim*	رحم

Directions:

Infront	*amaama*	أمَـام
Behind	*waraa'a, khalfa*	وَرآءَ، خَـلْف
Right	*yameen*	يَمـين
Left	*yasaar*	يَسَـار
South	*janoob*	جَـنُوب
North	*shimaal*	شـمَـال
East	*sharq*	شَـرْق
West	*garb*	غَـرْب

Prepositions:

From	*min*	مِـن
To	*ilaa*	إلـى
On	*'alaa*	عَـلـى
Near	*'inda*	عِـنْدَ
In	*fee*	فيَ
About	*'an*	عَـن
With	*bi*	ب
For/has	*li*	ل
With	*ma'a*	مَـعَ
After	*ba'ada*	بَـعْـدَ
Before	*qabla*	قَبْـلَ
Between	*bayna*	بَـيْنَ

The professions المهن والوظائف

Doctor	*tabeeb/doctor*	طبيب/دكتور
Dentist	*tabeeb asnan*	طبيب أسنان
ophthalmologist	*tabeeb oyoon*	طبيب عيون
Veterinary	*tabeeb baytaree*	طبيب بيطري
Surgeon	*jarrah*	جراح
Engineer	*mohandis*	مهندس
Writer	*katib*	كاتب
Editor	*moharrir*	محرر
Lawyer	*mohamee*	محامي
Judge	*qadee*	قاضي
Photographer	*mosawwir*	مصوّر

Poet	*shair*	شاعر
Actor	*momaail*	ممثل
Journalist	*sahafee*	صحفي
Dancer	*raqis/ raqisa*	راقص/ راقصة
Producer	*mukharij/ muntij*	مخرج/ منتج
Musician	*moseeqiy*	موسيقي
Dyer	*sabbag*	صبّاغ
Calligrapher	*khatat*	خطاط
Singer	*mugnee/matrab*	مغني/ مطرب
Carpenter	*najjar*	نجّار
Porter	*hammal/shayyal*	حمال/ شيال
Porter	*shayyal*	شيال
Bricklayer	*banna*	بناء
Chemist / Pharmacist	*saydaliy*	صيدلي
Drawer / Artist	*rassam*	رسام
Butcher	*lahham*	لحّام
Accountant	*mohasib*	محاسب
Baker	*khubaz*	خباز
Guard	*haris*	حارس
Money Changer	*sarraf*	صرّاف
Manager	*mudeer*	مدير
Translator	*motarjim*	مترجم
Jeweller	*jawharry*	جوهري
Gold Smith	*sayig*	صايغ
Barber/Hair dresser	*hallaq*	حلّاق

Black-smith	*haddad*	حداد
Teacher	*Muallim/ mudarris*	معلّم/ مدرّس
Analyst	*muhallil*	محلل
Administration Manager	*mudeer idaree*	مدير اداري
Auditor	*al mudaqqif*	المدقف
Finance manager	*al muddral malee*	المدير المالي
General manager	*al mudeerul aam*	المدير العام
Production Manager	*mudderul intaj*	مدير الانتاج
Marketing manager	*mudeerul tasweeq*	مدير التسويق
Office manager	*mudeer maktab*	مدير مكتب
Pilot	*tayyar*	طيّار
Engineer	*muhandas*	مهندس
Civil engineer	*muhandis madanee*	مهندس مدني
Electronic engineer	*muhandis electronee*	مهندس الكتروني
Electric engineer	*muhandis kaharbaee*	مهندس كهربائي
Mechanical engineer	*muhandis mechanikee*	مهندس ميكانيكي
Mechanic	*mikaneeky*	ميكانيكي
Electrician	*kaharbaee*	كهربائي
Plumber	*sabbak/samkary*	سباك/ سمكري
Tailor	*khayyat*	خياط
Salesman	*baaia*	بائع
Worker	*amel*	عامل
Architect	*muhandis miemariyy*	مهندس معماري
Interior designer	*muhandisu dicor*	مهندس ديكور

Agronomist	*muhandis ziraeyy*	مهندس زراعي
Flight engineer	*muhandisu tayaran*	مهندس طيران
Officer	*dabit*	ضابط
Soldier	*jundy*	جندي
Employer	*muwadhaf*	موظف
Fire fighter	*rajulul itfaa*	رجل الإطفاء
Merchant	*tajir*	تاجر
Nurse	*mumarred*	ممرض
Student	*taleb*	طالب
Painter	*dahhan*	دهان
Driver	*saek*	سائق
King	*malik*	مالك
Queen	*malika*	ملكة
President	*raess*	رئيس
Minister	*wazeer*	وزير
Ambassador	*safeer*	سفير
Author	*muallef*	مؤلف
Director	*mukhrij*	مخرج
Shoe-maker	*saniol ahdhiya*	صانع الأحذية
Miller	*tahhan*	طحان
Watchmaker	*saaty*	ساعاتي
Hostess	*mudeefatu tayran*	مضيفة طيران
Grocer	*baqqal (samman)*	بقال(سمان)
Baby sitter	*murbbiyatu atfal*	مربية أطفال
Programmer	*mubamij*	مبرمج

Clown	*muharrij*	مهرج
Warehouseman	*ameen mustawdaa*	أمين مستودع
Private Secretary	*ameen sirr*	أمين سر
Bookkeeper	*katibul hisbat*	كاتب الحسابات
Garbage collector	*amelu tandeefath*	عامل تنظيفات
Thief	*liss*	لص
Headmaster	*nadhirul madrasa*	ناظر المدرسة
Football player	*laebo kurati qadam*	لاعب كرة قدم
Arbitrator	*hakam*	حكم
Scientist	*alim*	عالم
Geologist	*geologyy*	جيولوجي
Astronaut	*raedo fadaa*	رائد فضاء
Politician	*siyassy*	سياسي
Contractor	*muqawal*	مقاول
Builder	*bannaa*	بناء
Knight	*fares*	فارس
Mayor	*mukhtaar*	مختار
Coach	*mudarreb*	مدرب
Warrior	*muhareb*	محارب
Principal	*mudeeru madrasa*	مدير مدرسة
Bellboy	*khadimu fondoq*	خادم فندق
Captain	*qubtan*	قبطان
Housekeeper	*mubarridathu manzil*	مبردة منزل
Sniper	*qannas*	قنّاص
Sergeant	*raqeeb*	رقيب

Teller	*ammenus sandouk (fil masref)*	أمين الصّندوق (في المصرف)
Beekeeper	*nahhal*	نحّال
Fortune-Teller	*qareeol bakht*	قارئ البخت
Postman	*sael bareed*	ساعي البريد
Leader	*qaed*	قائد
Prime minister	*raeesol wuzaraa*	رئيس الوزارء
Professor	*ustad/professor*	بروفسور/ استاد
Chemist	*keemayaee*	كيمائي
Physicist	*feezayee*	فيزائي
Cook	*tahee*	طاهي
Designer	*musammem*	مصمّم
Representative	*mandoub*	مندوب
Actor	*mumathel*	ممثل
Actress	*mumathela*	ممثلة
News broadcast	*mudheea*	مذيع
Reporter	*murasel*	مراسل
Fisher	*sayyadu samak*	صيّاد السّمك
Hunter	*sayyad tuyyour*	صياد الطيور
Athlete	*riyadi*	رياضي
Shepherd	*raey*	راعي
Farmer	*muzarea*	مزارع
Prince	*ameer*	أمير
Princess	*ameera*	أميرة
Writer	*kateb*	كاتب
Model	*aridatu azyaa*	عارضة أزياء

Upholstered	*munajjed*	منجد
Undertaker	*hanouty*	حانوتي
Wrestler	*musarea*	مصارع
Sculptor	*nahhat*	نحّات
Painter	*rassam*	رسّام
Servant	*khadem*	خادم
Lather/Turner	*kharrat*	خرّاط
Taxi driver	*saequ taxi*	سائق تاكسي
Tax collector	*gabee*	جابي
Midwife	*qabilatun qanouniyya*	قابلة قانونية
Brigadier	*ameed*	عميد
Legal Consultant	*mustashar qanouny*	مستشار قانوني
First aid man	*musef*	مسعف
Matchmaker	*khatiba*	خاطبة
Sweeper	*kannass*	كنّاس
Paver	*ballat*	بلاط

Stationary

Stationery	*al qirtasiyya*	القرطاسية
Book	*kitab*	كتاب
Paper	*waraqa*	ورقة
Ballpoint pens	*aqlam hibr jaaf*	أقلام حبر جاف
Signature pens	*aqlam tauqeeh*	أقلام توقيع
Pencils	*aqlam rasas*	أقلام رصاص
Sharpener	*barraya qalamurasas*	براية قلم رصاص
Paper clip	*mushbik awraq*	مشبك أوراق

Post pads	*lasiq awraq*	لاصق أوراق
Marker pen	*qalamussaoora*	قلم سبورة
Highlighter	*qalamu fasfoora*	قلم فسفوري
Stapler	*dabbasa*	دباسة
Gum/Glue	*samag*	صمغ
Box file	*malaffat box*	ملفات بوكس
Paper divider	*fasil awraq*	فاصل أوراق
Calculator	*ala hasine*	آلة حاسبة
Ruler	*mistara*	مسطرة
Punching machine	*kharama*	خرامة
Sticky notepad	*noota bilasiq*	نوتة بلاصق
Eraser	*mahaya rasas*	محاية رصاص
Transparent tap	*tap shafaf*	تيب شفاف
Double sticker	*lasiq wajatayn*	لاصق وجهتين
Scissors	*maqass*	مقص
Envelope opener	*fattaha muglafat*	فتاحة مغلفات
Staple remover	*khalla dababees*	خلاعة دبابيس
Envelope	*darf*	ظرف
Diary	*aganda*	أجندا
Note book	*daftor*	دفتر
Ball	*kurra*	كرة
Volley ball	*kurratulyad*	كرة اليد
Basket ball	*kurratussela*	كرة السلة
Rope	*habl*	حبل
Toy	*luaba*	لعبة
Slate/Board	*lawha*	لوحة

Coloured papers	*awraq mulawwana*	أوراق ملونة
Drawing sheets	*awraq rrasam*	أوراق الرسم
Wholesale	*bil jumla*	بالجملة
Retail	*bil mafraq*	بالمفرق
Bag	*haqeeba*	حقيبة
File	*malaff*	ملف
Newspaper	*jareeda*	جريدة
Magazine	*majalla*	مجلة
Stories	*qisas*	قصص
Computer	*hasoub (computer)*	حاسوب (كمبيوتر)
CDs	*alaqrasul mudmaja*	الأقراص المدمجة
Books/Resources	*kutub/marajea*	كتب / مراجع
Napkin	*ulbathu maharem*	علبة محارم
Perforator	*kharramatu waraq*	خرامة ورق
Headphone	*samatur raas*	سماعة الرأس
Telephone	*hatif*	هاتف
Garbage can	*sallatu muhamalaat*	سلة المهملات
Drawer	*durj*	درج
Calendar	*taqweem (ruznama)*	تقويم (رزنامة)
Correction pen	*musahheh*	مصحح
Timer	*saa*	ساعة
Cutter	*qatea*	قاطعة
Compass	*birkar*	بركار
Air conditioner	*mukayyeful hawaa*	مكيف الهواء
Map	*khareeta*	خريطة
Stamp	*tabea*	طابع

CD holder	*hamilatul aqrassil mudmaja*	حاملة الأقراص المدمجة
Globe	*al kuratul ardiyya*	الكرة الأرضية
Lamp	*misbah*	مصباح
Sharpener	*mibrat*	مبراة
Adhesive tape	*ashshareetul lasiq*	الشريط اللاصق
Khitm	*stamp*	ختم

Hotel, Restaurant, Food

Hotel	*funduq*	فندق
Room	*gurfah*	غرفة
Bath attached room	*gurfa bil hamam*	غرفة بالحمام
Room without bathroom	*gurfabidooon hamam*	غرفة بدون حمام
Lounge	*swala*	صالة
Balcony	*shurfa*	شرفة
Is there a telephone in the room?	*fee telephone filgurfa*	في تليفون في الغرفة ؟
Is there a TV in the room?	*fee talfiziyoon fil gurfa*	في تلفزيون في الغرفة ؟
Is there a heater in the room?	*fee musakhin fil gurfa*	في مسخن في الغرفة ؟
Is the room air conditioned?	*hal gurfa mukayyafa*	هل الغرفة مكيفة ؟
How much is the room rate per day?	*ma hiya ujrathul gurfa fil laylah*	ماهي أجرة الغرفة في الليلة ؟
Please don't disturb	*arrajaa adamil izaj*	الرجاء عدم الإزعاج
No smoking please	*alrijah adam al tadkheen*	الرجاء عدم التدخين
I want a cup of coffee	*ureedu finjan qahwah*	أريد فنجان قهوة

I want a cup of tea without milk	*ureedu koob shay bidoona haleeb*	اريد كوب شاي بدون حليب
With sugar or without sugar	*bissukkar aw bidoon sukkar*	بسكر او بدون سكر
I want to change the bed sheets	*ureedu tabdeelassharashef*	أريد تبديل الشراشف
I want to change the room	*ureedu tabdeelal gurfa*	أريد تبديل الغرفة
I want to change the key	*ureedu tabdeel al miftah*	أريد تبديل المفتاح
I want an orange juice	*ureedu aseer burthugal*	أريد عصير برتقال
I want cold water	*ureedu mae barid*	أريد ماء بارد
What is my room number ?	*ma huwa raqamu gurfatee ?*	ما هو رقم غرفتي؟
I want you to wake me up at 7 o' clock in the morning	*arjoo an tooqizanee fis sabi'ah sabahan*	أرجو أن توقظني في السابعة صباحا
I want the bus to lift me early to the airport	*ureedu an yoosilani lbaso ila lmatari bakiran*	أريد أن يوصلني الباص إلى المطار باكرا
Please drop me at the airport early	*arjoo wadanee al matar mubakkira*	ارجو ودعني المطار مبكرا
Bathroom	*hammam*	حمام
Shower	*doosh*	دوش
Room service	*khidmato gorfah*	خدمة الغرفة
Lobby	*albahow*	البهو
Visitor	*zair*	زائر
Single room	gorfa mofaridah	غرفة مفردة

Double room	gorfa mozdawajah	غرفة مزدزجة
Servant	*khadim*	خادم
First class	*darajah* oola	درجة أولى
Second class	*darajak* thaniyah	درجة ثانية
Restaurant	*mat'am*	مطعم
Breakfast	*fotoor*	فطور
Lunch	*gadaa*	غداء
Dinner	*ashaa*	عشاء
Fork	*shawkah*	شوكة
Knife	*sikkeen*	سكين
Cup	*finjan*	فنجان
Dish	*sahn*	صحن
Table	*tawilah/ maeda*	طاولة / مائدة
Waiter	*nadil/ garson*	نادل / غرسون / جرسون
Bill	*fatoorah*	فاتورة
Meat	*lahm*	لحم
Chicken	*dajaj*	دجاج
Fish	*samak*	سمك
Menu	*laihato ttaam/ kaimath alttam*	لائحة الطعام/قائمة الطعام
Soup	*shoorbah*	شوربة
Chick-peas	*hommos*	حمص
Peas	*bazilaa*	بازلاء
Cake	*kaak*	كعك
Napkin	*mahramah*	محرمة
Glass	*kaas*	كأس
Spoon	*milaqah*	ملعقة

Cook	*tabbakh*	طباخ
Vegetarian	*nabatee*	نباتي
Non vegetarian	*gairnabatee*	غيرنباتي
Fry	*mushwe*	مشوي
I'm a vegetarian I don't eat meat	*ana nabatiy la akolo llohoom*	أنا نباتي لا آكل اللحوم
I prefer fish meals	*ana uhibbual asmak*	أنا أحب الأسماك
Don't put salt in my food	*la tada milhan ala taami*	لا تضع ملحاً على طعامي
Salad without oil	*assalta bidoon zayt*	السلطة بدون زيت
Feast	*maedaba*	مأدبة
Party	*wajba*	وجبة
Fried Chicken	*dajaj Mushavee*	دجاج مشوي
Juice	*aseer*	عصير
meal	*wajabah ta'am*	وجبة طعام
Soops	*ashoorbat*	الشوربات
Vegetable soup	*shoorbal khudar*	شوربة الخضار
Cream of chicken soup	*shoorbat kremal dajaj*	شوربة كريمة الدجاج
Mushroom soup	*shoorba mashroom*	شوربة مشروم
Lentil soup	*shoorba adas*	شوربة عدس
Onion soup	*soorbal basel*	شوربة البصل
Sweet corn chicken soup	*shoorba dajaj biddurel halwa*	شوربة دجاج بالذرة الحلوة
Sweet corn vegetable soup	*shoorbal khudar biddural halwa*	شوربة الخضار بالذرة الحلوة

Hot and sour chicken soup	*shoorba dajaj har wa hamid*	شوربة دجاج حار و حامض
Cold apetizers	*al miqbalata barida*	المقبلات الباردة
Green salad	*salata khadrae*	سلطة خضراء
Hammoos	*hammas*	حمص
Mutabbel	*mutabbel*	متبل
Vine leave	*warq* inab	ورق عنب
Brains salad	*salata nakhaat*	سلطة نخاعات
Olives salad	*salata Zaytoon*	سلطة زيتون
Beans in oil	*bamiya bizzay*	بامية بالزيت
Youghurt with cuccumber	*roob khiyar*	روب خيار
French Fries	*batata muqalis*	بطاطا مقلية
Pickle	*mukhallil mushakkil*	مخلل مشكل
Mixed vegetable	*khudar mushakkal*	خضار مشكل
Rocket salad	*salata jirjeer*	سلاطة جرجير
Russian salad	*salata roosiyya*	سلاطة روسية
Greek salad	*salata yoonaniya*	سلطة يونانية
Mixed appetizers	*muqabbalat mushakkal*	مقبلات مشكل
Shrimp cocktail	*roban cocktail*	روبيان كوكتيل
Hot appetizers	*muqabbalat assakhina*	المقبلات الساخنة
Hamous with meat	*hammas billahma*	حمص باللحمة
Hammous with shawarma	*hammas shawarma*	حمص شورما
Fried wings	*jawanih* muqliya	جوانح مقلية
Chicken liver	*kabda dajaj*	كبدة دجاج
Fried mutton kidney	*beed ganam magala*	بيض غنم مقلي

Brain pane	*nakhaat baniyya*	نخاعات بانية
Fried Kebbeh	*kebbah mukliya*	كبة مقلية
Cheese pastry	*barak janba*	برك جبنة
Pastries	*alfatair*	الفطائر
Cheese	*jubna*	جبنة
Meat	*lahma*	لحمة
Zaatar	*zaatar*	زعتر
Spinach	*spinakh*	سبانخ
Labnah	*labneh*	لبنة
Eastern grills	*al musawee alsarqiyya*	المشاوي الشرقية
Kabab	*kabab*	كباب
Indian kabab	*kabab hindi*	كباب هندي
Chicken fry special	*dijaj maqlee khas*	دجاج مقلي خاص
Grilled chicken wings	*gawanh dijaj maswiyya*	جوانح دجاج مشوية
Kabab hot gril	*kabab khaskhas*	كباب خشخاش
Shish tawook	*seesh thaooq*	شيش طاووق
Boneless chicken	*dijaj mushab ala alfahm*	دجاج مسحب على الفحم
Grilled chicken	*dijaj muswee balihadm*	دجاج مشوي بالعظم
Meat hirayas	*arayes balilhama*	عرايس باللحمة
Mix grill	*masawee mushkil*	مشاوي مشكل
Main dish	*alatbak alraeesiyya*	الاطباق الرئيسية
Majboos	*magboos/ Makboos*	مجبوس / مكبوس
Western dish	*alitbakh alarabiyya*	الاطباق الغربية
Escalope chicken	*saklob dijaj*	سكلوب دجاج
Escalope meat	*saklob lahma*	سكلوب لحمة

Steek mushroom	*stayk mushroom*	ستيك مشروم
Steek with peper	*stayk balilfulful*	ستيك بالفلفل
Slice chicken	*sarihat dijaj balisos*	شرحات دجاج بالصوص
Pastries	*almuhganat almahasee*	المعجنات والمحاشي
Sea food	*mawkoolath bahriya*	مأكولات بحرية
Prawn chilly	*robayan balifulful*	روبيان بالفلفل
Prawn garlic	*robayan balithowm*	روبيان بالثوم
Prawn ginger	*robayan balizinjeel*	روبيان بالزنجبيل
Prawnmanchoorian	*robayan mansooreen*	روبيان منشورين
Grilled hamour	*hamoor fayla mushawee*	هامور فيلية مشوي
Prawn fried or grill	*robayan maqlee aw mushawee*	روبيان مقلي او مشوي
Sandwiches	*alsandoyathshat*	السندويتشات
Club sandwiches	*klob sandothash*	كلوب سندوتش
Toast chicken	*tosth dijaj*	توست دجاج
Toast cheese	*tosth jubna*	توست جبنة
Kabab sandwiches	*sandoyatsh mushawee*	سندويتش مشاوي
Shaworma sandwiches	*sandoyatsh shawarma*	سندويتش شاورما
Routy sandwiches	*sandosh rothee*	سندويتش روتي
Rubian sandwiches	*sandosh robiyaan*	سندويتش روبيان
Juices	*alasaer*	العصائر
Orange juice	*aseer burtuqal*	عصير برتقال
Mango juice	*aseer manjoo*	عصير مانجو
Strawberry juice	*aseer faravala*	عصير فراولة
Cocktail juice	*cocktal*	كوكتيل

Mix vegetables	*kidrwath musakal*	خضراوات مشكل
Veg Kuruma	*kuruma kidrwath*	قورمة خضراوات
Daal fry	*daal muqlee*	دال مقلي
Fast food	*wajba sareea*	وجبة سريعة
Appricot	*mishmish*	مشمش
Peach	*durraq*	درّاق
Pears	*ijas*	اجاص
Muskmelon	*shammam*	شمام
Peach	*khoukh*	خوخ
Raddish	*fijl*	فجل
Corriandor	*kuzbara*	كزبرة
Popcorn	*fishar*	فشار
soft drinks	*martabat*	مرطبات
milk	*haleeb*	حليب
youghurt	*laban*	لبن
cheese	*jobnah*	جبنة
salt	*milh*	ملح
sugar	*sokkar*	سكر
fish	*samak*	سمك
nuts	*jawz*	جوز
salad	*salatah*	سلطة
mint	*nahnah*	نعناع
orange	*bortoqal*	برتقال
Apple	*Tuffaha*	تفاحة
beans	*fasoolya*	فاصوليا

peas	*bazillah*	بازيلاء
lentil	*adas*	عدس
chick-peas	*hommos*	حمص
beans	*fool*	فول
wheat	*qamh*	قمح
rice	*arozz*	أرز
cherries	*karaz*	كرز
fig	*teen*	تين
melon	*bateex*	بطيخ
lemon	*laymoon*	ليمون
almond	*lawz*	لوز
cabbages	*malfoof*	ملفوف
carrot	*jazar*	جزر
onion	*basal*	بصل
garlic	*aoom*	ثوم
banana	*mawz*	موز
dates	*tamr*	تمر
pomegranate	*romman*	رمان
cucumber	*xiyar*	خيار
lettuce	*xass*	خس
Honey	*asal*	عسل
Croissant	*krwassan*	كرواسان
Do you have change?	*indaka fakka*	عندك فكّة؟
Did you like it ?	*hal Aejabaka*	هل اعجبك؟
I really like it	*aejabanee haqqan*	اعجبني حقّا

I am hungry	*ana jaeh*	انا جائع
I am thirsty	*ana atshan*	انا عطشان
I am angry	*ana zaelan*	انا زعلان
I am angry	*ana gadban*	انا غضبان
I am happy	*ana farhan*	انا فرحان
Call me tomorrow	*kallimanee bukra*	كلمني بكرة
We are honoured It was an honour to meet you	*tasharrafna*	تشرفنا
OK	*hasanan*	حسناً
Nice to meet you	*saedatu billiqaeka*	سعدت بلقائك
water	*maa*	ماء
Kitchen Ware	*advat mathbaka*	أدوات المطبخ
Home Appliances	*advat manziliyya*	ادوات منزلية
plate	*sahn*	صحن
spoon	*milaqah*	ملعقة
table-spoon	*milaqat taam*	ملعقة طعام
tea - spoon	*milaqat shay*	ملعقة شاي
fork	*shawkah*	شوكة
Cooker	*tanjarah*	طنجرة
tray	*sayniyyah*	صينية
tea-pot	*ibreeq shay*	ابريق شاي
tea - cup	finjan *shay*	فنجان شاي
frying pan	*miqlat*	مقلاة
electric fan	*mirwahah*	مروحة
flat-iron	*mikwat*	مكواة
electric razor	*alat hilaqah*	آلة حلاقة

sewing machine	*makanat ziyatah*	مكنة خياطة
television	*tilfizyon*	تلفزيون
radio	*almudyah/radiyo*	المذياع/راديو
door	*bab*	باب
oven	*forn*	فرن
pot	*qidr*	قدر
kitchen	*matbax*	مطبخ
bath sponge	*leefah*	ليفة
refrigerator	*barrad*	براد
carpet	*sajjad*	سجاد
curtain	*sitar*	ستار
cot	*sareer*	سرير
sofa	*areeka*	اريكة
bronze	*bronz*	برونز
steel	*foolath*	فولاذ
platinum	*platen*	بلاتين
nickel	*neekel*	نيكل
lead	*rasas*	رصاص
Washing machine	*ghassala*	غسّالة
Microwave	*microwave*	مايكروايف
Dryer	*nashafa*	نشّافة
Dishwasher	*jallaya*	جلّاية
Washing gloves	*qoffazan liljaly*	قفازان للجلي
Washing – up liquid	*saeel liljaly*	سائل للجلي
Washing sponge	*leefaton liljaly*	ليفة للجلي
Wooden spoon	*milaqatu tabkh*	ملعقة طبخ

Tablecloth	*ghataaon liltawil*	غطاء للطاولة
Kettle	*ibreeq*	إبريق
Storage jar	*bartaman*	برطمان
Rolling pin	*shawbak*	شوبك
Pestle	*medaqqatu thoum*	مدقة ثوم
Juicer, Squeezer	*assara*	عصارة
Mixing bowl	aniya/ *wiaa*	آينة/وعاء
Strainer	*misfaat*	مصفاة
Coffeepot	*rakwatu qahwa*	ركوة قهوة
Bread pack	*ulbathu khubzan*	علبة خبز
Cookbook	*kitabu tabkhen*	كتاب طبخ
Apron	*miezer* (*maryala*)	مئزر (مريلة)
Freezer	*thallaja*	ثلاجة
Balance	*meezan*	ميزان
Coffee maker	*saniul qahwa*	صانع القهوة
Toaster	*muhammisa*	محمصة
Tea towel	*menshafatus suhon*	منشفة الصحون
Worktop	*khashabatut taqteea*	خشبة التقطيع
Mixing bowl	*wiaaul khalt*	وعاء الخلط
Detergents	*munadhifat*	منظفات
Thermos	*tirmus*	ترمس
Whip	*khaffaqa*	خفاقة
Funnel	*qimaa*	قمع

Invitations الدعوات

Welcome	*ahlan wa sahlan*	أهلاً وسهلاً
Please come	*tafaddal*	تفضل
You are invited to	*anta maduwn ilal*	أنت مدعو إلى العشاء

dinner	*ashae*	
You are invited to lunch	*anta madwuww ila algidah*	انت مدعو الى الغداء
You are invited to breakfast	*anta maduww ila al futhoor*	انت مدعو الى الفطور
You are invited to a party	*anta maduww ila hafla*	انت مدعو الى حفلة
You are invited to tea	*anta maduww ila sshay*	انت مدعو الى الشاي
You are invited to a party	*anta maduww ila valeema*	انت مدعو الى وليمة
I missed you	*laqad ishtaqtu ilayk*	لقد اشتقت إليك
It's a long time since we've met	*lam araka mundu zaman/ma shuftuka min zaman*	لم أرك منذ زمن/ ما شفتك من زمان
You are invited with all friends to party tonight	*innaka maduww wa jameea l asdiqa iilalhaflat illayah*	إنك مدعو وجميع الأصدقاء إلى الحفلة الليلة
Are you busy tonight ?	*hal anta mashgool allaylah ?*	هل أنت مشغول الليلة ؟
Are you busy today?	*hal anta masgool alyawm ?*	هل أنت مشغول اليوم ؟
Are you busy now ?	*hal anta masgool alheen*	هل أنت مشغول الحين ؟
Is he busy now ?	*hal huwa masgool alheen ?*	هل هو مشغول الحين ؟
Are you busy tomorrow ?	*hal anta masgool bukra ?*	هل أنت مشغول بكرة ؟
I want to introduce you to my family members	*ureedu an uarrifaka ala afradi ailathi*	أريد أن أعرفك على أفراد عائلتي
I want to introduce	*ureedu an ahrfaka*	أريد ان اعرفك على

you to the members of my organisation	*ala ahdah jameeathi*	اعضاء جمعيتي
I want to introduce you to the members of my team	*ureedu an ahrfaka ala ahdae fareeqee*	اريد ان اعرفك على اعضاء فريقي
I want to introduce you to the members of my company	*ureedu an ahrfa ala ahdahi sarikathee*	اريد ان اعرفك على اعضاء شركتي
How about a cup of tea ?	*ma raeyaka fe koobi shay*	ما رأيك في كوب شاي؟
How about a cup of coffee ?	*ma raayoka bifinjani qahwa ?*	ما رأيك بفنجان قهوة ؟

Family العائلة

Family		العائلة
Grandfather	*jadd*	جد
Grandmother	*jaddah*	جدة
Father	*ab*	أب
Mother	*um*	أم
Son	*ibn*	إبن
Daughter	*ibnah*	إبنة
Baby Boy	*sabiyy*	صبي
Baby Girl	*sabiyya*	صبية
Girl	*bint*	بنت
Uncle	*amm*	عم
Aunt	*ammah*	عمة
Uncle	*khal*	خال
Aunt	*khala*	خالة

Nephew	*ibn alakh*	إبن الأخ
Niece	*ibnathi alakh*	إبنة الأخ
Cousin	*ibnalamm*	إبن العم
Cousin	*ibnathiamm*	إبنة العم
Cousin	*ibnalkhal*	إبن الخال
Cousin	*ibnathilkhal*	إبنة الخال
Neighbours	*jeeran*	يران
Son in law/Brother in law	*sihr*	صهر
Daughter in law	*kannah*	كنة
Friends	*asdiqaa*	أصدقاء
Relatives	*aqarib*	أقارب
Kinsman	*qareeb*	قريب
Brother	*akh*	اخ
Sister	*ukth*	اخت
Grand son	*hafeed*	حفيد
Grand daughter	*hafeeda*	حفيدة
Father-in-law	*hamoo*	حمو
Mother-in-law	*hamat*	حماة

At the Tailor عند الخياط

I need a shirt for my son	*ureedu qamees livalade*	اريد قميص لولدي
Do you need a readymade shirt ?	*tabgee qamees jahiz*	تبغ قميص جاهز ؟
I don't want	*la abgee*	لا ابغي
I want you to stich a	*abgee takheetu lahu*	ابغي ان تخيط له قميص

good shirt for him	*qamees zany*	زين
Big size	*hajm kabeer*	حجم كبير
Small size	*hajm sageer*	حجم صغير
Shirt	*qamees*	قميص
Pants	*bantaloon*	بنطلون
Pants/Trousers	*sirval*	سروال
Size	*maqas*	مقاس
Measurement	*qiyas*	قياس
Towel	*minshafah*	منشفة
Swimming suit	*mayyoh*	مايوه
Girdle	*mishadd*	مشد
Wool	*soof*	صوف
Silk	*hareer*	حرير
Linen	*kittan*	كتان
How much is the meter of this fabric?	*ma taaman mithril qimash?*	ما ثمن متر القماش ؟
Give me two meters of this cloth	*atinee mithrayani min hatha nnawe*	أعطني مترين من هذا النوع
Don't you have another colour ?	*ala yoojado ladayka lawn akhar ?*	ألا يوجد لديكم لون آخر ؟
Handkerchief	*mindeel*	منديل
Dress	*fostan*	فستان
Blouse	*blooz*	بلوز
Skirt	*tannora*	تنورة
Jacket	*jakeet*	جاكيت
Coat	*mitaf*	معطف

Belt	*zinnar*	زنار
Gloves	*qoffazat*	قفازات
Socks	*jawarib*	جوارب
Button	*zirr*	زر
Sweater	*kanzah*	كنزة
Tie	*kravat*	كرافات
Do you have shirts ?	*hal indaka qumsan ?*	هل عندك قمصان ؟
Women's wears	*albisaton nisaiyyah*	ألبسة نسائية
Men's wears	*albiston rrijaliyyah*	ألبسة رجالية
I want a sweater	*ureedu kanzata soof*	أريد كنزة صوف
Napkin	*mindeel Sofrah*	منديل سفرة
I want you to shorten my pants	*ureedu an toqassira lee albintal*	أريد أن تقصر لي البنطال
I want you to make for me a long coat	*ureedu an tasnaa lee litafan taweelan*	اريد أن تصنع لي معطفا طويلاً
I want you to let out the waist	*ureedu an towassi lee al kasr*	أريد أن توسع لي الخصر
Can I try it on ?	*hal astateeo an ajrabaha*	هل أستطيع أن أجربها
I want long sleeves	*ureedu akmaman taweelah*	أريد أكماماً طويلة
Where is the measuring room?	*ayna gorfatol qiyas*	أين غرفة القياس؟
Where is the mirror?	*aynal mirrah*	أين المرآة ؟
I want another colour	*ureedu lawnan akhar*	أريد لوناً آخر
I like this style	*yohiboni hatha ttasmeem*	يعجبني هذا التصميم

At the Shoes Shop عند محل الاحذية

Shoes	*hidae*	حذاء
I want a pair of men's shoes	*ureedu hidae rijjaliyya*	أريد حذاء رجالية
I want a black shoe	*ureedu hithahan aswad*	أريد حذاء أسود
I want a bigger size shoes	*ureedu hidae akbara qiyasan*	أريد حذاء اكبر قياساً
I want a women's shoes	*ureedu hithana nisaiyyan*	اريد حذاء نسائياً
High heeled	*kaab alee*	كعب عال
Low heeled	*kaab monkhafad*	كعب منخفض
Black shoe lace	*shareet aswad*	شريط أسود
Slipper	*nael*	نعل
Leather slipper	*nael mind jild*	نعل من الجلد
Sandal	*sandal*	صندل
Medium priced	*mutawassitussier*	متوسط السعر
Expensive shoe	*hidae galee*	خذاء غالي
Cheap shoe	*hidae rakea*	خذاء رخيص
Do you have Italian shoe?	*indak akhdiya italiya*	عندك اخذية ايطالية ؟
Do you have an original Indian shoe?	*indak akhdiya hindiyya asliyya*	عندك اخذية هندية اصلية ؟
I want women's shoe	*ureedu hidae nisaiyya*	اريد حذاء نسائية
From high quality	*min nowayyal aliya*	من النوعية العليا ؟

At the Bank في المصرف

Bank	*masrif/bank*	مصرف/بنك

Money	*mal*	مال
Draft/ Money order	*hawalah*	حوالة
Cash	*naqdee*	نقدي
Account	*hisab*	حساب
Current Account	*hisab jaree*	حساب جاري
Saving Account	*hisab toufeer*	حساب توفير
Credit	*dayn*	دين
Loan	*qard*	قرض
Instalment	*aqsat*	اقساط
Interest	*faeda*	فائدة
I want to collect this check	*ureedo an asrifa hadha al shek*	أريد أن أصرف هذا الشيك
Signature	*imda*	إمضاء
Where is the exchange office?	*ayna maktabu ssayrafah*	أين مكتب الصيرفة ؟
When does the bank open?	*mata yaftahu imasrif*	متى يفتح المصرف ؟
Statement	*kashfo hisab*	كشف حساب
I want to open an account here	*ureedu an aftaha hisab ladaykum*	أريد أن أفتح حساباً لديكم
What is the interest rate today ?	*ma qeematul faidah alyowm*	ما قيمة الفائدة اليوم ؟
What is the balance of my account?	*ma huwa raseedu hisabi?*	ما هو رصيد حسابي ؟
I want to renew my credit card	*ureedu an ujaddida bitaqatal iatiman*	أريد أن أجدد بطاقة الائتمان
Account type	*nauwul hisab*	نوع الحساب
Account Number	*raqamul hissab*	رقم الحساب
Statement date	*tareequl kashf*	تاريخ الكشف

Currency	*al umla*	العملة
Credit Card / ATM Card	*bataqatussarafil aalee*	بطاقة الصراف الألى
Without Interest	*bidoon faeda*	بدون فائدة
Narration	*al eedah*	الايضاح
Value date	*tareequl istiqaq*	تاريخ الاستحقاق
(Debit) Withdrawal	*sahb*	سحب
(Deposit) Credit	*eedae*	ايداع
Balance	*raseed*	رصيد
Check	*sheck*	شيك

In the City في المدينة

City	*madeenah*	مدينة
City centre	*markazil madeenah*	مركز المدينة
District	*mantiqah*	منطقة
Building	*binayah*	بناية
Station	*mahattah*	محطة
Shop	*dukkan*	دكان
Shop	*mahall*	محل
Factory	*masna*	مصنع
Telephone office	*markaz ittisalat*	مركز اتصالات
Museum	*mathaf*	متحف
Police station	*markaz alshurtah*	مركز الشرطة
Coffee shop	*maqha*	مقهى
Bar	*hanah*	حانة
Butchery	*malhamah*	ملحمة

Restaurant	*mat'am*	مطعم
Roads	*torqat*	طرقات
Car	*sayyarah*	سيارة
Train	*qitar*	قطار
Ship	*bakhira*	باخرة
Bus	*bas*	باص
Library	*maktabah*	مكتبة
Street	*sharih*	شارع
Bus stop	*mawqif*	موقف
Bridge	*jisr*	جسر
Park	*hadeeqah*	حديقة
Minaret	*manarah*	منارة
Foot path	*raseef*	رصيف
Letter	*risalah*	رسالة
Urgent letter	*risala mostajalah*	رسالة مستعجلة
Registered letter	*risal madmoonah*	رسالة مضمونة
Telegram	*barqiyyah*	برقية
Postal card	*bitaqa bareediyyah*	بطاقة بريدية
Telephone	*hatif*	هاتف
Post box	*sondooqo bareed*	صندوق بريد
Parcel	*tared bareedee*	طرد بريدي
Telephone call	*ittisal*	اتصال

Commerce التجارة

Sales represenative	*mandoob mabeaat*	مندوب مبيعات
Salesman	*baie*	بائع

Dollar	*dolar*	دولار
Money-changing	*sirafah*	صرافة
Partner	*shareek*	شريك
Broker	*simsar*	سمسار
Loss	*khisara*	خسارة
Gain	*ribh*	ربح
Tariff	*tareefah*	تعريفة
Receipt	*wasl*	وصل
How much is the kilo ?	*bikam al keelo?*	بكم الكيلو؟
How much is this ?	*kam hada ?*	كم هذا ؟
It's expensive	*innahoo galee*	إنه غالي
It's cheap	*innahoo rakhees*	إنه رخيص
I want a bigger size	*ureedu qiyasan akbar*	أريد قياسا أكبر
How much is this ?	*kam siro hatha ?*	كم سعر هذا ؟
Let me see this, please	*arinee hatha min fadlik*	أرني هذا من فضلك
I want to try this on	*ureedu an ojarriba hathihi*	أريد أن أجرب هذه
I'll take from this	*atinee min hatha*	أعطني من هذا

Taxi / Bus الاجرة / الباص

Stop	*mawqif*	موقف
Driver	*saiq*	سائق
Fare	*ujrah*	أجرة
I am little hurry	*ana mustajil shuway*	أنا مستعجل شوي

Slow down	*khaffif min suratika*	خفف من سرعتك
Please, stop the car for a while	*min fadlika towaqqaf qaleelan*	من فضلك ، توقف قليلا
I arrived, let me get down here	*laqad wasalt, anzilnee huna*	لقد وصلت ، أنزلني هنا
How much is the fare?	*kam alujra*	كم الاجرة
I want a taxi please	*ureedu sayyara ujra min fadlika*	اريد سيارة اجرة من فضلك
Bus	*hafila*	حافلة
Taxi	*sayyarathul ujra*	سيارة الاجرة
AC	*mukayyef*	مكيف
Speed/Fast	*sura*	سرعة
Bicycle	*darraja*	درّاجة
Motorcycle	*darraja nariyya*	درّاجة نارية
Bus stop	*mawqiful bas*	موقف الباص
Where is the bus stop?	*ayna mawqiful bas ?*	أين موقف الباص ؟
Where are the tickets?	*ayna qatao ttadakir?*	أين قطع التذاكر ؟
How much is the ticket ?	*kam thamano ttadkirah ?*	كم ثمن التذكرة ؟
Give me a ticket Please	*ureedu thadkirat min fadlik*	أريد تذكرة من فضلك
I want to go to Delhi	*ureedu an adhaba ila delhi*	أريد أن أذهب إلى دلهي
How many hours does it take ?	*kam saatan tastagriqu ila hounak ?*	كم ساعة تستغرق إلى هناك ؟
When shall we reach there ?	*mata nasil hinak ?*	متى نصل هناك؟

Drop me here please	*anzilnee huna min fadlik*	انزلني هنا، من فضلك
Can you turn on the AC please	*hal yumkinuka tashgeelol mokayyif?*	هل يمكنك تشغيل المكيف ؟
Is there any empty seat ?	*hal yoojad makan shagir?*	هل يوجد مكان شاغر؟

The Jewellery المجوهرات

Jeweller	*jawhary*	جوهري
Goldsmith	*saig*	صائغ
Gold	*dahab*	ذهب
Silver	*fidda*	فضة
Gold Souq/ Gold market	*souqu ddahab*	سوق الذهب
What is the gold rate today?	*ma seura dahab ela youm*	ما سعر الذهب اليوم ؟
Bracelet	*siwar*	سوار
Where is the jewellery shop?	*ayna mahallul mujawharat*	أين محل المجوهرات؟
Can you guide me to it ?	*hal bi imakatina an tadullanee alayhi ?*	هل بإ مكانك أن تدلني عليه ؟
I want a silver ring	*ureedu khatam fiddah*	أريد خاتم فضة
I want a golden ring	*ureedu khatam dahab*	أريد خاتم ذهب
Can I try it ?	*hal bi imkanee an ujarribahu ?*	هل بإمكاني أن أجربه
I want to buy this bracelet	*sa ashtaree hadihil oswarah*	سأشتري هذه الاسوارة
I want to gift it to my girl friend	*sauqaddimuha hadiyya lisadeeqatee*	سأقدمها هدية لصديقتي

How much is this necklace ?	*ma thamanu hadal iqd ?*	ما ثمن هذا العقد ؟
How many grams does it weigh?	*kam graman yazin ?*	كم غراماً يزن ؟

At the Travel Agency في مكتب السفريات

Tourism	*siyahah*	سياحة
Travel	*safar*	سفر
Passport	*jawaz safar*	جواز سفر
Ticket	*bitaqat safar/tadkira*	بطاقة سفر / تذكرة
Visa	*viza*	فيزا
Airlines	*khuotoot jawwiyah*	خطوط جوية
Airplane	*tairah*	طائرة
I want to travel to London	*ureedo an usafira ila landon*	أريد أن أسافر إلى لندن
How much is the ticket ?	*ma tamanu ttatdkirah*	ما ثمن التذكرة ؟
Where is the enquiry office ?	*ayna maktabul isteilamat ?*	اين مكتب الاستعلامات؟
Is the visa ready ?	*hal alveeza jahizah*	هل الفيزا جاهزة ؟
Is the visa ready?	*hal altaeshheerath jahizath*	هل التأشيرة جاهزة ؟
When shall we reach India?	*mata sansail al hind*	متى سنصل الهند ؟
What are the flights available with you?	*ma hiya mawaeedur rihalatil mutawaffi ladaykum*	ماهي مواعيد الرحلات المتوفر لديكم ؟

I want a return ticket to London	*ureedu tadkira dihab wa iyab ila london*	اريد تذكرة ذهاب واياب الى لندن
International airport	*matar dowalee*	مطار دولي
Domestic airport	*matar dakhilee*	مطار داخلي
What is the time of the flight?	*mata mawidurrihalah ?*	متى موعد الرحلة ؟
When will we arrive?	*mata nasil ?*	متى نصل ؟
Is there any other flight this evening?	*hal minrihla okhra hadal masaa ?*	هل من رحلة أخرى هذا المساء ؟
What is the allowed weight?	*ma howa al waznul masmooh bihee ?*	ما هو الوزن المسموح به؟
I have three bags only	*ladayaa talatu haqaeiba faqat*	لدي ثلاث حقائب فقط
Can you help me with my luggage?	*hal yumkinoka musaadatee fee hamil amtiah ?*	هل يمكنك مساعدتي في حمل الأمتعة ؟
Is there any tourist guide?	*hal yoojado daleel siyahiyee ?*	هل يوجد دليل سياحي ؟
Reception	*istiqbal*	استقبال
Landing	*haboot*	هبوط
take off	*iqlae*	اقلاع
Booking	*hajz*	حجز
Waiting list	*qaematul intidar*	قائمة الانتظار
Emigration	*hijra*	هجرة

Travelling by Sea السفر بالبحر

The marine travel company	*sharikat safar bahriyah*	شركة سفر بحرية

I want a return ticket	*ureedu tadkira dihab wa iyab*	أريد تذكرة ذهاب وإياب
Is it safe to travel by sea today ?	*hal albahru munasib lissafaril yawm ?*	هل البحر مناسب للسفر اليوم ؟
How many days does it take to India?	*kam yawm yastaqriqu ssafar ilalhind*	كم يوم يستغرق السفر إلى الهند ؟
How many points to stop at during our journey?	*kama mahattat woqoof toojado ala tareeqina*	كم محطة وقوف توجد على طريقنا ؟
Do you have a marine passport ?	*hal ladayka jawaz safar bahree ?*	هل لديك جواز سفر بحري ؟
Do you have life boats on the ship?	*hal yoojad qawarib najat ala matni ssafeenah?*	هل يوجد قوراب نجاة على متن السفينة ؟
I can't swim	*la astateeu an asbah*	لا أستطيع أن أسبح
When does the ship leave?	*mata tantaliqul bakhira ?*	متى تنطلق الباخرة ؟
I feel dizzy	*ashure biduwwar fee raesee*	أشعر بدوار في رأسي
ship	*safeena*	سفينة
Navigation	*mullaha*	ملاحة
Is lunch included in the ticket?	*hal tadkira tatadammanu wajabatil gadae ?*	هل التذكرة تتضمن وجبات الغداء ؟
customs	*jamrak*	جمرك
luggage	*amtiah / haqaib*	أمتعة/حقائب
hand bag	*haqeebat yad*	حقيبة يد
check-in	*tafteesh*	تفتيش
This is my bag	*hathihee haqeebatee*	هذه حقيبتي
Open your bag	*iftah alhaqeebah*	افتح الحقيبة

I lost my bag	*daat haqeebatee*	ضاعت حقيبتي
do you have any dangerous things?	*hal ladayka adwat khatirah?*	هل لديك أدوات خطرة؟
Have you got gold?	*hal ladayka dahab*	هل لديك ذهب
Have you got silver?	*hal ladayka fidda*	هل لديك فضة
Have you got any American Dollar?	*hal ladayka dollor amreekee*	هل لديك دولار امريكي
How many baggages have you got?	*kam haqeeba indak*	كم حقيبة عندك
What is the cost of the items?	*kam qeemal badaaeh*	كم قيمة البضائع ؟
Have you got anything to declare?	*indaka shaye tuelin anhu*	عندك شئ تعلن عنه ؟
You have to pay customs duty	*lazim tadfae rusoomal jamrak*	لازم تدفع رسوم الجمرك
Can I get exemption from customs duty?	*mumkin hasal istisnae min rusoom jamrakiyya*	ممكن حصل استثناء من رسوم جمركية ؟

Courtesy المجاملات

Welcome	*marhaban bik*	مرحباً بك
Thank you	*shokran lak*	شكراً لك
Can I help you?	*hal astateeul mosaadah*	هل أستطيع المساعدة ؟
Can I help you?	*mumkin usahadik*	ممكن اساعدك ؟
nice to meet you	*sarirtu biliqaeik, liqae saeed*	سررت بلقاءك / لقاء سعيد
Good morning	*sabahalkhair*	صباح الخير
Good evening	*masaolxayr*	مساء الخير
Good night	*tosbihoalxayr*	تصبح على خير

Congratulations	*tahaneat*	تهنئة
Happy birthday	*meeladon saeed*	ميلاد سعيد
Good bye	*maassalamah*	مع السلامة
I am sorry	*ana asif*	أنا آسف
Please come	*tafaddal*	تفضل
I apologize	*anaathathir*	أنا أعتذر
Excuse me	*ismehnee/ samihnee/ hafuvan*	اسمحني / سامحني / عفوا
I love you	*ana uhibbuka*	انا احبك
Do you want to come with me?	*hal toreedo an ta'atiya maee/ thabgee ta'atiya maee?*	هل تريد أن تأتي معي؟/ تبغى تأتي معي؟
Thank you	*shokran lak*	شكراً لك
Do you have an address ?	*hal ladayka onwan?/ hindaka unwan?*	هل لديك عنوان ؟/ عندك عنوان ؟
What's your name ?	*ma smuka? susmaka*	ما اسمك ؟ / شسمك
welcome	*marhaban bik/ marhaban/ ahlan vasahlan*	مرحبًا بك/ مرحباً/ اهلاً وسهلاً
How are you?	*kayfa halok?kaifak? shlonak? shakhbarak*	كيف حالك/كيفك/ شلونك/شخبارك

Diseases/Clinic/ Pharmacy الامراض / العيادة / الصيدلية

Disease	*marad (p) amrad*	مرض (ج) امراض
Dizziness	*dawkha*	دوخة
High temperature	*harara mourtafiah*	حرارة مرتفعة
Diarrhea	*ishal*	اسهال
Cold	*rashh*	رشح

Sweat	*araq*	عرق
Headache	*sudae*	صداع
General weakness	*daafaam*	ضعف عام
What's my Illness?	*ma huwa maradee*	ما هو مرضي؟
Ulcer	*qurhah*	قرحة
Conjunctivitis	*ramad*	رمد
Anemia	*faqrud dam*	فقر دم
Cough	*sual*	سعال
Cancer	*sartan*	سرطان
Cold	*zukam*	زكام
Constipation	*imsak*	امساك
Flu	*inflowanza*	انفلونزا
Rheumatism	*iltihab mafasil*	التهاب مفاصل
Insomnia	*araq*	أرق
Plague	*taoon*	طاعون
Malaria	*malaria*	ملاريا
Varicose	*dawalee*	دوالي
Gangrene	*angareena*	غنغرينا
Neuroglia	*alam ahsab*	ألم أعصاب
Stomach ache	*waja maidah*	وجع معدة
Heartache	*wajaa qalb*	وجع قلب
Headache	*waja raas*	وجع رأس
Sick	*mareed*	مريض
Earache	*waja othon*	وجع اذن
Meningitis	*sahaya*	سحايا
Rupture	*ftaq*	فتاق
Fix	*nawbah*	نوبة

Burn	*horq*	حرق
Fracture	*kasr*	كسر
Hypertension	*irtifa daqt*	ارتفاع الضغط
Blood pressure	*dagtuddam*	ضغط الدم
Diabetics	*sukkaree*	سكري
Clinic	*iyadah*	عيادة
What is your illness?	*mimma tashkoo*	مم تشكو؟
My leg pains	*saqee tue alimunee*	ساقي تؤلمني
Xray	*soorat ashiah*	صورة اشعة
Medicine	*dawaa*	دواء
Blood	*dam*	دم
Urine	*bawl*	بول
Analysis	*tahleel*	تحليل
Pulse	*nabad*	نبض
I will measure your temperature	*sa aqeesu hararataka*	سأقيس حرارتك
Allergy	*hasasiyyah*	حساسية
Male nurse	*mumarrid*	ممرض
Female nurse	*mumarrida*	ممرضة
Hospital	*mostashfa*	مستشفى
Thermometer	*meezan hararah*	ميزان حرارة
Injection	*ibrah/hoqnah*	إبرة / حقنة
Cotton	*qutun*	قطن
Tranquilizer	*mosakkin*	مسكن
Suppository	*tahmeelah*	تحميلة
Prescription	*wasfa tibbiyah*	وصفة طبية
Pain	*alam*	ألم

Give me an antiseptic	*aatinee motahhir liljurh*	أعطني مطهّر للجرح
Which doctor would you advise me?	*bi ayyi tabeeb tansahunee*	بأي طبيب تنصحني ؟
I want a medicine for diarrhea	*ureedu dawa lilishal*	أريد دواء للاسهال
Tablet	*habba*	حبة
Tonic	*muqawwe*	مقوي
You have to rest for 3 days	*alayka an tartah liaalaati ayyam*	عليك أن ترتاح لثلاثة أيام
Dentist	*tabeebul asnan*	طبيب الاسنان
General practitioner	*mumarris aam*	ممرس عام
Consultant	*mustashar*	مستشار
Specialist	*ikhsaee*	اخصائي

Recreation التسلية

Where is the restaurant?	*aynalmatam*	أين المطعم ؟
Where is the cinema?	*aynal sinema*	أين السينما ؟
How about going to the cinema?	*ma raayoka bidhahab ila ssinima*	ما رأيك بالذهاب إلى السينما ؟
How much is the ticket'	*bika attathkarah*	بكم التذكرة ؟
Where is the ticket counter ?	*ayna shobbako ttathakir*	أين شباك التذاكر ؟
When does the show begin?	*mata yabdao ardol feelm*	متى يبدأ عرض الفيلم ؟
Where is the casino?	*ayna yaqool kazino*	اين يقع الكازينو ؟
Theatre	*masrah*	مسرح
Night club	*nadi laylee*	نادي ليلي
Where is the club?	*wayn annade*	وين النادي؟

Where is the swimming pool ?	*wayn birkathussibaha*	وين بركة السباحة ؟
Where is the dance?	*wayn arraqsa*	وين الرقص ؟
Recreation centre	*markazuttarfeeh*	مركز الترافيه
Drama	*masrahiyya*	مسرحية
Magic	*khiffatal yed*	خفة اليد
Musical programme	*azf wa ginae*	عزف وغناء
Take a seat please	*tafaddal wastarih*	تفضل واسترح
Would you like to play?	*hal targab billulhab*	هل ترغب باللعب؟
Would you like to dance?	*hal tarqab birraqas*	هل ترغب بالرقص؟
What is the fare of journey ?	*ma hiya takaleefo ssafar*	ما هي تكاليف السفر؟
Would you like to travel?	*hal targab bissafar*	هل ترغب بالسفر؟
Would you like to reserve?	*hal targab bil hazj*	هل ترغب بالحجز؟

LESSON TWENTY THREE

SOME QUESTIONS

What is your name?	*shusmak?*	شُـسْـمَـك؟
Where are you from?	*min wayn inta?*	مـنْ وينْ انْت؟
Where is your car?	*wayn sayyaaratuk?*	وَيْنْ سَـيَّـارَتُـك؟
Where is your house?	*wayn baituk?*	وَيْنْ بَـيْـتُـك؟
Where is your office?	*wayn maktabuk?*	وَيْنْ مَـكْـتَـبُـك؟
Where is your school?	*wayn madrasatuk?*	يْنْ مَـدْرَسَـتُـك؟
Where do you work?	*wayn tashtagil?*	وَيْنْ تَـشْـتَـغـل؟
Where are you going?	*wayn taruh?*	وَيْنْ تَـرُحْ؟
Where is he from?	*min wayn huwa?*	مـنْ وينْ هُـو؟
Where is she from?	*min wayn hiya?*	مـنْ وينْ هـي؟
Who is that?	*meen dalik?*	مـين ذَلك؟
Who is this?	*meen hada?*	مـين هٰـذَا؟
How do you go home?	*kaifa taruh bait?*	كَيْفَ تَـرُحْ بَـيْت؟
Who goes with you?	*ma'a meen taruh?*	مَـعَ مـينْ تـرُحْ؟
How is he?	*kaifa huwa?*	كَيْفَ هُـو؟
How is she?	*kaifa hiya?*	كَيْفَ هـي؟
Can I go now?	*mumkin aruh alheen?*	مُـمْـكن رُحْ الْحـين؟
Can I speak to the manager, please?	*min fadhlik, mumkin kallamal mudeer?*	مـنْ فَـضْـلك مُـمْـكنْ كَلَّم الْمُـدير؟
When will he come?	*mata yajee?*	مَـتٰى يَجـيء؟
When will you go?	*mataa taruh?*	مَـتٰى تَـرُحْ؟

How much is this?	*kam haada?*	كَمْ هٰـذَا؟
Are you busy?	*hal inta mashgool?*	هَـلْ أَنْتَ مَـشْـغُـول؟
Are you married?	*hal inta mutazawwij?*	هَـلْ أَنْتَ مُـتَـزَوِّج؟
How many children have you got?	*kam walad indak?*	كَمْ وَلَدًا عِـنْدَكَ؟
Have you got a car?	*hal indaka sayyaara?*	هَـلْ عِـنْدَكَ سَـيَّارَة؟
Have you got a house?	*hal indaka bait?*	هَـلْ عِـنْدَكَ بَـيْت؟
What is this?	*shunu haada?*	شُـنُ هٰـذَا؟
What do you want?	*eash tabgi?*	ايشْ تَـبْـغِ؟
Can you drop me at the airport?	*mumkin khallinee almataar?*	مُـمْـكِنْ خَـلِّـنِي الْمَـطَّارْ؟
Can you try for me once more?	*mumkin tuhaawil lee marra thaniya?*	مُـمْـكِنْ تُـحَـاوِلْ لِي مَـرَّة ثَانِيَة؟
How long are you in Doha?	*kam sana inta fiddoha?*	كَمْ سَـنَة أَنْتَ فِي الدُّوحَـة؟
Why you did not attend the meeting?	*laysh lam tahdhur alhafla?*	لَيْشْ لَمْ تَـحْـضُـر الْحَـفْـلَة؟
Why are you tired?	*laysh inta ta'ubaan?*	لَيْشْ أَنْتَ تَـعْـبَـانْ؟
Why did you go early?	*laysh ruh mubakkir?*	لَيْشْ رُحْ مُـبَـكِّـرْ؟
Why didn't you contact?	*laysh lam tattasil?*	لَيْشْ لَمْ تَـتَّـصِـلْ؟
How can I go there?	*kaifa aruh hunaak?*	كَيْفَ أَرُحْ هُـنَاك؟
When does the manager come?	*mataa yajee almudeer?*	مَـتٰـى يَجِـيئ الْمُـدِير؟
When will you come from the office?	*mataa tarji'u minal maktab?*	مَـتٰـى تَـرْجِـع مِـنَ الْمَـكْـتَـب؟
When will you speak to him?	*mataa tukallimahu?*	مَـتٰـى تُـكَـلِّـمُـهُ؟
What time is it?	*saa'a kam?*	سَـاعَـةُ كَمْ؟

What time do you go?	*saa'a kam taruh?*	سَاعَةُ كَمْ تَرُحْ؟
What time do you come?	*saa'a kam tajee?*	سَاعَةُ كَمْ تَجِيئ؟
What time does it open?	*saa'a kam battal?*	سَاعَةُ كَمْ بَطَّلْ؟
What time does it close?	*saa'a kam sakkir?*	سَاعَةُ كَمْ سَكِّرْ؟
What time is the flight?	*saa'a kam ataa'ira?*	سَاعَةُ كَمْ الطَّائِرَة؟
Where are you now?	*wayn inta alheen?*	وَيْنْ أَنْتَ الْحين؟
Can you come over here?	*mumkin tajee hinee?*	مُمْكن تَجِيئ هني؟
Which market do you go?	*ayyu sooqun taruh?*	أيُّ سُوق تَرُحْ؟
Which Airline do you want?	*ayyu taa'ira tabgi?*	أيُّ طَائِرَة تَبْغ؟
When do you go to the office?	*saa'a kam taruh maktab?*	سَاعَةُ كَمْ تَرُحْ مَكْتَب؟
What is the price of this clock?	*kam haadihissaa'a?*	كَمْ هٰذه السَّاعَة؟
What is the last price?	*aakhir kam?*	آخر كَمْ؟
How much did you buy this for?	*bikam ishtarayta haadihee?*	بكَمْ إشْتَرَيْتَ هٰذه؟
What is the discount?	*khasm kam?*	خَصْمُ كَمْ؟
Where can I find a bank?	*wayn ajid bank?*	وَيْنْ أجدْ بَنْك؟
Where can I find a hotel?	*wayn ajid funduq?*	وَيْنْ أجدْ فُنْدقْ؟
Where can I find an interpreter / translator?	*wayn ajid mutarjim?*	وَيْنْ أجدْ مُتَرجمْ؟
Where can I find a house?	*wayn ajid bait?*	وَيْنْ أجدْ بَيْت؟
Where can I find a school?	*wayn ajid madrasa?*	وَيْنْ أجدْ مَدْرَسَة؟

Where is the general manager?	*wayn al mudeer al 'aam?*	وَيْنْ الْمُـدير الْعَـام؟
What would you like to drink?	*tuhib tashrab eash?*	تُـحب تَـشْرَب ايش؟
Is he experienced? / Has he got experience?	*hal 'indahu tajrba?*	هَـلْ عِـنْدَهُ تَـجْربَـة؟
Why did he leave early?	*laysh ruh mubakkir?*	لَيْشْ رُحْ مُـبَـكِّرْ؟
Who came late, yesterday?	*meen yajee muta'akhir ams?*	مِـينْ يَـجِـيئ مـتَـأخِّـر أمْـس؟
Who closed the door?	*meen sakkiril baab?*	مِـينْ سَـكِّر الْبَـاب؟
Who is going to Dubai today?	*meen yaruh dubai alyawm?*	مِـينْ يَرُحْ دُبَـيْ الْيَوْم؟
Whose duty is tomorrow?	*dawaam meen bukra?*	دَوَامُ مِـينْ بُـكْرَة؟
When should I contact you?	*mataa attasil bik?*	مَـتٰـى أتَّـصِـلْ بِـكَ؟
Is this costly?	*hal haada gaalee?*	هَـلْ هٰـذَا غَـالي؟
Is this cheap?	*hal haada rakhees?*	هَـلْ هٰـذَا رَخِـيص؟
How is his conduct?	*kaifa khulquhu?*	كَيْفَ خُـلُقُه؟
How is he in work?	*kaifa huwa fishugl?*	كَيْفَ هُـوَ في الشُّـغَـل؟
What do you think about him?	*maa ra'uyuka 'anhu?*	مَـا رأيُـكَ عَـنْهُ؟
Where is the file?	*wayn al mulf?*	وَيْنْ المـلف؟
Where are the documents?	*wayn almustanadaat?*	وَيْنْ المُـسْـتَـنَدَات؟
Where is the accomodation?	*wayn assakan?*	وَيْنْ السَّـكَنْ؟
What is the number?	*raqmu kam?*	رَقَم كَمْ؟

Can I see you tomorrow?	*mumkin ashoofak bukra?*	مُـمْـكِنْ أشُـوفَـكَ بُـكْرَة؟
Can I call you back after sometime?	*mumkin attasil bika ba'ada shuway?*	مُـمْـكِنْ أتَّـصِـلْ بِـكَ بَـعْـدَ شُـوَيْ؟
Can you give me an hour?	*mumkin tu'utinee saa'a?*	مُـمْـكِنْ تُـعْـطني سَـاعَـة؟
Can you help me in this?	*mumkin tusaa'idnee fee haada?*	مُـمْـكِنْ تُـسَـاعِـدْني في هٰـذَا؟
How can I help you?	*kaifa usaa'iduk?*	كَيْفَ أُسَـاعِـدُكَ؟
Can I help you?	*mumkin usaa'iduk?*	مُـمْـكِنْ أُسَـاعِـدُكَ؟
What is the rent?	*eaajaar kam?*	إيجَـارُ كَمْ؟
Is the flat furnished?	*halishuqqa mafroosha?*	هَـلْ الشُّـقَّة مَـفْـرُوشَـة؟
Are the water and electricity free?	*halil kahrbaa wal maa majjaan?*	هَـلْ الْكَهرُبَـاء والْمَـاءُ مَـجَّـانًا؟
How many rooms are there?	*kam gurfa feeh?*	كَمْ غُـرْفَـة فـيه؟
How many toilets are there?	*kam hammaam feeh?*	كَمْ حَـمَّـام فـيه؟
Do you understand Arabic?	*hal tafham arabi?*	هل تفهم عربي؟
Do you speak Arabic?	*hal tatakallam arabi?*	هَـلْ تَـتَـكَلَّمُ عَـرَبـي؟
How old is he?	*kam 'umruhu?*	كَمْ عُـمْـرُهُ؟
How old is she?	*kam 'umruhaa?*	كَمْ عُـمْـرُهَـا؟
What is his height?	*kam tooluhu?*	كَمْ طُولُهُ؟
What is her height?	*kam tooluhaa?*	كَمْ طُولُهَا؟
What is his weight?	*kam waznuhu?*	كَمْ وَزْنُهُ؟
What is her weight?	*kam waznuhaa?*	كَمْ وَزْنُهَا؟

How is the weather?	*kayfa taqs?*	كَيْفَ طَقس؟
What is the temperature?	*kayfal haraara?*	كَيْفَ الْحَرَارَة؟
Is he sick?	*hal huwal mareedh?*	هَلْ هُوَ الْمَرِيض؟
Are you angry?	*hal inta za'ulaan?*	هَلْ أَنْتَ زَعْلاَن؟
Would you like to drink something?	*tuhib tashrab shay?*	تُحِبُّ تَشْرَبُ شَيْء؟
Who is your sponsor?	*meen kafeeluk?*	مِينْ كَفِيلُكَ؟
Who is your partner?	*meen shareekuk?*	مِينْ شَرِيكُكَ؟
Which company are you from?	*min ayyi sharika inta?*	مِنْ أيِّ شَرِكَة أَنْتَ؟
Which city are you from?	*min ayyi madeena inta?*	مِنْ أيِّ مَدِينَة أَنْتَ؟
Is your car new?	*hal sayyaaratuk jadeeda?*	هَلْ سَيَّارَتُكَ جَدِيدَة؟
What is the colour of your car?	*eash lawn sayyaaratik?*	ايشْ لَوْن سَيَّارَتكَ؟
Have you got change for 100/- Riyals?	*indak qurda limi'a riyal?*	عِنْدَكَ قِرْدَة لِمائَة رِيَالْ؟
Have you got a mobile phone?	*'indaka jawwaal?*	عِنْدَكَ جَوَّالْ؟
What are you doing there?	*shusawwee hinak?*	شُسَوِّي هِنَاكَ؟
Who made a call?	*meen sawwee talifoon?*	مِينْ سَوِّي تَلِيفُون؟
How many cars have you got?	*kam sayyaara 'indak?*	كَمْ سَيَّارَة عِنْدَكَ؟
How many drivers have you got?	*kam sawwaaq 'indak?*	كَمْ سوَاق عِنْدكَ؟

What time do you sleep?	*saa'a kam tanaam?*	سَاعَةُ كَمْ تَنَامْ؟
Where is the car parking?	*wayn mooqif sayyaara?*	وَيْنْ مُوقَف سَيَّارَة؟
Try	*hawil*	حَاولْ
Try again	*hawil marra thaniya*	حَاولْ مَرَّة ثَانيَة
Try once more	*hawil marra ukhra*	حَاولْ مَرَّة أُخْرٰى
Try later	*hawil ba'edayn*	حَاولْ بَعْدَيْنْ
Try after some time	*hawil ba'uda shuway*	حَاولْ بَعْدَ شُوَيْ
I will try	*uhawil*	أُحَاولْ
Can you try for me again?	*mumkin tuhawil lee marra thaniya*	مُمْكِنْ تُحَاولْ لي مَرَّة ثَانيَة
How can I try?	*kayf uhawil?*	كَيْفَ أُحَاولْ؟
Never mind	*ma leysh*	مَا لَيْشْ
Not difficult (No problem)	*ma fee mushkila*	مَا في مُشْكلَة
Don't speak	*ma fee kalaam*	مَا في كَلاَمْ
Keep quiet	*uskut*	أُسْكُتْ
Who will you go with?	*ma'a meen taruh?*	مَعَ مينْ تَرُحْ؟
I am going with my father	*aruh ma'a baaba*	أرُحْ مَعَ بَابَا
I am going with my mother	*aruh ma'a mama*	أرُحْ مَعَ مَامَا
I am going with my husband	*aruh ma'a zawj*	أرُحْ مَعَ زَوْج
I am going with my friend	*aruh ma'a rafeeq*	أرُحْ مَعَ رَفيقْ

Who is with you?	*meen ma'ak?*	مـيـنْ مَـعَـكْ؟
You should keep right	*ilzam yameen*	إلْزَمْ يَمـين
You should keep left	*ilzam yasar*	إلْزَمْ يَسَـارْ
You should keep the law	*ilzam alqanoon*	إلْزَمْ الْقَانُون
After one week	*ba'uda usboo'e*	بَـعْـدَ أُسْـبُـوع
Check after 3 days	*muraja'a ba'uda thalatha ayyam?*	مُـرَاجَـعَـة بَـعْـدَ ثَلاَثَة أيَّامْ
Renewal of Residence permit	*tajdeedul iqama*	تَـجْـدِيدُ الإقَامَـة
Congratulations	*mabrook*	مَـبْرُوكْ
1000 congratulations	*alf mabrook*	ألْف مَـبْرُوكْ
May God bless you	*baarakallaah feek*	بَارَكَ الله فِـيك
Contract	*aqd*	عَـقْد
License / Permission	*rukhsa*	رُخْـصَـة
What is today's exchange rate?	*sa'iritahweela kam alyawm?*	سَـعـر التَّـحْـويلَة كَمْ الْيَوْم؟
Exit	*Khurooj*	خُـرُوج
Entry	*dukhool*	دُخُـول
Passport	*jawaaz*	جَـوَاز
Change of sponsorship	*naql kafaala*	نَقْل كَفَـالَة
Release	*tanaazil*	تَـنَازل
Visa	*ta'esheera*	تَأشِـيرَة
Visit visa	*ta'esheera ziyaara*	تَأشِـيرَة زيَارَة
Residence visa	*ta'esheera iqaama*	تَأشِيرَة إقَامَـة
Tourist visa	*ta'esheera siyaaha*	تَأشِـيرَة سِـيَاحَـة

Transit visa	*ta'esheera muroor*	تَأشِـيرَة مُـرُور
Work visa	*ta'esheera 'amal*	تَأشِـيرَة عَـمَـلْ
Business visa	*ta'esheera rijaal a'umaal*	تَأشِـيرَة رِجَـال أعْـمَـالْ
Application	*talab*	طَلَب
Commercial registration (CR)	*sijil attijaari*	سِـجِـلْ التِّـجَـاري
Reservation	*hajz*	حَـجْـزْ
Police	*shurta*	شُـرْطَة
Traffic police	*shurtal muroor*	شُـرْطَة الْمُـرُور
Please	*arjook*	أرْجُـوك
(Request) Please give me time	*arjook an tu'utinee waqt*	أرْجُـوك أنْ تُـعْـطِينِي وَقْت
Perhaps / Possible / May be	*mumkin*	مُـمْـكِنْ
Telephone	*haatif*	هَـاتِـفْ
Possible, for you to give me your telephone no home/office	*mumkin tu'utinee raqm hatif / bayt am maktab*	ممكن تعطيني رقم هاتف/بيت أم مكتب
If you don't mind, give me all	*law smaht a'utwinee kul*	لَوْ سَـمَـحْـت أعْـطني كُل
Have you got a mobile?	*'indaka jawwaal?*	عِـنْدَكَ جَـوَّالْ؟
What is the number?	*raqm kam?*	رَقَمْ كمْ؟
Have you got a car?	*'indaka sayyara?*	عِـنْدَكَ سَـيَّارَة؟
Have you got a servant?	*'indaka khaadim?*	عِـنْدَكَ خَـادمْ؟

Have you got a maid?	*'indaka khaadima?*	عِنْدَكَ خَادِمَة؟
Have you got a house?	*'indaka bayt?*	عِنْدَكَ بَيْتْ؟
Come	*ta'aal*	تَعَالْ
Come after a little while	*ta'aal ba'uda shuway*	تَعَالْ بَعْدَ شُوَي
Come after one hour	*ta'aal ba'uda saa'a*	تَعَالْ بَعْدَ سَاعَة
Where is the file?	*wayn al malaf?*	وين الْمَلَفْ؟
Present	*mawjood*	مَوجُود
Let me see	*khallinee shuf*	خَلِّني شُفْ
Leave it on the table	*kallee 'ala ttaawila*	خَلِّي عَلَى الطَّاولَة
Secretary	*ameen*	أمينْ
Leave it with the secretary	*khallee ma'alameen*	خَلِّي مَعَ الأمين
See how?	*shuf kayf?*	شُفْ كَيْفَ؟
You must help	*lazim musa'ida*	لأَزِمْ مُسَاعِدَة
Make	*sawwee*	سَوِي
What are you doing there?	*shoo sawwee hinaak?*	شُو سَوِّي هِناك؟
Make a copy	*sawwee nuskha*	سَوِّي نُسْخَة
Hurry up	*ya allaah sur'a*	يَا ألله سُرْعَة

LESSON: TWENTY FOUR

CONVERSATIONAL PRACTICE

Introduction

Jabir: Good morning.	*jabir: sabahal khair*	جابر: صباح الخير.
Khalid: Good morning, How are you?	*khalid: sabahannoor, kaifa halak?*	خالد: صباح النور، كيف حالك؟
Jabir: Good, Thanks, And how are you?	*jabir: bi khair, shukran, wa kaifa halak?*	جابر: بخير، شكراً، وكيف حالك؟
Khalid: Fine praise be to Allah.	*khalid: zayn, al-hamdu lillah.*	خالد: زين، الحمد لله.
Jabir: What is your name?	*jabir: shusmak?*	جابر: شسمك؟
Khalid: Khalid, What is your name?	*khalid: khalid, shusmak inta?*	خالد: خالد، شُسمك انت؟
Jabir: I'am Jabir.	*jabir: ana jabir.*	جابر: انا جابر.
Khalid: Where are you from?	*khalid: min ayyi baladin inta?*	خالد: من اي بلد انت؟
Jabir: I'am from India, and you?	*jabir: ana minal hind, wa inta?*	جابر: انا من الهند، وانت؟
Khalid: I'am from Pakistan.	*khalid: ana min bakistan.*	خالد: انا مِن باكستان.
Jabir: What do you do here?	*jabir: shu sawwee hinee?*	جابر: شُسوِّي هِني؟
Khalid: I'am a businessman, and what do you do?	*khalid: ana tajir, wa inta shu sawwee?*	خالد: انا تاجر، وانت شُسوِّي؟
Jabir: I'am a teacher.	*jabir: ana mudarris.*	جابر: انا مُدَرِّس.

Khalid: Who is this lady with you?	*khalid: wa man hadihi ssayyida ma'ak?*	خالد: ومَن هذه السيدة معك؟
Jabir: This is my wife Rasheeda.	*jabir: hiya zawjatee rasheeda.*	جابر: هي زوجتي رشيدة.
Khalid: Is she also a teacher?	*khalid: ahiya aydan mudarrisa?*	خالد: اهي ايضاً مُدَرِّسة؟
Jabir: Yes, she is a Science teacher in the Government school.	*jabir: ay. hiya mudarrisla uloom fil madrassa hukoomiyya.*	جابر: اي، هي مُدرِّسة العلوم في المدرسة الحكومية.
Khalid: Hello.	*khalid: marhaba.*	خالد: مرحبا.
Rasheeda: Hello.	*rasheeda: marhabatain.*	رشيدة: مرحبتين.
Khalid: And who is this boy with you?	*khalid: waman hada ssabab ma'ak?*	خالد: ومَن هذا الشباب معك؟
Jabir: He is my son Mubarak.	*jabir: hada ibnee mubarak.*	جابر: هذا ابني مبارك.
Khalid: Where do you live in India?	*khalid: wayn inta sakin fil hind?*	خالد: وين انت ساكن في الهند؟
Jabir: I live in Mumbai.	*jabir: ana sakin fee mumbai.*	جابر: انا ساكن في مُمباي.
Khalid: When did you arrive in Doha?	*khalid: mata wasalta doha?*	خالد: متى وصلت الدوحة؟
Jabir: Last week, and when did you arrive?	*jabir: al usboo'ul madee, wa inta wasalta mata?*	جابر: الأسبوع الماضي، وانت وصلت متى؟
Khalid: Day before yesterday.	*khalid: awwal amsi.*	خالد: اوَّل امس.
Jabir: How long do you want to stay here?	*jabir: wa kam tabgee tabqa hinee?*	جابر: وكم تبغ تبق هني؟

Khalid: Two weeks.	*khalid: usboo'ayn.*	خالد: أسبوعين.
Jabir: Have you got a car?	*jabir: indaka sayyara?*	جابر: عندك سيارة؟
Khalid: Yeah. I rented out a car today.	*khalid: ay. istaejartu sayyara al-yawm.*	خالد: اي استأجرت سيارة اليوم.
Jabir: What is the rent here?	*jabir: eejar kam hinee?*	جابر: ايجار كم هني؟
Khalid: 100 Riyals per day.	*khalid: miatu riyal lil-yawm.*	خالد: مائة ريال لليوم.
Jabir: Have you got a driving license?	*jabir: indaka rukhsa qiyada?*	جابر: عندك رُخصة قيادة؟
Khalid: Yes.	*khalid: aywa, mawjood*	خالد: ايوا، موجود.
Jabir: Howmany children have you got?	*jabir: kam waladan indak?*	جابر: كم ولداً عندك؟
Khalid: I have two sons. They are studying in the school.	*khalid: indee waladani, huma talibani fil-madrasa.*	خالد: عندي ولدان، هما طالبان في المدرسة.
Jabir: What would you like to drink?	*jabir: tuhib tashrab aysh*	جابر: تحب تشرب ايش؟
Khalid: Let us have a coffee.	*khalid: khali nasrab al-qahwa.*	خالد: خل نشرب القهوة.
Jabir: OK. Let us go to a restaurant.	*jabir: aywa, hayya bina naruh ilal mat'am*	جابر: ايوا، هيا بنا نرح الى المطعم.
Khalid: OK.	*khalid: aywa.*	خالد: ايوا.
Jabir: Nice to meet you, give me your address and telephone number.	jabir: *liqae sa'eed, a'itinee unwanak wa raqamal hatif.*	جابر: لقاء سعيد، اعطني عُنوانك ورقم الهاتف.
Khalid: Fine. Here is my address.	*khalid: zayn, hada unwanee.*	خالد: زين، هذا عنواني.

Jabir: Thank you so much.	*jabir: shukran jazeela.*	جابر: شكراً جزيلاً.
Khalid: Good bye.	*khalid: ma'assalama*	خالد: مع السلامة.
Jabir: See you.	*jabir: ila-lliqa.*	جابر: الى اللقاء.

At the Air-Port

Airport Officer: May I help you?	*mu'addaful matar: mumkin usaedak?*	مؤظف المطار: ممكن أُساعدك؟
Passenger: Thanks.	*al-musafir: Shukran.*	المسافر: شكراً.
Airport Officer: Which flight are you travelling by?	*mu'addaful matar: inta musafir bi ayyi taera?*	مؤظف المطار: انت مسافر بأيِّ طائرة؟
Passenger: I'am travelling by Qatar Air-ways.	*al-musafir: Ana musafir bil-qatariyya.*	المسافر: انا مسافر بالقطرية.
Airport Officer: Go there.	*mu'addaful matar: ruh hinak.*	مؤظف المطار: رُح هناك.
Passenger: Thanks.	*al-musafir: Shukran.*	المسافر: شكراً.
Airline Officer: Come on. Give me your ticket and passport.	*mu'addafuttayran: faddal, Aitinee tadkiratuk wa jawazu ssafar.*	مؤظف الطيران: فضل اعطني تذكرتك وجواز السفر.
Passenger: Here is my ticket and passport.	*al-musafir: Ha huwa da tadkiratee wa jawazu ssafar.*	المسافر: ها هو ذا تذكرتي وجواز السفر.
Airline Officer: Howmany baggages have you got?	*mu'addafuttayran: kam haqeeba indak?*	مؤظف الطيران: كم حقيبة عندك؟

Passenger: I have two baggages.	*al-musafir: Indee haqeebatayn.*	المسافر: عندي حقيبتين.
Airline Officer: Leave it on the balance. Let me see in weight.	*mu'addafuttayran: khalli alal meezan, ashuf al-wazn.*	مؤظف الطيران: خلي على الميزان، اشف الوزن.
Passenger: OK.	*al-musafir: zayn.*	المسافر: زين.
Airline Officer: Fine. Take your boarding pass and go to the immigration.	mu'addafuttayran: *zayn, khud bitaqatu su'ood, waruh ilal jawazat.*	مؤظف الطيران: زين، خذ بطاقة صعود ورح الى الجوازات.
Passport Officer: Which country are you from sir?	dabitul jawazat: *min ayyi baladin inta ya sayyidee?*	ضابط الجوازات: من ايِّ بلدٍ انت يا سيدي.
Paasenger: From India.	al-musafir: *minal hind.*	المسافر: من الهند.
Passport Officer: What is your name?	*dabitul jawazat: shusmak?*	ضابط الجوازات: شُسمك؟
Paasenger: Jabir	*al-musafir: Jabir.*	المسافر: جابر
Passport Officer: Where is the passport and exit permit?	*dabitul jawazat: wayn tasreehul khurooj? wayn al-jawaz?*	ضابط الجوازات: وين تصريح الخروج؟ وين الجواز؟
Paasenger: Please take.	*al-musafir: faddal.*	المسافر: فضَّل
Passport Officer: Fine, go to the waiting hall.	*dabitul jawazat: zayn, ruh ila salatil intizar.*	ضابط الجوازات: زين، رُح الى صالة الإنتظار.

[Jabir meets his friend Ahmed in the waiting hall]

[Jabir yuqabilu sadeeqahu Ahmed fee salatil intizar.]

[جابر يقابل صديقه أحمد في صالة الإنتظار]

Ahmed: Most welcome my brother. How are you?	*ahmed: ahlan wa sahlan wa marhaban bika ya akhee. wa kayfa halak?*	أحمد: أهلاً وسهلاً ومرحباً بك يا أخي. وكيف حالك؟
Jabir: Fine, Praise be to Allah. And you?	*jabir: zayn, al-hamdu lillah. wa inta?*	جابر: زين، الحمد لله. وانت؟
Ahmed: Well, Thanks.	*ahmed: Bi khayr shukran.*	أحمد: بخير شُكراً.
Jabir: Where are you travelling to?	*jabir: wayn tusafir?*	جابر: وين تُسافر؟
Ahmed: To Dubai.	*ahmed: Ila Dubai.*	جابر: إلى دبئي.
Jabir: Is it an official trip or personal?	*jabir: hal hadihee rihla rasmiyya aw shakhsiyya?*	جابر: هل هذه رحلة رسمية او شخصية؟
Ahmed: Official trip. And where are you going to?	*ahmed: rihla rasmiyya. wa inta ruh wayn?*	أحمد: رحلة رسمية، وانت رُح وين؟
Jabir: I'am travelling to India. This is my annual vacation.	*jabir: ana musafir ilal hind. Hadihee ijazatee assanawiyya.*	جابر: انا مسافر الى الهند، هذه إجازتي السنوية.
Ahmed: When will you return from India?	*ahmed: mata tarjiu minal hind?*	أحمد: متى ترجع من الهند؟
Jabir: God willing, after two months. And howmany days do you want to stay in Dubai?	*jabir: baeda shahrayn insha allah. wa kam yawm tureedu an tabq fee dubai?*	جابر: بعد شهرين ان شاء الله، وكم يوم تريد ان تبقى في دُبي؟
Ahmed: Perhaps two weeks.	*ahmed: mumkin usbooayn.*	أحمد: ممكن أسبوعين
Jabir: Which flight are you travelling?	*jabir: ayya taera tusafir?*	جابر: اي طائرة تسافر؟
Ahmed: I'am flying	*ahmed: ana musafir*	أحمد: أنا مسافر

by Emirates and you?	*bil imarat wa inta?*	بالإمارات وانت؟
Jabir: Qatar Airways.	*jabir: al qatariyya.*	جابر: القطرية.
Ahmed: What time is your flight?	*ahmed: sa'a kam taeratuk?*	أحمد: ساعة كم طائرتك؟
Jabir: 9.30 pm. And what time is the Emirates?	*jabir: assa'a ttasi'a wannisf laylan, wa sa'a kam al-imarat?*	جابر: الساعة التاسعة والنصف ليلاً. وساعة كم الإمارات؟
Ahmed: At 10 pm.	*ahmed: assa'al ashira laylan.*	أحمد: الساعة العاشرة ليلاً.
Jabir: More than two hours are left. Let us have a cup of tea.	*jabir: fa baqiya aksaru min sa'atayn, khalee nashrab shay.*	جابر: فبقي اكثر من ساعتين، خل نشرب شاي.
Ahmed: Good idea. Let us go to the Coffee shop.	*ahmed: fikra tayyiba, hayya bina ilal maqhee.*	أحمد: فكرة طيبة، هيا بنا إلى المقهى.
Jabir: Do you like to eat anything.	*jabir: tabea taekul shaye.*	جابر: تبع تأكل شيئ؟
Ahmed: No, I'm not hungry. Only tea will do for me.	*ahmed: la, ana mub jaw'an, bas shay yakfeenee.*	أحمد: لا، أنا مُب جوان، بس شاي يكفيني
Jabir: As you wish.	*Jabir: ala kayfak?*	جابر: على كيفك.
Ahmed: Good bye.	*ahmed: ma'a ssalama.*	أحمد: مع السلامة.
Jabir: See you.	*jabir: ilal liqae.*	جابر: الى اللقاء.

In the Hotel

Receptionit: Most welcome sir, what can I do for you?	*mu'addaful istiqbal: ahlan wa sahlan ya sayyidee, ayyu khidma?*	مؤظف الإستقبال: أهلاً وسهلاً يا سيدي، أيُّ خدمة؟
Khalid: I would like	*khalid: ureedu an*	خالد: أريد أن احجز

to book a room.	*ahjuza gurfa.*	غرفة.
Receptionist: Do you want a room for one person or for the family.	*mu'addaful istiqbal: hal tureedul gurfa lilwahid aw lillaaela?*	مؤظف الإستقبال: هل تُريد الغرفة للواحد او للعائلة؟
Khalid: I want a room for one person.	*khalid: ureedul gurfa lilwahid.*	خالد: أريد الغرفة للواحد.
Receptionist: How long do you like to stay here?	*muaddaful istiqbal: kam tabgi tabqa hinee?*	مؤظف الإستقبال: كم تبغ تبقي هني؟
Khalid: I do not know exactly, may be five days. What is the rent for a day?	*khalid: la adree bizzabt, mumkin khamsata ayyam. kamil eejar lil-yawm?*	خالد: لا ادري بالضبط، مُمكن خمسة ايام. كم الإيجار لليوم؟
Receptionist: Two hundred riyals.	*mu'addaful istiqbal: miatayn riyal.*	مؤظف الإستقبال: مائتين ريال.
Khalid: What are the facilities available in the hotel?	*khalid: wama ttasheelatal mawjooda fil-funduq?*	خالد: وما التسهيلات الموجودة في الفندق.
Receptionist: Toilet, heater, telephone and television in each room in addition to the restaurants, coffee shop, club and library on each floor.	*mu'addaful istiqbal: hammam, wa musakhin, wa telephone, wa telefiziyoon fee kulli gurfa, fazlan anil mata'am wal maqhee wannadee wal maktaba fee kulli dawr.*	مؤظف الإستقبال: حمام ومسخن وتليفون وتلفيزيونٍ في كل غرفة فضلا عن المطعم والمقهى والنادي والمكتبة في كل دورٍ.
Khalid: Fine.	*khalid: zayn.*	خالد: زين
Receptionist: On which floor do you like to stay?	*mu'addaful istiqbal: fee ayyi dawrin tabgee an tuqeema?*	مؤظف الإستقبال: في أي دورٍ تبغ ان تُقيم؟

Khalid: On the ground floor.	*khalid: fiddowril ardee.*	خالد: في الدور الأرضي.
Receptionist: Sorry sir, All the rooms on the ground floor are occupied now.	*mu'addaful istiqbal: asif ya sayyidee, kulla gurfa fiddowril ardee mashgoola haliyan.*	خالد: آصف يا سيدي، كل غرفة في الدور الأرضي مشغولة حالياً.
Khalid: Is it possible in the first floor?	*khalid: mumkin fiddowril awwal?*	خالد: ممكن في الدور الأول؟
Receptionist: Possible, Insha Allah.	*mu'addaful istiqbal: mumkin insha allah.*	مؤظف الإستقبال: ممكن ان شاء الله.
Khalid: When shall the room be ready?	*khalid: mata takoonul gurfa jahiza?*	خالد: متى تكون الغرفة جاهزة؟
Receptionist: In half an hour.	*mu'addaful istiqbal: binisfi sa'a.*	مؤظف الاستقبال: بنصف ساعة.
Khalid: Please make it fast.	*khalid: min fadlika sur'a*	خالد: من فضلك سرعة.
Receptionist: What is your name? Give me your address.	*mu'addaful istiqbal: shusmak? aitinee unwanak.*	مؤظف الإستقبال: شسمك؟ اعطني عُنوانك.
Khalid: This is my card. All details are there.	*khalid: hadihee bitaqatee, feehal bayanat kullaha.*	خالد: هذه بطاقتي، فيها البيانات كلها.
Receptionist: Thanks.	*mu'addaful istiqbal: shukran.*	مؤظف الاستقبال: شكراً.
Khalid: Welcome.	*khalid: afwan.*	خالد: عفواً.
Receptionist: The room is ready. Your room number is150. and here is the room	*mu'addaful istiqbal: al gurfa jahiza, raqmu gurfatika mia wa khamseen, wa hada*	مؤظف الإستقبال: الغُرفة جاهزة، رقم غرفتك ١٥٠، وهذا هو مفتاح الغرفة.

key.	*huwa miftahul gurfa.*	
Khalid: Thanks.	*khalid: mashkoor.*	خالد: مشكور.
Receptionist: We wish you a pleasant stay with us.	*mu'addaful istiqbal: natamanna laka sakan saleem indana.*	مؤظف الإستقبال: نتمنى لك سكن سليما عندنا.
Khalid: Thank you very much.	*khalid: shukran jazeela.*	خالد: شكراً جزيلاً

At A Restaurant

Khalid: Peace be up on you.	*khalid: assalamu alaykum.*	خالد: السلام عليكم
Waiter: Peace be up on you too, Please come.	*aljarasoon: wa alaykumussalam, faddaloo.*	الجرسون: وعليكم السلام، فضلوا.
Khalid: Where is the family section?	*khalid: wayn qismul aaelee?*	خالد: وين قسم العالي؟
Waiter: Upstairs.	*aljarasoon: fowq.*	الجرسون: فوق.
Khalid: Fine.	*khalid: zayn.*	خالد: زين.
Waiter: Welcome sir, What would you like to have?	*aljarasoon: ahlan wa sahlan ya sayyidee shunu tabgi an tatanawal?*	الجرسون: أهلاً و سهلاً يا سيدي شُنُ تبغ ان تتناول؟
Khalid: First let me see the menu.	*khalid: awwalan khallinee ashuf qaematutta'am.*	خالد: اولاً خلني اشف قائمة الطعام.
Waiter: Here is the menu sir. What would you prefer to have sir?	*aljarasoon: ha huwa da qaematu tta'am ya sayyidee. shunu tufaddilu ya sayyidee.*	الجرسون: ها هُو ذا قائمة الطعام يا سيدي. شُنُ تُفَضِّل يا سيدي؟
Khalid: Have you got	*khalid: hal indakum*	خالد: هل عندكم دجاج

fried chicken?	*dajaj mushfee?*	مشوي.؟
Waiter: Yeah. It is there, You want half or full?	*waiter: mawjood, tabgee nisf aw kamil?*	الجرسون: موجود، تبغ نصف اور كامل؟
Khalid: Half will be enough for me.	*khalid: nisf yakfeenee*	خالد: نصف يكفيني.
Waiter: Wait a little.	*aljarasoon: intadir shuway.*	الجرسون: انتظر شُوي.
Khalid: No problem.	*khalid: ma lay.*	خالد: ما لي.
Waiter: Do you want anything else?	*aljarasoon: tabgee ayyu shai'en ba'edu?*	الجرسون: تبغي أي شيئ آخر؟
Khalid: Give me a bowl of chicken soup and a plate of salad also.	*khalid: aitinee shurba dajaj wa tabaqin min salate aydan.*	خالد: اعطني شربة دٍجاج وطبق مِن سلطه ايضاً.
Waiter: OK, Do you want anything else?	*aljarasoon: hadireen, tabgee ayya shai'in aakhar?*	الجرسون: حاضرين، تبغي أي شيئ آخر؟
Khalid: Give me a cup of tea also.	*khalid: aitinee shay ba'ed.*	خالد: اعطني شاي بعد.
Waiter: I will bring it now.	*aljarasoon: aatee halan.*	الجرسون: آتِي حالاً.
Khalid: Thanks.	*khalid: shukran.*	خالد: شُكراً.
Waiter: Welcom	*aljarsoon: afwan.*	الجرسون: عفواً.

In the Hospital

Khalid: What are you suffering from, my brother?	*khalid: mimma tashkoo ya akhee?*	خالد: مِمَّ تشكو يا اخي؟
Nasir: Body pain. Too much pain.	*nasir: alamul jism, alam wajid.*	ناصر: الَمُ الجسم، الَمُ واجد.

Khalid: Let us go to the hospital.	*khalid: hayya bina ilal mustashfa.*	خالد: هيَّا بنا الى المستشفى.
Nasir: How shall we go? Have you got a car?	*nasir: kayfa naruh? indaka sayyara?*	ناصر: كيف نرُح؟ عندك سيَّارة؟
Khalid: The hospital is near. Let us walk.	*khalid: al mustashfa qareeb, khallee namshee.*	خالد: المستشفى قريب، خل نمشي.
Nasir: I am verymuch tired. I can't walk. Let us rent out a car	*nasir: ana ta'eben wajid, la aqdir amshee nastaejira sayyara.*	ناصر: انا تعبان واجد، لا اقدر امشي نستأجر سيّارة.
Khalid: No problem.	*khalid: ma laysh.*	خالد: ما ليش.
Nasir: Where can we find a car?	*nasir: wayn najidu sayyara?*	ناصر: وين نجد سيَّارة؟
Khalid: We may get it on the road.	*khalid: mumkin nuhassil fi-sharih.*	خالد: ممكن نحصِّل في الشارع.
Nasir: Have you got the number of car rental office?	*nasir: indaka raqam maktab taejeeru sayyarat?*	ناصر: عندك رقم تأجير سيَّارات؟
Khalid: Yes.	*khalid: ee. mawjood.*	خالد: اي موجود.
Nasir: It is better you contact the office.	*nasir: ittasil bil maktab ahsan.*	ناصر: اتصل بالمكتب احسن.
Khalid: OK. give me your mobile. I will contact.	*khalid: zayn aitinee jawalak attasil.*	خالد: زين اعطني جوالك اتصل.
Nasir: Please take.	*nasir: faddal.*	ناصر: فضِّل.

[Khalid contacts the car rental office]

[*khalid yattasil bimaktab taejeer sayyarat*]

[خالد يتصل بمكتب تأجير سيّارات]

Khalid: Peace be upon you.	*khalid: assalamu alaykum.*	خالد: السلام عليكم
Office: Peace and Mercy of Allah be upon you too. Who is calling. May I help you?	*maktab: wa alaykumussalam wa rahmatullah. meen ma'ee? mumkin usa'edak?*	المكتب: وعليكم السلام ورحمة الله. مين معي؟ ممكن اُساعدك؟
Khalid: Khalid with you. I would like to rent out a car.	*khalid: khalid maek, abgee astaejiru sayyara*	خالد: خالد معك، ابغ استأجر سيّارة.
Office: Which car do you want?	*maktab: ayyu sayyara tabgee?*	مكتب: ايُّ سيارة تبغ؟
Khalid: A small car	*khalid: sayyara sageera.*	خالد: سيارة صغيرة
Office: For how many days?	*maktab: likam yawm?*	مكتب: لكم يوم؟
Khalid: For one day only.	*khalid: liyawm wahid faqat.*	خالد: ليوم واحد فقط.
Office: 200 Riyals for one day.	*maktab: miatayn riyal li-yawm wahid.*	مكتب: مائتين ريال ليوم واحد.
Khalid: OK. No problem, What time does your office open in the morning?	*khalid: zayn, ma laysh, sa'a kam battal maktabukum sabahan?*	خالد: زين ما ليش، ساعةٍ كم بطل مكتبكم صباحاً.
Office: At 10 AM.	*maktab: assa'a al'ashira sabahan.*	مكتبٍ: الساعة العاشرة صباحاً.
Khalid: OK. I will reach your office at 10 O clock.	*khalid: zayn, asil maktabukum assa'al 'ashira?*	خالد: زين، اصل مكتبكم الساعة العاشرة.
Doctor: What are you suffering from, my brother?	*attabeeb: mimma tashkoo ya akhee?*	الطبيب: ممَّ تشكو يا اخي؟

Nasir: Severe pain throughout the body.	*nasir: alam wajid fee sa'eril jism.*	الم واجد في سائر الجسم.
Doctor: When did it start?	*attabeeb: mata bada?*	الطبيب: متى بدأ؟
Nasir: Day before yesterday.	*nasir: awwal amsi.*	ناصر: أول أمس.
Doctor: What did you do?	*attabeeb: shu sawwayt?*	الطبيب: شسوّيت؟
Nasir: I did n't do any thing.	*nasir: ma sawwayta shay'an.*	ناصر: ما سويت شيئاً.
Doctor: OK. Let me see it. Lay down on the cot.	*attabeeb: zayn, khallinee shuf. idtajih ala ssareer.*	الطبيب: زين خلني شف. اضطجع على السرير.
Nasir: Ready.	*nasir: hazir.*	ناصر: حاضر.
Doctor: Breath powerfully.	*attabeeb: tanaffas biquwwa.*	الطبيب: تنفس بقوة.
Nasir: OK.	*nasir: zayn.*	ناصر: زين.
Doctor: OK. I will give you medicine. This is simple. It is due to the weather change. Take this three times a day for one week.	*attabeeb: zayn, aiteeka dawa. hada baseet. hada min tagyeerittaqs. tanawal thalatha marrat fil-yawm li-usboo'e.*	الطبيب: زين، اعطيك دواء. هذا بسيط. هذا من تغير الطقس. تناول هذا ثلاثة مرات في اليوم لاسبوع.
Nasir: Where shall I get the medicine from?	*nasir: wayn hassal ddawa?*	ناصر: من وين حصل الدواء؟
Doctor: From the pharmacy on the ground floor.	*attabeeb: mina ssaydaliyya fi-ddowril ardee.*	الطبيب: من الصيدلية في الدور الأرضي.
Nasir: Thank you doctor.	*nasir: shukran ya daktoor.*	ناصر: شكراً يا دكتور.

Doctor: May Allah cure you brother.	*attabeeb: allah yashfeeka ya akhee.*	الطبيب: الله يشفيك يا اخي.
Nasir: Hello Jamal, How are you? What is the matter?	*nasir: ahlan jamal, kayfa halak? aysh fee?*	ناصر: اهلاً جمال، كيف حالك؟ ايش في؟
Jamal: My brother met with an accident. I took him to the emergency.	*jamal: qad useeba akhee bi haditha, akhadathu ilat tawaree.*	جمال: قد اصيب اخي بحادثة، اخذته الى الطوارئ.
Nasir: When was the accident and how?	*nasir: mata kanatil haditha, wa kayfa?*	ناصر: متى كانت الحادثة، وكيف؟
Jamal: Today morning. He was going to the office. Then a motor cycle hit him at grand road.	*jamal: sabahal yawm. kana yaruh ilal maktab fasadamathu darraja nariyya fee sharihil kabeer.*	جمال: صباح الخير. كان يروح الى المكتب. فصدمته دراجة نارية في الشارع الكبير.
Nasir: Has he suffered any seriuos injuries?	*nasir: a useeba bi juroohin khatara?*	ناصر: اصيب بجروح خطرة؟
Jamal: No, small injuries only. I don't know whether there is any fracture or not?	*jamal: la, jurooh sageera faqat. la adree fee kasoor am la?*	جمال: لا، جروح صغيرة فقط. لا ادري فيه كسور ام لا؟
Nasir: And what about his family?	*nasir: wa kayfa halu usratihi?*	ناصر: وكيف حال أُسرته؟
Jamal: They are safe by the grace of Allah.	*jamal: hum salimoona bi fazlillah.*	جمال: هم سالمون بفضل الله.
Nasir: Where is he now?	*nasir: wayn huwa al-heen?*	ناصر: وين هو الحين؟
Jamal: With the doctor in the Emergency.	*jamal: ma'a ddaktoor fi-ttawaree.*	جمال: مع الدكتور في الطوارئ.
Nasir: Do you need any help?	*nasir: tabgee ayyu khidma?*	ناصر: تبغ ايُّ خدمة؟

Jamal: Thanks.	*jamal: mashkoor.*	جمال: مشكور.
Nasir: How do you go home?	*nasir: kayfa taruh bayt?*	ناصر: كيف ترح بيت؟
Jamal: By Bus.	*jamal: fil bas.*	جمال: في الباص.
Nasir: No, I have got a car with me. I shall wait and drop you home.	*nasir: la, indee sayyara. intazir wa waddi'eka byt.*	ناصر: لا، عندي سيارة. انتظر وودعك بيت.
Jamal: I may be late.	*jamal: mumkin ata akhar?*	جمال: ممكن اتأخر؟
Nasir: No problem, I will wait. I'm free today.	*nasir: ma laysh. antazir. ana fadee al-yawm.*	ناصر: ما ليش، انتظر. انا فاضي اليوم.
Jamal: Emergency section of this hospital is open 24 hours.	*jamal: qismuttawaree fee hadal mushtasfa maftooh arba'en wa ishreena sa'a.*	جمال: قسم الطوارئ في هذا المستشفى مفتوح اربعاً وعشرين ساعة.
Nasir: Have you taken X-ray?	*nasir: hal akhadtal ashi'aa?*	ناصر: هل اخذت الأشعَّة؟
Jamal: Ya.	*jamal: aywa.*	جمال: ايوا.
Nasir: Did you speak to the doctor after X-ray?	*nasir: kallamta ddaktoor ba'edaa ashi'aa?*	ناصر: كلّمت الدكتور بعد الأشعَّة؟
Jamal: No, I'm waiting for him.	*jamal: la, ana fee intizarihee.*	جمال: لا انا في انتظاره.
Nasir: Where is he now?	*nasir: wayn huwa alheen?*	ناصر: وين هُو الحين؟
Jamal: He is examining a patient inside.	*jamal: huwa yakshifu ala mareed fee dakhil.*	جمال: هو يكشف على مريض في داخل.
Nasir: Where is the nurse?	*nasir: wayn al-mumarrida?*	ناصر: وين الممرِّضة؟

Jamal: She is also with the doctor.	*jamal: hiya aydan ma'a ddaktoor,*	جمال: هي أيضاً مع الدكتور.
Doctor: Jamal come and take your seat.	*attabeeb: ta'al ya jamal, istarih.*	الطبيب: تعال يا جمال، استرح.
Jamal: Thank you doctor.	*jamal: shukran daktoor.*	جمال: دكتور.
Doctor: By the grace of Allah, your brother is safe. There is no fracture or anything in the X-ray. Take him home after some time.	*attabeeb: bi fadlillah akhooka salim. ma fee kasra wala shay'e fil-ashi'aa. khudhu ilal bayt ba'eda qaleel.*	الطبيب بفضل الله اخوك سالم. ما في كسرة ولا شيئ في الأشعَّة. خذه الى البيت بعد قليل.
Jamal: I praise Allah and thank Him.	*jamal: ahmadulla wa ashkuruhu.*	جمال: احمد الله واشكره.
Doctor: May Allah give you comfort.	*attabeeb: allah yu'eteekal 'afiya.*	الطبيب: الله يعطيك العافية.
Jamal: May Allah save you.	*jamal: allah yusallimak.*	جمال: الله يسلّمك.
Nasir: Come on. Let us go home.	*nasir: hayya naruh bayt.*	ناصر: هيا نرح بيت.
Jamal: Just a minute. Let me take the medicine from the Pharmacy.	*jamal: daqeeqa, khalli aakhudu ddawae mina ssaydaliyya.*	جمال: دقيقة، خل آخذ الدواء من الصيدلية.
Nasir: Yes, I'm near the main gate.	*nasir: zayn, ana ladal bab rraeesee.*	ناصر: زين، انا لدى الباب الرئيسي.
Jamal: I will reach there now.	*jamal: asil hinaka halan.*	جمال: اصل هناك حالاً.
Nasir: Come on fast.	*nasir: ya allah sur'a.*	ناصر: يا الله سرعة.

Jamal: Who is this young man?	*jamal: meen hada shabab?*	جمال: مين هذا الشباب؟
Nasir: This is my friend Khalid. He came with me to the hospital.	*nasir: hada sadeeqee kahlid, ja'a ma'ee ilal- mustashfa.*	ناصر: هذا صديقي خالد، جاء معي الى المستشفى.
Jamal: Hello Khalid, How are you?	*jamal: ahlan khalid, kayfa halak?*	جمال: اهلاً خالد، كيف حالك؟
Khalid: Hello.	*khalid: ahlan wa sahlan.*	خالد: اهلاً وسهلاً.
Nasir: Shall we move?	*nasir: naseer?*	ناصر: نسير؟
Jamal: Yeah, In the name of Allah.	*jamal: ee, bismillah.*	جمال: اي بسم الله.
Khalid: Where is your house, brother?	*khalid: wayn baytuka ya akhoy?*	خالد: وين بيتك يا اخوي؟
Jamal: Near the central school, Stop infront of the boys section.	*jamal: qareeb minal madrasatil markaziyya waqqif amama qismil baneen.*	جمال: قريب من المدرسة المركزية وقف امام قسم البنين.
Khalid: Fine.	*khalid: zayn.*	خالد: زين.
Jamal: Would you like to buy something.	*jamal: tabgee tashtaree shay'e.*	جمال: تبغ تشتري شيئ.
Nasir: No, it is late.	*nasir: la, alwaqtu muta akhir.*	ناصر: لا، الوقت متأخر.
Khalid: We have reached your house. Get down.	*khalid: wasalna baytakum. inziloo.*	خالد: وصلنا بيتكم انزلوا.
Jamal: Come on, We shall drink something.	*jamal: faddaloo nashrab shay'e.*	جمال: فضلوا. نشرب شيئ.
Nasir: Not now, on	*nasir: laysa alheen,*	ناصر: ليس الحين، في

another occasion, Insha Allah.	*fee munasabatin ukhra insha allah.*	مناسبة أُخرى، ان شاء الله.
Jamal: May Allah give you good reward.	*jamal: jazakumullahu khayra.*	جمال: جزاكم الله خيراً.
Nasir: May Allah bless you.	*nasir: barakallahu feekum.*	ناصر: بارك الله فيكم.
Jamal: Good bye.	*jamal: ma'a ssalama.*	جمال: مع السلامة.
Nasir: See you.	*nasir: ila-lliqae.*	ناصر: الى اللقاء.

In the Bank

Khalid: Hello	*khalid: halla.*	خالد: هلا.
Jamal: Hello, How are you? Where are you? I have not seen you for a long time.	*jamal: halla. kayfa halak? waynak? ana ma shuftaka min zaman.*	جمال: هلا كيف حالك؟ انا ما شفتك من زمان.
Khalid: Praise be to Allah. I was very busy in the office, that is why I could not visit you. How are you? How is your family?	*khalid: alhamdu lillah, kuntu mashgool wajid fil maktab. falida ma qadartu ziyaratak. kayfak? wa kayfal a'ela?*	خالد: الحمد لله، كنت مشغول واجد في المكتل، فلذا ما قدرت زيارتك. كيفك؟ وكيف العائلة؟
Jamal: All are fine. Praise be to Allah.	*jamal: kulluhum tayyiboon. alhamdu lillah.*	جمال: كلهم طيبون، الحمد لله.
Khalid: Where are you going?	*khalid: ila wayn?*	خالد: إلى وين؟
Jamal: To the bank.	*jamal: ilal bank.*	إلى البنك.
Khalid: What is the matter?	*khalid: aysh fee?*	خالد: ايش فيه؟

Jamal: I would like to open an account in the bank.	*jamal: abe'u aftahul hisab fil bank.*	جمال: ابغ افتح الحساب في البنك.
Khalid: Would you like to have the account in your name or a joint account	*khalid: tabe'ul hisab bimika awil hisab al mushtarika?*	خالد: تبغ الحساب باسمك او الحساب المشترك؟
Jamal: A joint account in my name and my wife's name.	*jamal: hisabul mushtarik bismee wabismi zawjatee.*	جمال: حساب مشترك باسمي وباسم زوجتي.
Khalid: What does your wife do now?	*khalid: shusawwee zawjatuka al-heen?*	خالد: شُوي زوجتك الحين؟
Jamal: She is a teacher in a private school.	*jamal: hiya mudarrisa fee madrasa khusoosiyya.*	جمال: هي مُدرّيسة في مدرسة خصوصية.
Khalid: Have you got an account in any bank?	*khalid: indaka hisab fee ayyi bank?*	خالد: عندك حساب في ايِّ بنك؟
Jamal: Yeah, In Doha Bank.	*jamal: ey, fee bankuddoha.*	جمال: اي، في بنك الدوحة.
Khalid: In which bank you would you like to open the new account.	*khalid: wafee ayyi bank tabgee an taftah al-hisab al-jadeed?*	خالد: وفي ايِّ بنك تبغ ان تفتح الحساب الجديد؟
Jamal: Commercial Bank, Are you free now? Can you drop me at the bank?	*jamal: bank attijaree, hal inta fadee al-heen? mumkin waddi'enee al bank.*	جمال: بنك التجاري، هل انت فاضي الحين؟ مُمكن ودعني البنك؟
Khalid: No problem, I want to draw some	*khalid: ma laysh abgee ashab ba'eda*	خالد: ما ليش ابغ اسحب بعض النقود من

amount from my account in the main branch.	*nnuqood min hisabee minal far'erraeesee.*	حسابي من الفرع الرئيسي.
Jamal: Then come fast, we shall go together.	*jamal: ta'al sur'a fa naruh ma'an.*	جمال: تعال سُرعة فنرح معاً.
Khalid: Wait a little, I will come at once.	*khalid: intadir shuway, ajee halan.*	خالد: انتظر شُوي، اجي حالاً.
Jamal: I'am waiting for you.	*jamal: ana fintizarik.*	جمال: أنا في انتظارك.
Bank officer: Good morning. May I help you?	*muaddaful bank: sabahal khayr, ayyu khidma?*	مؤظف البنك: صباح الخير، اي خدمة؟
Jamal: I woul like to open an account in your bank.	*jamal: abgee aftahu hisaban fee bankikum.*	جمال: ابغ افتح حساباً في بنككم.
Bank officer: Fill the details in this form and come.	*muaddaful bank: zayn, imla el bayanat fee hadihil istimara wa ta'al.*	مؤظف البنك: زين، املأ البيانات في هذا الإستمارة وتعال.
Jamal: Fine, I will come now.	*jamal: zayn, ajee al-heen.*	جمال: زين اجيئ الحين.
Bank officer: Bring your passport copy and a photograph also.	*muaddaful bank: jib sooral jawaz wa ssoora shakhsiyya ba'ed.*	مؤظف البنك: جب صورة الجواز والصورة الشخصية بعد.
Jamal: Everything is ready me.	*jamal: kullu mawjood ma'ee.*	جمال: كل موجود معي.
Bank officer: Sir, you didn't sign in the	*muaddaful bank: inta ma waqa'ata fil*	مؤظف البنك: أنت ما وقعت في الإستمارة يا

form, sign here and there.	*istimara ya sayyidee, waqa'a hinee, wahinak*	سيدي، وقع هني، وهناك.
Jamal: Excuse me. I forgot to sign.	*jamal: ismahnee naseetu an uwaqi'a.*	جمال: اسمحني نسيت ان اوقع.
Jamal: Thanks.	*jamal: mashkoor.*	جمال: مشكور.
Jamal: Of course.	*jamal: tab'an.*	جمال: طبعاً.
Jamal: Well.	*jamal: hasanan.*	جمال: حسناً
Bank officer: The account will be ready within one hour.	*muaddaful bank: ma laysh nusawwee ttarteebat wal hisab yakoon jahiz ba'eda sa'a.*	مؤظف البنك: ما ليش نسوي الترتيبات والحساب يكون جاهزا بعد ساعة.
Bank officer: Do you need cheque books also?	*muaddaful bank: hal tabge daftarisheekat ba'ed?*	مؤظف البنك: هل تبغ دفتر الشيكات بعد؟
Bank officer: Fine come after one hour.	*muaddaful bank: zayn, ta'al ba'eda sa'a.*	مؤظف البنك: زين، تعال بعد ساعة.
Khalid: I want to encash this cheque sir.	*khalid: abgee sarf hadasheeku ya sayyidee.*	خالد: ابغ صرف هذا الشيك يا سيدي.
Bank officer: Have you got an account in the bank?	*muaddaful bank: hal laka hisab fil bank?*	مؤظف البنك: هل لك حساب في البنك؟
Khalid: Yeah.	*khalid: aywa.*	خالد: ايوا.
Bank officer: No problem, submit it at counter number 5.	*muaddaful bank: ma fee mushkila, qaddimhu fee shubbak raqm khamsa.*	مؤظف البنك: ما في مشكلة، قدمه في شباك رقم ٥.
Khalid: I want to encash some foreign currency also.	*khalid: ureedu tahweela ba'edal 'umla alkharijiyya ba'ed.*	خالد: أُريد تحويل بعض العملة الخارجية بعد.
Bank officer: Which currecy have you got?	*muaddaful bank: ayyu 'umla 'indak?*	مؤظف البنك: اي عُملة عندك؟

Khalid: American Dollar, What is the exchange rate today?	*khalid: doolar amreekee, wa ma si'eru ttahweel al-yawm?*	خالد: دولار امريكي. وما سعر التحويل اليوم؟
Bank officer: 3.5 riyal for a Dollar.	*muaddaful bank: thalathu riyal wanisf li-doolar wahid.*	مؤظف البنك: ثلاث ريال ونصف لدولار واحد.
Khalid: Exchange for me 100 Dollars.	*khalid: hawil lee mi'a doolar.*	خالد: حول لي مائة دولار.
Bank officer: No problem, Go to counter No. 2	*muaddaful bank: ma laysh ruh shubbak raqm ithnayn.*	مؤظف البنك: ما ليش رح شباك رقم ٢.
Khalid: Thanks.	*khalid: shukran.*	خالد: شكراً.
Bank officer: Welcome.	*muaddaful bank: afwan.*	مؤظف البنك: عفواً.

In the Garden

Jabir: What shall we do this evening Khalid?	*jabir: ma da naf'alu hadal masae ya khalid?*	جابر: ما ذا نفعل هذا المساء يا خالد؟
Khalid: I have got an idea. We shall go to the park.	*khalid: indee fikra, nadhab ilal hadeeqa.*	خالد: عندي فكرة، نذهب الي الحديقة.
Jabir: Which park?	*jabir: ayyu hadeeqa?*	جابر: ايُّ حديقة؟
Khalid: City Park.	*khalid: hadeeqatul madeena.*	خالد: حديقة المدينة.
Jabir: I think the zoo is better.	*jabir: adunnu hadeeqal hayawanat ahsan.*	جابر: اظن حديقة الحيوانات احسن.
Khalid: Zoo is closed on Sunday.	*khalid: hadeeqal hayawanat sakkar yawmal ahad.*	خالد: حديقة الحيوانات سكَّر يوم الأحد.

Jabir: Then we will go to the city park.	*jabir: idan naruh hadeeqal madeena.*	جابر: إذن نرُح حديقة المدينة.
Khalid: How shall we go? Have you got a car?	*khalid: kayfa naruh? indaka sayyara?*	خالد: كيف نرح؟ عندك سيَّارة؟
Jabir: I don't have a car, We shall go by bus.	*jabir: ma indee sayyara, naruh bil bas.*	جابر: ما عندي سيّارة، نرُح بالباص.
Khalid: It is difficult by bus, better we shall rent out a car.	*khalid: bas mushkila, ahsan nasta'ejiru sayyara.*	خالد: باص مشكلة، احسن نستأجر سيّارة.
Jabir: No. Wait a little. Let me ask my brother. He has got a car.	*jabir: la, sabr shuway. khallinee as'al akhee. 'indahu sayyara.*	جابر: لا، صبر شُوي. خلني اسأل اخي. عنده سيّارة.
Khalid: Leave it. It is better we rent it out.	*khalid: khallihee, nasta'ejir ahsan.*	خالد: خله، نستأجر احسن.
Jabir: As you like it.	*jabir: ala kayfak.*	جابر على كيفك.
Khalid: Dinner from where? Let us have it in the park.	*khalid: al'ashae min wayn? kahlli naekuduha fil-hadeeqa.*	خالد: العشاء من وين؟ خلِّ نأخذه في الحديقة.
Jabir: Today we shall dine out at my expense.	*jabir: al-yawm naekula barra ala hisabee.*	جابر: اليوم نأكل برًّا على حسابي.
Khalid: Fine.	*khalid: zayn.*	خالد: زين
Jabir: Are you coming with your family?	*jabir: inta qadim ma'al 'aela?*	جابر: انت قادم مع العائلة؟
Khalid: Of course, and what about you?	*khalid: taba'an, wa inta kayf?*	خالد: طبعاً، وأنت كيف؟
Jabir: My wife is	*jabir: zawjatee*	جابر: زوجتي تعبانة

tired today, She may not come, Let me ask her.	*ta'ebana al-yawm, mumkin la taetee, khalli as'aluha.*	اليوم، ممكن لا تأتي، خلّ اسألها.
Khalid: What time shall we go out.	*khalid: sa'a kam nakhruj?*	خالد: ساعة كم نخرج؟
Jabir: After Magrib prayer.	*jabir: ba'eda salatil magrib.*	جابر بعد صلاة المغرب.
Khalid: It is better before magrib. We shall watch the sun set from the park.	*khalid: ahsan qablal magrib. nushahidul guroob minal hadeeqa.*	خالد: احسن قبل المغرب، نشاهد الغروب من الحديقة.
Jabir: No problem, What is the time now?	*jabir: ma fee mushkila, sa'a kam al-heen?*	جابر: ما في مشكلة. ساعة كم الحين؟
Khalid: The time now is 5.45, Half an hour is left.	*khalid: assa'a al-heen sitta illa rubu'e. baqiya nisfu sa'a.*	خالد: الساعة الحين ستتة الا رُبع يقي نصف ساعة.
Jabir: Fast, Let us go to the park.	*jabir: sur'a, hayya bina ilalhadeeqa.*	جابر: سُرعة، هيّا بنا الى الحديقة.
Khalid: Is there a canteen in the park.	*khalid: maqsaf mawjood fil-hadeeqa, am la?*	خالد: مقصف موجود في الحديقة، ام لا؟
Jabir: Yes, There is one.	*jabir: ee mawjood.*	جابر: اي موجود.
Khalid: Have you got a Camera?	*khalid: indaka kamera?*	خالد: عندك كاميرا؟
Jabir: Yeah, I have got a nice camera.	*jabir: ee. indee kamera zayn.*	جابر: اي عندي كاميرا زين.
Khalid: The car is coming, come on fast.	*khalid: assayyara qadima, ta'alou sur'a.*	خالد: السيّارة قادمة، تعالوا سُرعة.
Jabir: What shall we do in the park?	*jabir: ma da nusawwee fil-hadeeqa?*	جابر: ما ذا نسوِّي في الحديقة؟

Khalid: We shall relax, enjoy, play and spend time with children.	*khalid: nartah, natamatta'e, nal'ab wa naqdee waqt ma'al awlad.*	خالد: نرتاح، نتمتع، نلعب ونقضي وقت مع الأولاد.
Jabir: The weather is moderate today.	*jabir: al-jawwu mu'etadil al-yawm.*	جابر: الجوُّ معتدل اليوم.
Khalid: Yesterday the humidity was too much.	*khalid: ams kanati rrutooba wajida.*	خالد: امس كانت الرطوبة واجدة.
Jabir: The park is filled with families today.	*jabir: al-hadeeqa al-yawm mamloo'a bil-'a'elat.*	جابر: الحديقة اليوم مملوءة بالعائلات.
Khalid: Sunday is the family day for the park.	*khalid: yawmul ahad, yawmul 'a'elat fil-hadeeqa.*	خالد: يوم الأحد، يوم العائلات في الحديقة.
Jabir: Do you come here on every Sunday?	*jabir: inta ta'etee hinee kulla yawmul ahad?*	جابر: انت تأتي هني كل يوم الأحد؟
Khalid: Most often. and some times we go to the Cornish.	*khalid: katheeramma wabaedal ahyan naruh ilal koornish.*	خالد: كثيراً ما، وبعض الأحيان نرح الى الكورنيس.
Jabir: Look. The sun is about to set.	*jabir: shuf ashams kadat tagrab.*	جابر: شف الشمس كادت تغرب.
Khalid: Nice, Sun set is a beautiful scene.	*khalid: huluwu, guroobushams manzar jameel.*	خالد: حُلو، غروب الشمس منظر جميل.
Jabir: Come on, let us go to the restaurant, we are hungry.	*jabir: hayya naruh al-mat'am, nahnu jaw'aa.*	جابر: هيّا نرح المطعم، نحن جوعى.
Khalid: After half an hour, Insha Allah.	*khalid: ba'eda nisfu sa'a, insha allah.*	خالد: بعد نصف ساعة، ان شاء الله.

Jabir: What shall we do after dinner?	*jabir: ba'edal 'ashae shusawwee?*	جابر: بعد العشاء شوِّي؟
Khalid: We shall walk a little.	*khalid: namshee shuway.*	خالد نمشي شُوي.
Jabir: Good idea.	*jabir: fikra tayyiba.*	جابر: فكرة طيبة.

At a Pharmacy

(Khalid is sick. His father calls a doctor. The doctor comes, inspects and prescribes some medicine for him)

Doctor: It is simple. It is due to the change in weather, Don't worry my brother.	*doctor: hada baseet, bisababi tagyeeri ttaqas la taqlaq ya akhoy.*	الطبيب: هذا بسيط، بسبب تغيير الطقس لا تقلق يا اخوي.
Khalid: Some time I feel weakness in my heart.	*khalid: ahissu bidu'efil qalbi ahyanan.*	خالد: أُحسُّ بضُعفِ القلب احَيانا.
Doctor: Do you smoke?	*doctor: hal inta mudkhin?*	الطبيب: هل انت مُدخن.
Jabir: Yeah.	*khalid: ee.*	خالد: اي.
Doctor: It is the cause of your disease and there is no treatment for it except giving up smoking.	*doctor: hada huwa sababu maradika. wala 'ilaja lahu illa tarku ttadkheen.*	الطبيب: هذا هُو سبب مرضك، ولا علاج له إلاّ تركُ التدخين.

(The doctor orders Khalid to give up smoking and prescribes some tonics. Khalid goes with the prescription to a near by pharmacy and on the way he meets his friend Jabir)

Jabir: Where are you going my brother?	*jabir: ila wayn ya akhoy?*	جابر: الى وين يا اخوي؟
Khalid: To the pharmacy.	*khalid: ila ssaydaliyya.*	خالد: الى الصيدلية.

Jabir: What is the matter?	*jabir: aysh fee?*	جابر: ايش فيه؟
Khalid: I was very tired and the doctor prescribed some medicine for me.	*khalid: kuntu ta'eban wajid, wawasafa lee attabeeb ba'edal adwiya.*	خالد: كنت تعبان واجد، ووصف لي الطيب بعض الأدوية.
Jabir: Which pharmacy would you like to buy the medicine from?	*jabir: min ayya saydaliyya tabgi tashtaree al adwiya?*	جابر: من أي الصيدلية التي أمام المدرسة.
Khalid: From the pharmacy in front of the school.	*khalid: mina ssaydaliya allatee amamal madrasa.*	خالد: من الصيدلية التي أمام المدرسة.
Jabir: How do you go? Can I drop you?	*jabir: kayfa taruh? mumkin waddi'ek?*	جابر: كيف تَرح؟ ممكن ودعك؟
Khalid: No, the pharmacy is near, I will walk, No problem	*khalid: la, assaydaliya qareeba, amshee, mafee mushkila*	خالد: لا، الصيدلية قريبة، امشي، ما في مشكلة.
Jabir: Fine, may Allah cure you. I will see you tomorrow.	*jabir: zayn, allah yashfeek, ashoofaka bukra.*	جابر: زين، الله يشفيك. أشوفك بُكرة.

(Khalid walks and reaches the pharmacy)

Pharmacist: Welcome, may I help you?	*assaydalee: marhaban, mumkin usa'edak?*	الصيدلي: مرحباً، ممكن أساعدك؟
Khalid: I want some medicine.	*khalid: ureedu ba'edal adwiya.*	خالد: أريد بعض الأدوية.
Pharmacist: Where is the prescription?	*assaydalee: wayn al wasfa?*	الصيدلي: وين الوصفة؟
Khald: Here is it.	*khalid: mawjood.*	خالد: موجود.

Pharmacist: Take a tablet each three times a day.	*assaydalee: khud habba thalatha marra fil-yawm.*	الصيدلي: خُذ حبة ثلاث مرات في اليوم.
Khalid: How much is this?	*khalid: kam hada?*	خالد: كم هذا؟
Pharmacist: Twenty riyals. Do you want invoice also?	*assaydalee: 'eshroon riyal, tabgil fatoora ba'ed?*	الصيدلي: عشرون ريال، تبغ الفاتورة بعد؟
Khalid: If you don't mind.	*khalid: law samaht.*	خالد: لو سمحت.
Pharmacist: Here you are.	*assaydalee: faddal.*	الصيدلي: فضّل.
Khalid: Thanks.	*khalid: mashkoor.*	خالد: مشكور.
Pharmacist: We wish you fast recovery.	*assaydalee: natamanna laka shifa al-'ajil.*	الصيدلي: نتمنى لك الشفاء العاجل.
Khalid: Good bye.	*khalid: ma'a ssalama.*	خالد: مع السلامة.
May Allah protect you.	*assaydalee: fee amanillah.*	الصيدلي: في أمان الله.

At the Market

Babu: Good evening, Raju.	*babu: masaal khayr, raju.*	بابو: مساء الخير، راجو.
Raju: Good evening, How are you?	*raju: masaannoor, kayf halak?*	راجو: مساء النور، كيف حالك؟
Babu: Good, and you?	*babu: bikhayr, inta kayf?*	بابو: بخير أنت كيفك؟
Raju: All right.	*raju: kullish tamam.*	راجو: كلش تمام.
Babu: How is your family? How are children?	*babu: kayf aaela? kayfal awlad?*	بابو: كيف عائلة، كيف أولاد؟

Raju: All are fine, Praise be to Allah.	*raju: kulluhum twayyiboon, alhamdu lillah.*	راجو: كلهم طيبون، الحمد لله.
Babu: What do you do here Raju.	*babu: shu sawee hinee ya raju.*	بابو: شو سوي هني يا راجو.
Raju: I want to buy a watch.	*raju: abeu ashtaree saa.*	راجو: أبغ أشتري ساعة.
Babu: What watch you want to buy?	*babu: ayyu saa tabeu?*	بابو: أي ساعة تبغ؟
Raju: I want to buy a Continental watch.	*raju: abeu saa continental.*	راجو: أبع ساعة كانتيننتل.
Babu: Fine, Go straight, See the first shop on your left, there is sales promotion.	*babu: zain, ruh seeta, shuf awwal mahal fil yasar, feehi tanzeelat.*	بابو: زين، رح سيتا شف أول محل في اليسار فيه تنزيلات.
Raju: Thank you babu, What do you do here?	*raju: shukran ya babu, inta aysh sawee hinee?*	راجو: شكرا يا بابو، أنت ايش سوي هني؟
Babu: I'am travelling after one week, I want to buy some clothes for my children.	*babu: ana musafir baeda usbooe, ashtaree baedal malabis lil awlad.*	بابو: أنا مسافر بعد أسبوع أشتري بعض الملابس للأولاد.
Raju: Where are you staying now?	*raju: inta sakin wayn al heen?*	راجو: أنت ساكن وين الحين؟
Babu: At Muntaza.	*babu: fee muntaza.*	بابو: في منتزه.
Raju: How did you come here?	*raju: kayf jeata hinee?*	راجوا: كيف جئت هني؟
Babu: By taxi.	*babu: fee taksee.*	بابو: في تاكسي.
Raju: Can I drop you home?	*raju: mumkin khalleeka fil bayt?*	راجو: ممكن خليك في البيت؟
Babu: Thanks, I will be little late. I have	*babu: shukran, ana mutaakhir shuway,*	بابو: شكرا، أنا متأخر شوي، عندي عمل واجد

too much work in the market.	*indee amal wajed fissooq.*	في السوق.
Raju: What time do you want to go home?	*raju: saa kam tabeu taruh bayt?*	راجو: ساعة كم تبغ ترح بيت؟
Babu: May be at 9 O'clock.	*babu: mumkin saa tis'a.*	بابو: ممكن ساعة تسعة.
Raju: No problem, I will be there infront of the mosque, We shall go together.	*raju: mafee mushkila. akoon mawjood amamal masjid, naruh maen.*	راجو: ما في مشكلة، أكون موجود أمام المسجد، نرح معاً.
Babu: Thank you brother.	*babu: shukran ya akhoya.*	بابو: شكراً يا أخويا.
Raju: Welcome.	*raju: afwan.*	راجو: عفواً.
	[With the shop keeper]	
Raju: Have you got continental watch?	*raju: fee saa continental maekum?*	راجو: في ساعة كانتينينتل معكم؟
Shop keeper: Yes, it is there.	*sahibulmahal: bala, mawjood.*	صاحب المحل: بلا، موجود.
Raju: How much is this?	*raju: hada kam?*	راجو: هذا كم؟
Raju: How much?	*raju: kam?*	راجو: كم؟
SK: Come and see whic model do you want?	*sm: fadhal, shuf, ayy model tabeu?*	ص. م: فضل، شف، أي مودل تبغ؟
SK: This is three hundred.	*sm: hada thalathu mia.*	ص. م: هذا ثلاث مائة.
Raju: This is expensive brother?	*raju: hadi gali ya akhoy?*	راجو: هذه غالية يا أخوي؟
SK: Of course, Continental is little expensive. You want cheaper one.	*sm: tabaan, continental shuway gali. tabeu rakhees?*	ص. م: طبعا، كانتينينتل شوي غالي. تبغ رخيص؟

Raju: No, I want only Continental.	*raju: la, abeu bas continental.*	راجو: لا، أبغ بس كانتيننتل.
Raju: What is the last price?	*raju: akhir kam?*	راجو: آخر كم؟
SK: I will give you for 280 Riyal.	*sm: ueteeka li miatayn wa thamaneen riyal.*	ص. م: أعطيك لمائتين وثمانين ريال.
Raju: 250 will be OK?	*raju: mumkin miatayn wa khamseen?*	راجو: ممكن مائتين وخمسين.
SK: No way. It is loss, anyway I will give you for 270.	*sm: la yaseer, ya akhoy, hada khasara ala kulli hal jib meatayn wa sab'een*	ص. م: لا يسير، يا أخوي، هذا خسارة، على كل حال جب مائتين وسبعين.
Raju: Is there guarantee?	*raju: feeh dhaman?*	راجو: فيه ضمان؟
SK: Yes.	*s m: aywa.*	ص. م: أيوا.
Raju: For how many years?	*raju: li kam sana?*	راجو: لكم سنة؟
SK: For 5 years.	*sm: li khamsa sana.*	ص. م: لخمس سنوات.
Raju: Fine, give me this.	*raju: zain, aietinee hada.*	راجو: زين، أعطني هذا.
SK: You want invoice?	*sm: tabeu fatoora?*	ص. م: تبغ فاتورة.
Raju: Ofcourse, give me the guarantee card also.	*raju: tabaan, aitinee bataqatudhaman baed.*	راجو: طبعا، أعطني بطاقة الضمان بعد.
SK: No problem.	*sm: mafi mushkila.*	ص. م: ما في مشكلة.
Raju: Have you got change for 500/-?	*raju: indaka qurda li khamsu mia?*	راجو: عندك قردة لخمس مائة؟
SK: Yes, No problem.	*sm: mawjood, ma fee mushkil.*	ص. م: موجود، ما في مشكل.

Raju: Have you got watch for ladies also?	*raju: indak saat li ssayyidat baed?*	راجو: عندك ساعة للسيدات بعد؟
SK: Yes, look there, these all are for ladies.	*sm: mawjood. shuf minak. hada kullaha lissayyidat.*	ص. م: موجود، شف مناك، هذا كلها للسيدات.
Raju: Give me a nice watch.	*raju: aetinee saa zayn.*	راجو: أعطني ساعة زين.
Raju: For my daughter.	*sm: li zawjatik aw bintik?*	ص. م: لزوجتك أو بنتك؟
SK: For your wife or daughter?	*raju: li bintee.*	راجو: لبنتي.
SK: How old is she?	*sm: kam umruha?*	ص. م. كم عمرها؟
Raju: 15 years.	*raju: khamsa ashra sana.*	راجو: خمسة عشرة سنة.
SK: Take this.	*sm: khud hada.*	ص. م: خذ هذا.
Raju: How much is this?	*raju: kam hada?*	راجو: كم هذا؟
SK: 200 Riyal only.	*sm: miatayn riyal bas.*	ص. م: مائتين ريال بس.
Raju: What is the discount?	*raju: kam khasm?*	راجو: كم خصم؟
SK: This is the last price.	*sm: hada akhir.*	ص. م: هذا آخر.
Raju: You must give me discount. So that I may come here again.	*raju: lazim tueteenee khasm, asa ajeu marra thani hinee.*	راجو: لازم تعطيني خصم، عسى أجيئ مرة ثاني هني.
SK: I will give it you for 190 Riyals.	*sm: ueteek li mea wa tiseen.*	ص. م: أعطيك لمائة وتسعين.
Raju: OK, give me the invoice.	*raju: zayn, aetinee al fatoora.*	راجو: زين، أعطني الفاتورة.
SK: Fine, Go to the	*sm: zayn, ruh ila*	ص. م: زين، رح إلى

cashier, Thank you Raju, hope you visit us again.	*ameenu ssundooq. shukran raju. narjoo tazorana marra ukhra.*	أمين الصندوق، شكرا راجو، نرجو تزورنا مرة أخرى.
Raju: I will visit you shortly.	*raju: shukran, azoorukum qareeban. insha allah.*	راجو: شكرا، أزوركم قريبا. إن شاء الله.
SK: Good bye.	*sm: maa ssalama.*	ص.م: مع السلامة.
Raju: See you.	*raju: ila lliqa.*	راجو : إلى اللقاء.

(10) AT THE TRAVEL AGENTS OFFICE

You: Good evening.	*anta* : *masaal khayr.*	انت: مساء الخير
Travelling Agent: Good evening, Please come, take your seat.	*wakeelussafariyat: masaanoor, fadhal istarih.*	وكيل السفريات: مساء النور، فضل إسترح.
You: Thanks, How are you?	*anta: shukran, kayf halak?*	انت: شكراً كيف حالك؟
T.A.: Praise be to Allah, May I help you?	*w.s.: alhamdu lillah, mumkin usaaeduk?*	و. س: الحمد لله ممكن أساعدك؟
You: Yeah, I want to travel to India.	*anta: ureedu an usafira ilal hind.*	انت: إي أريد أن أسافر إلى الهند.
T.A.: Where in India?	*w.s.: wayn fil hind?*	و. س: وين في الهند؟
You: Mumbai.	*anta: ila mumbai.*	انت: إلى ممبئي.
T.A.: You want to travel by Air or Sea?	*w.s.: hal tureedussafar jawwan aw bahran?*	و.س: هل تريد السفر جوّا أو بحراً؟
You: I want to travel by Air.	*anta: ureeduhu jawwan.*	انت: أريده جوًّا.
T.A.: Are you travelling alone?	*w.s.: hal inta musafir wahdak?*	و.س: هل أنت مسافر وحدك؟
You: No, I'am travelling with family.	*anta: la, ana musafir mael aela.*	انت: لا، أنا مسافر مع العائلة.

T.A.: When do you want to travel?	*w.s.: mata tabeu tusafir?*	و.س: متى تبغ تسافر؟
You: I want to travel on 30th July.	*anta: abeu usafir fee 30 yooliyoo.*	انت: أبيع أسافر في ٣٠ يوليو.
T.A.: Which flight do you want?	*w.s.: ayyu taira tabeu?*	و.س: أي طائرة تبغ؟
You: Is there any difference in fair.	*anta: fee farq fil ujoor?*	انت: في فرق في الأجور؟
T.A.: Little.	*w.s.: shuway.*	و.س: شوي.
You: What is the difference in fair?	*anta: shunul farq fil ujoor?*	انت: شن الفرق في الأجور؟
T.A.: Indirect flight there is 10% discount. You want Kuwait Air ways or Oman Air?	*w.s.: taira gair muwajaha fee khasm ashra fil mia. tabeu alkuwaitiya aw al omaniya?*	و.س: طائرة غير مواجهة في خصم عشرة في المائة. تبغ الكويتية أو العمانية؟
You: How many hours it will take?	*anta: kam saa taukhuduhu?*	انت: كم ساعة تأخذه؟
T.A.: Approximate 10 hours. 5 hours waiting in Kuwait.	*w.s.: taqreeban ashra saa. khamsa saa intidhar fil kuwait.*	و. س: تقريباً عشرة ساعة. خمسة ساعة إنتظار في الكويت.
You: Book a ticket for me in Kuwait Air ways.	*anta: ihjiz lee tadkira fil kuwaitiya.*	انت: إحجز لي تذكرة في الكويتية.
T.A.: Fine.	*w.s.: zayn.*	و. س: زين.
T.A.: What time is the departure from Doha?	*w.s.: saa kam almugadara min doha?*	انت: ساعة كم المغادرة من الدوحة؟
You: 6:30 in the evening.	*anta: saa sitta wannisf masaen.*	و.س: ساعة ستة والنصف مساء.
T.A.: What time shall we reach Kuwait?	*w.s.: saa kam nasil kuwait?*	انت: ساعة كم نصل الكويت؟

You: 7:30	*anta: saa sabeu wannisf.*	و. س: ساعة سبع والنصف.
T.A.: Dinner from where?	*w.s.: asha min wayn?*	انت: عشاء من وين؟
You: They may give you in Kuwait.	*anta: mumkin tuetoon fil kuwait.*	و. س: ممكن تعطون في الكويت.
T.A.: No problem.	*w.s.: ma fee mushkila.*	انت: ما في مشكلة.
You: What is your name, address, post box, telephone number.	*anta: shusmak, unwan, sundooq bareed, raqm hatif.*	و. س: شسمك، عنوان، صندوق بريد، رقم هاتف.
You: Fine, the ticket is booked. Take at any time you want.	*anta: zayn tazkira mahjooza, khud ayy waqt tabeu.*	و. س: زين تذكرة محجوزة خذ أي وقت تبغ.
T.A.: What time does your office open in the morning?	w.s.: *saa kam battal maktabukum sabahan?*	انت: ساعة كمٍ بطل مكتبكم صباحا؟
You: 8:00 O'clock.	*anta: saa thamaniya.*	و.س: ساعة ثمانية.
T.A.: What time does is close?	*w.s.: mata sakkar?*	انت: متي سكر؟
You: 12:30	*anta: saa ithna ashra wannisf.*	و.س: ساعة إثنا عشرة والنصف.
T.A.: No problem, I will come tomorrow or day after tomorrow. In sha Allah	*w.s.: ma lee. ajeu bukra aw baeda bukra, in sha allah.*	انت: ما لي. أجيئ بكرة أو بعد بكرة. إن شاء الله.
You: As you wish	*anta: ala kayfak?*	انت: على كيفك؟
T.A.: What is your telephone number?	*w.s.: kam talafoonak?*	و.س: كم تليفونك؟
You: Landline or Mobile?	*anta: aadee aw jawwal?*	انت: عادي أو جوال؟

T.A.: Give me all.	*w.s.: aeitinee kul.*	و.س: أعطني كل.
You: 4360363, Mobile: 5814379	*anta: 4360363, aljawwal: 5814379*	انت: ٤٣٦٠٣٦٣ الجوال: ٥٨١٤٣٧٩
T.A.: I will call you before I come.	*w.s.: sa attasil bik qabla an ajeu.*	و.س: سأتصل بك قبل أن أجئ.
You: Most welcome. Glad to help you.	*anta: ahlan wa sahlan. masroor li nusaedak.*	انت: أهلاً وسهلاً. مسرور لنساعدك.
T.A.: Thank you very much.	*w.s.: shukran jazeela.*	و.س: شكرا جزيلاً.
You: You are welcome.	*anta: afwan.*	و.س: عفواً.
T.A.: Good bye.	*w.s.: maa ssalama.*	و.س: مع السلامة.
You: See you.	*anta: ila lliqa.*	و.س: إلى اللقاء.

LESSON TWENTY FIVE

DICTIONARY

A

Abbreviation	اختصار	Abrupt	فجْأة
Absolute	مُطلق	Absolute value	القيمة المُطْلقة
Absorb	إمتصّ	Abundance	رفرة
Academy	مُجْمَع	Accelerate	سَارَعَ
Accident	حَادثَة	Accomplishment	إنجاز
Acountancy	مُحاسَبَة	Accountant	مُحَاسب
Accredited journalist	صُحفي مُعْتَمَد	Accuracy	دقة
Accuse	اتَّهم	Achieve	أدرك
Acidity	حمضية	Acquinted	مَطلَع
Activate	نشط	Addition	جمع/ إضافة
Additional	إضافي	Address	عُنوَان
Adhere	لصق/ التصق	Adhesive	لصوق
Adjoin	تلاصق/تَجَاور	Adjustments	سويات
Adolescence	مراهقة	Adorn	زَيّنَ
Advance	متقدم	Advantage	فائدة
Adverse	عكس	Advertisement	إعلان
Advise	نصيحة	Advisable	ملائم
Affair	شأن	Affinity	ألفة/قرابة
Affirmation	اثبات	Affuent	رافد
Afford	اطاق	Agency	واسطة/ وكالة
Agenda	جدول أعمال/مفكرة/مذكرة	Aggression	عدوان
Agitate	حرك/هيج	Agree	اتفق

Agreement	اتفاقية	Aim	هدف
Air conditioner	مكيف الهواء	Air force	سلاح الطّيران
Air mail	بريد جوّي	Alignment	تراصق
Allergy	حساسيّة	Aliance	حلف
Allocate	خصَّص/ عين	Allow	سَمَحَ
Allowance	سماح	Alter	بدّل
Alternate	تناوَبَ	Alternative	بديل
Amalgamation	ملغمة	Ambulance	سيَّارة الإسعاف
Amendment	تعديل	Amity	تفاهُم
Amplifier	مضخَّم	Anemia	فقرُ الدَّم
Anesthesia	خُدَار	Analgesic	مُسكن
Analogue	نَظير	Analyse	حلَّلَ
Analyst	مُحَلِّل	Anarchy	فوضى
Annex	مُلحَقة	Annihilation	إبادة
Annotation	تذييل	Antenna	هوائي
Anxious	قلق	Apology	إعتذار
Appendix	مُلحَق	Application	طَلَب
Approximate	تقريبي	Aptitude	أهليَّة
Aquarium	مَرْبي مضائيٌّ	Arcade	قنطرة
Archeologist	عالم الآثار	Argue	جادل
Arrange	رَتَّب/ نسّق/ هَيَّا	Arrangement	تنظيم
Arrest	أوقف/ كبج	Arrival	وُدُود/ وُصول
Artificial	صناعي	Ash tray	صحن سجائر
Assembly	إجتماع	Assert	مُوَافَقَة
Assort	أكَّدَ	Asset	مَوجُودَة
Assignment	مُهمَّة	Assimilation	تَمْثِيل
Assistant	مُسَاعد	Assume	افترض

Assurance	تَأكيد	Asthma	نسمة
Astonish	أَذْهَل/ أدهَشَ	Astry	شَارد
Astronomy	علْمُ الفَلَك	Atom	ذَرّة
Atomic bomb	قُنْبُلَة ذُرِّيَة	Attach	رَبطَ
Attack	هجوم	Attain	أدركَ
Attempt	محاولة	Attendant	مُرَافق
Attention	إنتباه	Attest	أكّد
Attorney general	النّائب العام	Attract	جذب
Auditorium	قاعة	Automatic	تلقائي
Auxiliary	إحتياطي	Available	متوفر
Avenue	شارع عريض	Average	معدّل/ متوسط
Avoid	تجنب	Award	منحة/ مكافأة
Awareness	وعي	Away	بَعيد عن
Awkward	بشع		

B

Back ground	خلفية	Badge	شارة/ شعار
Bag	حقيبة	Bakery	مَخْبَز
Balance	رَصيد	Balance	وازن
Balance sheet	ميزانية	Balcony	شُرفَة
Bamboo	خيزران	Bankrupt	مفلس
Bank note	عملة ورقية	Bandage	ضماد
Bargian	صفقة	Barley	شعير
Barren	عاقر	Barricade	متْرَاس
Barrier	عائق	Barter	مقابضة/ مبادلة
Basic	أساسي/ أصلي/ اولى	Basic data	المعطيات الأساسيَّة
Basic structure	بَنِيَّة الأسَاسي	Basic system	نظام أساسي

Basin	حوض/ طست/ قصعة	Bastard	نغل/ ذنيئ/ شاذ
Bath room	حَمَام	Battery	مَجْمُوعة متواحدة
Battle	معركة	Beacon	فنار
Beak	منقار	Beaker	منقار
Beam	شعاع/ أشعّة	Bearer	حامل
Bed room	غُرْفَة النَّوم	Behaviour	سيرة
Belt	حزام	Bend	لَوي/ حنى
Beneficial	مُفيد	Berth	مَرْسي
Betray	خان	Bias	انحياز
Bifurcate	تَشَعَّبَ	Bill	كَشْف الحساب/ فاتورة
Bind	حزم	Bio chemistry	الكيمياء الحيوية
Bio data	بيان حالة شخصية	Biology	علم الأحياء
Bi sexual	خُنثى	Black mail	ابتزار بالتّهديد
Blame	لاَمَ	Blank	خالي
Blanket	بطانية	Blast	نفخة
Blaze	لهيب	Bleach	بَيَّض/ قَصَّر
Bleaching powder	مَسْحُوق التبيض	Blind	أعمى
Blink	رَمَشَ	Blood pressure	ضَغْطُ الدَّمْ
Blood test	فحصُ الدَّم	Blossom	نُورة
Blotting paper	نشّافَة	Blow	نفخة
Board of Directors	مَجْلس امناء	Boat	قارب/ زورق
Boggy	سبخ	Boil	غلي
Boiler	غلاَبَة	Bond	سندة
Bonnest	قلنسوة	Bonus	إكراميَّة/ منحة
Booking office	مكتبُ الحجْز	Book keeper	ماسك دفاتر
Boom	رنين/ ازير/ طنين	Boost	عزز
Booster	معزز	Booth	مقصورة/ حجيرة

Booty	غنيمة	Bore well	بئر ارتوازية
Bootle	قارورة	Bound	مُتجه
Boundary	حد	Bow	حني
Bracket	حتيفة	Brain	دماغ
Brake	مكبح/ فرملة	Branch	شعبة/ فرع
Breast	صدر/ ثدي	Breath	نفس
Breed	نسل	Breeding	توليد
Breeze	نسمة	Brube	رَشَا/ بَرْطَلَ
Brick	طوبة/ لبنَة	Bridge	جسر
Bright	ساطع/باهر/ زاهر	Brilliant	لاَمع/ زَاه
Bring	حلب	Brochure	كتيب
Brow	حاجب	Bucket	سطل/ دلو
Bud	بُرْعُم	Buddle	حُفْرَة
Budget	ميزانية	Buffet	صدم/ صارع
Bulb	بصلة/ لمبة	Bulky	ضخم
Bullet	طلقة نارية	Burden	عبأ/ثقل
Bureau	مكتب	Burn	حرق
Burst	انفجار	Burry	دفن/ طمر
Bush	شُجيرة/ جلبة	Bus routes	خطوط الحافلة
Bus stop	موقف الحافلات	Button	زر/ازرار
Bylaw	قانون داخلي	Bypass	مجري جانبي

C

Cabin	مقصورة	Cabinet	خزانة
Calculate	حسب	Calcualtor	حاسبة
Calendar	تقويم/ روزنامة	Calendar year	سنة شمسية
Camp	معسكر	Campaign	حملة

Campus	حرم الجامعة او كُلِّيّة	Canal	قناة
Cancel	أبطل/ الغى	Cancellation	إلغاء
Cancer	سرطان	Candle	شمعة
Cane	عصا	Canteen	مطعم
Cap	قلنسوة	Capacitor	مكثّف
Capacity	سعة/ وسع/ قدرة	Capitalism	رأسماليّة
Captain	قائد/ ربان/ نقيب	Capture	اسرٌ/ احتجاز/ قبض
Cardinal	أساسي/ رئيسي	Cardinal number	عدد أصلي
Care	عناية	Careful	حريص/ حذرٌ
Careless	مهمل	Caretaker	مراقب
Cargo	شحنة	Carpenter	نجّار
Carpet	بساط/ حاملة	Catridge	طلقة/ خُرطوشة
Carve	نحت/ نقش	Cascade	ضلال/ مسقط/ مياه
Casting	سبك/ صب	Casual	عرضي/ طارئٌ
Casualty	أمرٌ طارئ/ إصابة	Catalysis	حفْزٌ
Catalyst	مادة حفازة	Catch	أمسك
Category	صنف	Caution	حذر
Cave	كهفٌ/ غارٌ	Cease	كفَّ/ أوقف
Ceilling	سقف	Celestial body	جرم سماويٌّ
Cell	خلية	Cellular	خلويٌّ
Cement	ملاطٌ	Censor	رقيب
Censorship	رقابة	Centenary	مئوي
Center	مركز	Centralise	ركّز
Certificate of fitness	شهادة لياقة	Chain	سلسلة
Chain surveyor	سلسلة المساح	Chalk	طباشير
Challenge	تحدي	Chamber	حجيرةٌ
Champion	بطَلٌ	Chance	فرصة/ صدفة/ نصيب

Change	غَيَّر/ حَوَّل	Changeability	قابلية التغير
Changeable	متغير	Channel	مجرى/ ممر
Chaos	تشويش/ فوضى	Chap	فلع/ فتى/ غلام
Char	احرق	Character	طابع/ سجيّة
Charge	حشا/ شحن/ حمل/ فرض	Charger	جهاز شحن
Charging ciruit	دائرة الشحن	Charging station	محطة التحميل
Chart	خارطة/ خريطة	Chartered	مجاز/ قانوني
Chartered accountant	مُحاسب قانوني	Chase	طارد/ لاحق/ تعقب
Chatter	صوّت/ اصطك/ ثرثر	Cheap	رخيص
Cheat	غشّ/ خدَعَ/ غَبَنَ	Check	صَدَّ/ كَبَحَ/ دَقَقَ
Check list	قائمة المراجعة	Check up	فحص
Cheek	خَدٌّ/ وجْنَة	Chemical process	طريقة كيمائية
Chemical action	تفاعل كيمَائي	Chiller	مبرد
Chimney	مدخنة	Chip	شنطيَّة
Chocker	مخنقة	Choose	اختارَ/ انتخبَ
Chord	وَتر	Chronic	مُزمنٌ
Chronological	مياقتي/ مرتب/ زمنيا	Cinders	رَمادٌ/ فحمٌ
Circle	دائرة/ حلقة	Circuit	دورة/ مدار
Circular	مستدير/ دائري	Circular function	دالة دائرية
Circularity	استدارة	Circulate	دار/ داول/ نشر
Circulation	دوران	Circulator	مُدوال/ مُوزَعٌ/ مُروجٌ
Citadel	حصنٌ/ قلعةٌ/ معقلٌ	Civic	مدني
Civil	مدني، أهلي	Civil Aviation	الطيران المدني
Civil engineer	مهندس مدني	Civilization	تمدن/ حضارة/ مدنية
Civil service	خدمة مدنية	Claim	إدّعى
Clap	تصفيق	Cleaner	منظف
Cleaning brush	فرجونُ تنظيف	Clear	صاف/ رائق/ دجلي/ خالص

Clearance certificate	شهادة تخليص	Cleaning	تصفية/ تخليص/ إزالة
Cleaning agent	عامل إزالة	Client	زبون/ عميل/ موكل
Climate	مناخ	Climatology	علم المناخ
Climax	ذروةٌ/ نهاية	Climb	تسلق/ ارتقى
Clip	شبك	Clipper	مجز
Close	أغلق	Clot	جمّد/ جلّط/ خثّر
Cloud	سحابة/ غَيْمة/ غَمَامَة	Club	هراوةٌ/ نادي
Clue	دليل	Cluster	عنقود
Clutch	قابض	Coconut	جوزُ الهند/ نارجيل
Code	شفرةٌ/ كلام رمزي	Co-existence	تعايش
Coherence	تماسك/ التصاق/ اتساق	Coil	لَفَّ
Coincide	تطابق/ تزامن	Coincidence	مطابقة
Collaborate	تعاوُن	Collapse	هبط/ انهار
Collation	مقارنة	Colleague	زميل/ رفيق
Collect	جمع/ ضم / حشد	Collection	مجموعة
Collector	حاشد/ مجمعٌ	Collide	صدم
Collision	تصادم	Colourful	زاه
Column	عَمودٌ/ رتلٌ/ طابورٌ	Comb	مُشطٌ/ محسّةٌ
Combination	جمعٌ/ ضمٌّ	Comfort	راحة/ انشراح
Comfortable	مريح/ مرتاح	Commandant	قائد
Commence	ابتدأ/ شرع/ باشر	Comment	تعليق/ ملاحظة
Commentator	معلّق/ معقّب	Commerce	تجارة
Commission	تفويض/ براءة	Commissioner	مندوب/ مفوض
Commit	ارتكب	Commitment	تعهد/ التزام
Committee	لجنة/ هيئة	Commodity	سلعة/ متاع/ بضاعة
Common	شائع/ عام/ عادي	Communicate	تبادل/ اتصل
Communism	الشيوعية	Commutation	تبديل/ تعديل

Compact مضغوط/ متضام
Comparable مقارن/ مماثل
Compartment حجيرة/ مقصورة
Compel أجبر/ أكره
Compete نافس/ بارى
Compile جمع/ نسق
Complement تتمَّة/ تَكْملَة/ تَمَامَة
Completion اكمال/ اتَمام
Complexion مظهر/ ملامح
Compliance قبول/ مطاوعة/ استجابة
Compose اَلَّفَ/ حرَّرَ
Comprehend فَهَمَ/ اَدْرَكَ
Compress ضغط/ شدَّ
Compromise تسوية/ مصالحة
Compute حسب/ قدّر
Concave lens عَدَسَة مُقَعَّرَة
Conceal أخفَى/ خَبَّا/ سَتَرَ
Concentrate رَكَزَ
Concession تَسليم/ تنازُل
Concise مَوجز/ مختصر
Concomitant ملازم/ مرافق
Concurrence تواخف/ تزامن
Condemn حكم علَى/ شجبَ/ دانَ
Condenser مكثف
Conditioning تكييف
Conduct سلوك
Conductor قاطعُ التَّذاكر/ مُوصل/ مُرشد
Company شركة/ رفقة/ عشرة
Comparatively نسبيا/ بالمقارنة
Compatable منسجم/ متوافق
Compensate عوَّض/ عادل
Competition مباراة/منافسة/ مسابقة
Complain شكا/ تذمَّر
Complete كامل/ تَام
Complex مُرَكَّب/ مُعَقَّد
Complexity تعقد
Compliment اطراء/ مدح ثناء
Composition تَرْكيب
Comprehensive شامل
Comprise شَمُلَ/ احتوَى
Compulsion اجباري/الزامي
Concave مقعَّر
Concavity تَقعَّرَة
Conceive أدرَكَ/ تَصَوَّرَ
Concept مَفْهُوم
Conciliation توفيق/ مُصالحَة
Conclusion نهاية/ ختام
Concrete صُلب/ مادي
Concussion ارتجاج
Condensation تكثيف/ تلخيص
Condition حال/ وضع/ ظرف/شرط
Conduce ساعدَ/ أدَّى/ أفضَى
Conductibility توصَّلِيَّة
Confine حَصَرَ/ حَدَّدَ

Confirm	أثبت/ أيَّدَ / أكَّدَ	Confiscate	صادر
Configration	حريق	Conflict	تضارب/ نزاع/ تناقض
Conformation	تطابق	Confound	ربَّكَ/ حَيَّرَ/ أدهلَ
Confront	واجه	Confusion	إختلاط/ اضطراب
Congest	زَحَمَ/ احْتَقَنَ	Congestion	إزْدحَام/ احتقان
Conglomeration	تَكتَّلَ/ تَراكُم	Conglutination	تلازُق/ تلزّج
Congratulate	هَنَّأ/ بَارَكَ	Congregation	احتشاد/ تجمهر
Congress	مؤتمر/ مجلس	Congruence	موافقة/ مطابقة
Conjoin	ضم/ زرَّجَ	Conjugate	زَوَّجَ/ صرَّفَ (الفعل)
Connect	وصل/ ربط	Connive	تغاضي عن/ تواطأ
Conquer	غَلَبَ/ فَتَحَ	Conscience	ضَمير/ وجدان
Consciousness	وعي	Consecutive	متتابع
Consent	رضي/ قبول	Consequence	نتيجة/ عاقبة
Conservation	صيانة/ حفظ	Consider	اعتبر
Consign	أودعَ/ أرْسَلَ	Consist	تَركَّبَ/ تَألَّفَ
Consolidate	ضَمَّ/ وَحَّدَ/ عَزَّزَ	Consolidation	تقوية/ تعزيز
Consonance	توافُق/ انسجام	Conspiracy	مُؤامَرَة
Constant	ثابت/ مستمر/ مُخْلص	Consituent	مُكوِّن
Constitution	تَكْوين/ بنية	Constrain	ألزَمَ/ أرغَمَ
Constraint	حَصَرَ/ تَفييد	Constriction	تضييق/ احتناق
Construct	بَنَى/ شَيَّدَ/ رَسَمَ/ أنشأ	Construe	فسَّرَ/ أوّلَ
Consult	استشارَ/ استطلَعَ	Consume	استهلك/ استنفقد
Consummate	تَمَّمَ/ أكمَلَ	Contact	إتَّصَلَ/ لامَسَ/ مَسَّ
Contain	احتَوَى / تَضَمَّنَ	Container	وِعَاء/ إنَاء
Contemplate	إعتَزَمَ/ تَأمَّلَ	Contemporary	مُعاصر/ مُزامن
Contend	قادَمَ/ جَادَلَ/ نَافَسَ/ كَافَحَ	Content	مُحْتَوَى/ مَضْمُون

Context	مُلاحَقَة/ تَجَاور/ تَلاَمس	Continent	قَارَة
Continuation	استمرار	Continue	استمَرَّ
Contort	عَوَّجَ/ لَوَّى	Contract	عقد
Contractor	متعهد/ مقاول	Contradiction	تناقضٌ
Contribution	تَبرَّع /مُسَاهَمَةٌ	Control	تحكم/ توجيه/ اشراف
Controversy	جدال/ مُناظرة	Convenience	مُلائمَةٌ/ سُهُولَة
Convention	اجتماع/ مؤتمر	Converge	تجمع/ تَقارُب
Converse	حدَّث/ كَلَّمَ	Convert	حَوَّلَ/ بَدَّلَ
Cooler	مُبَرَّد	Co-operate	تَعاوَنَ
Co-ordinate	نَسَّق/ رَتَّبَ	Corn	مسمَارٌ
Corner	قَرْنَةٌ/ رُكْنٌ/ زَاوِيَةٌ	Corrupt	أفسَدَ/ رَشَا
Count	عَدَّ	Counter	عدَاد
Counterpart	نسْخَة طبْقَ الأصل	Course	مجرى مسلك/ وجهة
Court	ساحة/ محكمة	Courtesy	لُطفٌ/ كباسة/ مُجَامَلَة
Crack	تشقُّق/ تَصَدُّع/ تَفلُّع	Crackle	طقطقة/ فرقع
Cradle	مَهْدٌ	Craft	مهنة/ حرفة
Cranck	ذراع/ تدوير/ مرفق	Crawl	زحف/ دبّ
Cream	قشدةٌ	Create	خلق/ أحَدث
Credit	ثقَةٌ/ تَصْديق	Crew	بَحَارَةٌ
Crib	مَهْدٌ/ مَذوَدٌ	Crime	جُرْمٌ/ جنَايَةٌ/ خَطِيئَةٌ
Cripple	كَسيحٌ/ مُقْعَدٌ	Critical	انتقادي/ مدقق
Criticize	انتقد	Crown	تاج/ اكليل
Crush	هَشم/ تحطّم	Crystal	بلَّور
Cube	مُكَعَّبٌ	Cure	داوَى/ عَالَجَ
Curfew	مَنع التجوُّل	Custom	عادةٌ/ عُرْف
Customs duty	رَسْمٌ جَمَركي	Customs	جَمْرَك

D

Dairy	مَلْبَنَة	Dam	سَدٌّ/ حَاجزٌ
Damage	خَسارَةٌ/ تَلَفٌ	Danger	خَطَرٌ
Data	مُعْطيَاتٌ/ بَيَانَاتٌ	Debate	مُنَاقَشَةٌ/ مُنَاظَرَةٌ
Decay	تَلفَ/ انحلال	Decide	قرَّرَ/ عَزَمَ/ صَمَّمَ
Declaration	إعلان/ تَصْريح	Declination	ميل/ انحراف
Decorate	زَيَّنَ/ زَخرَفَ/ نَمَّقَ	Decorator	مُزَخْرِفٌ
Decrease	نَقَصَ/ قَلَّ	Decree	قرار/ مرسوم
Deduce	استنتج/ استخلص	Deduct	اقتطع/ طرح
Deed	وثيقة/ مستند	Deep	عميقٌ/ معقدٌ/ عويص
Defeat	قهَّرَ/ هزَمَ/ احبَطَ/ خَيَّبَ	Defect	عَيْبٌ/ خَلَلٌ/ نَقْصٌ
Defense	دفاع/ حماية/ تحصين	Defer	أجّل/ أرجأ
Deference	احترام/ مراعاة/ إذعانٌ	Deficiency	عجزٌ/ قصور
Define	عَرَّفَ/ عَيَّنَ/ حَدَّدَ	Degenerate	انحطَّ/ تَدَنَّأ
Delay	أخَّرَ/ أجَّلَ	Delegation	تَفْويْضٌ/ إيفادٌ
Delete	حَذْفٌ/ شَطْبٌ	Deliberate	تَدبَّرَ/ تَأمَّلَ/ تَدَاوَلَ
Delivery	تَسْليْمٌ/ تَوريدٌ	Delude	ضَلَّلَ/ خَدَعَ
Deluxe	فَاخرٌ	Demand	طَلَبَ/ التَمَسَ/ أمَرَ
Demolish	دَمَّرَ/ هَدَّمَ/ خَرَبَ	Demonstration	بَيان عملي/ برهان
Denial	انكار/ نفي	Denote	دل على/ بين/ عنَى
Density	كثافة	Depart	انطلق/غَادَرَ
Depend	اعتمَدَ/ تَوَقَّفَ	Depict	تَأمينٌ/ وَديْعَةٌ
Depot	مُستَوْدَعٌ/ مَخزَنٌ	Depress	ضَغَطَ/ خَفَضَ
Deprive	حَرَمَ/ جَرَّدَ/ مَنعَ	Deputy	نائب/ وَكيْلٌ
Derive	اشتق من/ تفرّعَ/ نَشَأ عن	Describe	وَصَفَ/ رَسَمَ
Desert	صَحْرَاءٌ/ بَيْدَاء	Design	صَمَّمَ/ رَسَمَ
Destitute	مُعوزٌ/ مُعْدَمٌ	Detach	فَصَّلَ/ نَزَعَ

Detect	اكْتَشَفَ	Detention	حَبْسٌ/ توقيفٌ
Determination	عَزْمٌ/ تَحْدِيْدٌ	Detonation	تَفْجِيْرٌ/ صَعْقٌ
Develop	تطوَّرَ/نَمَى	Deviate	انحرَفَ/ مالَ
Devote	خَصَّصَ/ وَقَفَ	Diagnosis	تشخيص
Dialect	لَهْجَةٌ	Diary	يوميَّة/ مُذكَّرَة
Diet	غذاءٌ/ حمية	Differ	اختلف
Diffuse	نشر/ انتشر	Dig	حفر
Digest	هضمَ/ استوعب	Digit	رقم/ إصبع
Dilate	وسَّعَ	Dilemma	إحراج/ ورطة
Dilute	خَفَّفَ	Dim	عَتَمَ/ خفتَ
Dimension	بعد	Dip	غمس/ غطّ
Direct	وَجَّهَ/ أرْشَدَ	Directorate	إدارةٌ
Directory	دليل	Discard	نبذَ/ رَمَى/ طَرَحَ
Discern	مَيزَ/ أدْرَكَ	Discharge	فَرَّغَ
Disciplin	ضَبْط/ نظامٌ/ تأديب	Disclose	كَشْفَ
Disconnect	فك/ حَلَ	Discover	اكتشف
Discretion	فطنة/ تَعقُّلَ	Discriminate	مَيَّزَ
Disease	مرضَ/ داء	Disgrace	أهان/ أذل
Disguise	تنكَّرَ/ تَقَنَّعَ	Disc	قُرْص
Dismiss	سَرَحَ/ طَرَدَ	Dispensary	مستوصف
Display	بسطَ/ أظهَرَ/ عَرَضَ	Dispose	رتب/ دَبَّرَ
Dispute	نازعَ/ خاصَمَ/ جَادَلَ	Disseminate	بَثَّ/ نَشَرَ
Distant	بَعيد/ نَاء	Distill	قَطَّرَ
Distort	شدَّة/ ضيق	Distribute	وَزَّعَ/ قَسَّمَ/ فَرَّقَ
District	مقَاطَعَة/ نَاحيَة	Disturb	أزْعَجَ/ اَقْلَقَ
Dodge	تَهرَّبَ/ تَجنَّبَ	Dosage	جُرْعَةٌ
Douche	منضحةٌ/ حَمَّامٌ	Drainage	تجفيفٌ/ تصفيةٌ
Dry	جافٌ/ يابس	Duty	واجبٌ/ مُهِمَّةٌ

E

Ebb	جَزْرٌ	Eclipse	كُسُوف/ خُسُوف
Ecology	علمُ الْبَينَة	Edge	طَرْفٌ
Edit	حَرَّرَ	Effect	تأثير
Efficiency	فاعليَّةٌ	Elastic	مَطَّاط
Elect	انتخب/ اختار	Elegant	أنيق/ بَهي
Elevation	رَفْعٌ	Eliminate	حَذْفٌ
Emanation	انبثاقٌ	Emblem	شعَارٌ/ رمز
Embrace	إعتنقَ/ طوق/ حوَى	Emergency	ضَرورةٌ ملحة
Emotion	عاطفة	Employ	وَظَّفَ
Empty	فَرَغَ	Enclose	سَوَّرَ/ حَصَرَ
Endure	إحْتَمَلَ/ صَمَدَ/ دَامَ	Enemy	خَصم/ عدو
Energy	طاقة/ مَقدرَةٌ/ نَشاةٌ	Engage	شَغَلَ/ شَبَّكَ
Enrich	أغْنَى/ أخصَبَ/ زَوَّدَ	Enroll	سَجَّلَ
Entrap	اصطادَ	Envelop	غلاف/ ظرف
Environment	بيئة/ احاطة	Episode	واقعية/ حادثة
Equalize	ساوَى/ عادَلَ	Equation	مَعَادَلَة
Equilibrium	تَعَادَلَ/ تَوَازَنَ	Error	خَطأ/ غلطة
Escape	هرب/ تَخَلَّص	Escort	رَافِدٌ/ وَاكبٌ
Establish	أسَّس/ شيَّد	Estimate	قَدَّرَ/ ثَمَّنَ
Eternal	دَائم/ أزَلِيٌّ/ أبَدِيٌّ	Evoke	أثارَ/ استحضرَ
Evolution	توليد/ انبعاث	Examine	فحص/ اختبر/ إمتحن
Exchange	تبادل/ ابدل	Exclude	طرد/ نفى
Excuse	عذر/ أعفَى عَنْ	Existence	كَيَان/ بَقَاءٌ
Expand	مَدَّدَ/ وَسَّعَ	Expel	طَرَدَ/ أخْرَجَ
Expenditure	نفقة	Experience	خبرةٌ/ مرانةٌ/ ممارسةٌ
Expire	انتهى/ انقضى	Explode	انفجر

Exploit	استغل/ استثمر	Exploration	استكشاف/ استطلاع
Explosion	انفجار	Export	تصدير
Export duty	رسمٌ تصديرٌ	Express	عبّر/ صرّح
Exterior	خارجيٌّ/ ظاهريٌّ	Extra	زيادة
Extract	انتزع/ اقتلع	Extreme	أقصى / مُتناه
Exude	نتح/ نزَّ/ تَحلَّبَ	Eye witness	شاهد عيان

F

Fabric	نسيج/ قماشٌ	Facet	وُجيهٌ/ سُطَيْحٌ
Facilitate	سَهَّلَ/ يَسَّرَ	Facsimile transmission	نقل الصور الثابتة
Factor	منصٌ/ عاملٌ	Factory	مصنع
Fade	ذوي/ ذُبل/ تلاشَى	Fag	كَدَّ/ كدح
Fail	خابَ/ فشلَ	Faint	خاختَ/ بَاهتَ
Faith	ثقةٌ/ إيمانٌ	Fall	سُقوطٌ/ هُطُولٌ/ شَلالات
Family	عائلة/ اسرةٌ	Famine	مجاعةٌ/ جَدبٌ
Fan	مِرْوَحَةٌ	Fancy	خَيَال
Fantacy	وهمٌ/ تَخَيُّلٌ	Fare	أجر
Fashion	شَكْلٌ / اُسلُوبٌ	Fasten	أوثق/ شَدَّ/ ثَبطَ
Fatal	مُميتٌ/ مُهْلكٌ/ قَاتِلٌ	Fatigue	تعبٌ / مَشَقَّةٌ / جُهْدٌ
Fault	خَلَلٌ/ غلَطٌ	Feature	لَمْحَةٌ / سمةٌ
Feel	أحَسَّ/ شَعَرَ	Feign	تَظَاهَرَ / تَصنعَ
Fell	قَطَعَ / قَتَلَ	Fence	سياحٌ / سُورٌ
Ferry	معْبَرٌ / مَرْكَبٌ / عُبُورٌ	Fertilize	خَصَّبَ/ سَعَّدَ
Fettle	هَيَّا / أعَدَّ	Fiction	قَصَصٌ خَيالي
File	مَبْرَدٌ / ملفٌ	Filter	مَرَشحٌ/ جهاز ترشيح
Fire prevention	مَنْعُ الحرائق	Firm	راسخٌ/ حازمٌ / صُلْبٌ

First aid	إسعاف أولي	Fission	انشطارٌ / إنفلاق
Fit	لائق/ مناسب/ ملائم	Fix	ثبت / عيّنَ
Flag	عَلَمٌ / رايَة	Flake	نُدْفَةٌ / فُشَارَةٌ
Flame	لَهيبٌ / شَعْلَةٌ	Flap	رَفْرَفَ
Flash	وَميضٌ / بَريقٌ	Flat	مُسَطَّع / مُنْبَسطٌ
Flee	هَرَبَ / فَرَّ	Flexibility	لَدانَةٌ
Flexion / Flection	إنثناءٌ/ إلْتِواءٌ	Flow	سال/ فَاضَ
Fluctuate	تَراوَحَ / تَقَلَّبَ	Forge	كَوَّرَ/ طَرَّقَ / صَهَرَ
Formality	إجْراء شكليٌّ / عُرْف	Formation	تَكْوِيْنٌ / تَشْكيلٌ
Formulation	صِيَاغَةٌ	Fortune	ثَرْوَةٌ / حَظٌّ
Forum	سَاحَةٌ / نَدْوَةٌ	Foster	شَجَعَ / عَزَزَ
Foul	قَذْرٌ / وَسْخٌ	Fracture	كَسْرٌ
Fragment	كَسْوَةٌ / شَظَيةٌ	Fragrance	أريجٌ / رائحةٌ ذكيَّةٌ
Frail	هَزيلٌ / ضَعيفٌ	Frank	صَريحٌ / علنيٌّ
Freeze	جَمَّدَ / جَلَّدَ	Frequency	تَوَاتَرَ
Fresh	طَازَجٌ / عَذْبٌ / نَاخر	Frontier	حدٌّ / تُخْمٌ
Frost	صقيع	Function	وظيفة
Fund	إعتمادٌ ماليٌّ	Fundamental	أساسيٌّ / أصليٌّ
Furnish	زَوَّدَ / أَثَّثَ / فَرَّشَ	Fusion	إنصهارٌ / إندماج
Futility	جَدوَى / عَدْمُ فائدة		

G

Gauge	معيارٌ / مقياسٌ	Galaxy	كَوكَبَةٌ
Gap	ثغرة / فَجْوَة / فَرجَةٌ	Gargle	غرغر / تمضمَضَ
Garrison	حامية / موقع	Gauze	شَفٌّ
Gear	مُسَنَنَةٌ	Genealogy	سلسلة نسب/علم الأنساب
Genius	عَبْقَرِيٌّ / نَابَغ	Glance	لَمْحٌ/ وَمْضٌ

Glacial	جَليدي / مَصفُولٌ	Gland	غُدَّةٌ
Glide	إنزَلَقَ / إنحدَرَ	Glossary	مسرد / جدْوَلٌ
Glow	توهَّجَ / إحْمَرَّ	Goods	بضاعةٌ / سلَعٌ
Governor	والي / مُنَظِّمٌ	Graduate	تَخرَّجَ في/ دَرَّجَ
Grant	مَنْحَةٌ / عَطيَّةٌ	Graph	رَسْمٌ بَياني
Graze	حَكٌّ / كَشَطَ	Grinder	جَارِشٌ / طَاحِنٌ
Grip	قَبْضَةٌ / مقْبَضٌ	Gross	إجماليٌّ
Guardian	وَصيٌّ / وَليٌّ	Guide	دَليلٌ/ مُرْشِدٌ
Gun	مُسَدَّسٌ / بُنْدُقِيَّةٌ	Gush	تَدَفَّقَ / تَفَجَّرَ

H

Habit	عَادَةٌ	Habitat	مَوْطِنٌ / بِيئَةٌ / طَبِيعَةٌ
Hack	قَطَّع	Halt	وَقْفَةٌ
Hammer	مِطْرَقَة	Hamper	أعاقَ / عَرْقَل
Handicraft	صُنْعَةَ يَدَوِيَّة / بَرَاعَة يَدَوِيَّة	Handle	ممسك / مقبض
Hanger	مشجب / حمالة	Harass	أنهك/ ضايق
Harm	أضرّ / أذى	Harmony	تَنَاغُم / انسَجام / تَلاؤُم
Harrow	مسلفة / مُشط	Harvest	حصد
Hash	فرم / هرّم	Hawk	صقر / بازي
Head office	مَكْتَب رَئِيسي	Heal	شَفَى / أبرأ/ إندمل
Health certificate	شهادة صحِّيَّة	Health insurance	الضّمان الصِّحِّي
Heater	مسخَن / مدفاة	Heed	اهتَمَّ / رَاعى
Helmet	خُوذَة	Helper	مُساعد / مُعاون
Herb	عُشبٌ	Hide	خَبَّأَ/ أخفى
Hierarchy	درجاتٌ / مَرْتَبَةٌ	Highway	طَرِيقٌ عامٌ
Hint	لَمَّحَ / أشارَ	Hire	استجارَ/ اكترَى
Hobby	هِوَايَةٌ	Horizontal	أُفقِي

Host مُضيف

Hum ظَنَّ / أزَّ / دَنَّ

Hunt اصطاد / طَارَدَ

Hybrid هَجينٌ / نَغلٌ

Hydrology علمُ المياه

Hydro therapy معالجة بالماء

I

Ice جَمَّدَ/ ثلجٌ

Identification إثبات الشَّخْصية

Identification mark علامة تعدين

Identity علامة ذاتية/ شخصيّة

Igneous petrology علم الصخور النّارية

Igniter مشعلٌ/ جهازُ إشعال

Illuminate أضاء / أنار

Illusion توهَّمَ / تخيّل

Image خيالٌ / طيفٌ

Imbide شرب / تشبّع

Imitate قلّد

Immigration هجرةٌ

Immune حصينٌ/ مَنيعٌ

Impact وَقْعَ / صَدَمَةٌ

Impede عَاقَ / عَرْقَلَ

Import license إجازة استيراد

Impose فرضَ/ ألزَمَ

Impression تأثيرٌ

Improve أصلحَ/ حَسَّنَ/ قَوي

Impulse دافعٌ/ مُحَرِّكٌ/ باعثٌ

Inactivity خُمُول/ كَسَلٌ

Inauguration تَدْشين/ إفتتاح

Inclination مَيْلٌ/ رَغْبَةٌ

Inclusive مُتَضَمِّنٌ

Income إيرادٌ/ دَخلٌ

Income tax ضَرِيْبَةٌ الدَّخْل

Increment زيادة/ علاوة/ فضل

Incubation حضانَة

Independence إستقلالٌ

Index دليل/ فهرس

Indicate دَلَّ عَلى/ بَيَّنَ

Induce حَرَّضَ/ أغرَى

Induct أدخلَ/ قَادَ/ أفضَى

Indurate قَسَّ/ صَلَدَ/ صَلَبَ

Industrialize صَنَّعَ

Inevitable مَحْتومٌ/ حَتْمِي

Infection عَدْوَى/ تَلَوُّث

Inferiority دَنَاءَةٌ

Inflammation إلتهابٌ/ احتدامٌ

Inflation نَفْخٌ/ تَضَخمٌ

Influence تأثير

Informal غَيْرُ رَسْمِي

Infraction مُخَالَفَةٌ

Infrastructure أساسٌ

Infuse	نقَع/ صَبَّ	Inhale	استنشق/ شَهَقَ
Inherit	وَرَثَ	Inhibit	مَنَعَ/ نَهَى
Initiate	دَرَّبَ/ بَدَأَ	Inject	حَقَنَ
Innovate	استحدَثَ	Inquiry	أستعلام/ بَحْثٌ
Insanity	جُنُون	Insert	أولَجَ/ أدرجَ
Insulate	عَزَلِ	Insurance	تأمين
Integrity	نَزَاهَةٌ/ استقامَةٌ	Intelligent	ذَكِيٌّ/ فَطَنٌ/ لَبِيْبٌ
Intensity	شدَّةٌ/ قُوَّةٌ/ حِدَّةٌ	Intercept	إعترض
Interfere	تَدَخَّلَ	Intermidiary	مُتَخَلَّل/ وَسيْطٌ
Interpret	أَوَّلَ/ فسَّرَ	Interval	فَاصل/ بونٌ
Interview	مُقَابَلةٌ	Intimidation	تَخْوِيْفٌ/ إرهابٌ/ تَرْوِيجٌ
Intoxication	تَسْمِيمٌ/ سُكْرٌ	Intrigue	دسيسة/ مَكيدَةٌ
Intuition	حَدْسٌ/ بَديْهَة	Invalid	مُقْعَدٌ/ بَاطِلٌ
Invent	إختَرَعَ/ ابْتكرَ	Invest	استَشْمَرَ
Invoke	تَضَرَّعَ إلى/ توَسَّلَ	Involve	تَضَمَّنَ
Irony	تَهَكُّمٌ/ استهزاء	Irradiate	أشع/ تألَّقَ
Irrigate	رَوَى/ سَقَى	Irritate	أغضبَ/ أزعَجَ
Isolate	عَزَلَ/فَصَلَ/ أَفْرَدَ	Issue	صَدَرَ/ إنْبَثَقَ/ نَتجَ

J

Jab	نَخزَ/ طَعَنَ/ لَكزَ	Jacket	قميصٌ
Jail	سِجْنٌ	Jangle	تَشَاحَنَ/ تَشاجَرَ
Jape	مِزَاحَ	Jerk	رَجْفَةٌ/ هزَّةٌ
Jiggle	هَزَّ	Joint	مَفْصَلٌ/ وَصْلَةٌ
Jolt	رَجَّ/ هَزَّ	Jounce	إرْتَجَّ
Journalism	الصَّحافَة	Judicious	حَكِيمٌ/ حَصِيفٌ
Juice	عَصِيْرٌ	Jumble	خَلَطَ/ شَوْشَ

Jump	قفزَ/ وَثَبَ	Junction	مُلْتَقى/ مُفْتَرَقَ
Juxtaposition	مُقَارَبَة/ تَجَاوُر		

K

Keep	حفظَ/ دَاوَمَ/ صَانَ	Kick	رَكَل/ رَفس
Kindle	أشعَلَ/ أضْرَمَ	King	مَلِكٌ
Kink	عُقْدَةٌ/ التِوَاءٌ	Kiss	قَبَّلَ
Kitchen	مَطْبَخ	Knack	مَهَارَةٌ/ بَرَاعَةٌ
Knee	رَكْبَةٌ	Knife	سكِّيْنٌ
Knit	حَبَطَ/ حَاكَ	Knock	دَقَّ/ طَرَقَ
Knot	عُقْدَةٌ/ أُنْشُوطَةٌ	Know	عَلَمَ/ عَرَف
Knowledge	عِلْمٌ	Kudos	شَهْرَةٌ/ شُمْعَةٌ حَسَنَةٌ

L

Laboratory	مُخْتَبَرٌ	Label	بطَاقَةٌ/ رُقْعَةٌ
Laborious	شَاقٌ/ مُتعَبٌ	Lace	شَرِيطٌ/ رِبَاطٌ
Lacerate	مَزَّقَ/ نَهَشَ	Lad	صَبِيٌّ/ غُلاَمٌ
Ladder	سُلَّمٌ	Lady	سَيِّدَةٌ
Lag	تَبَاطَأ/ تَخلَفَ	Lake	بُحَيْرَةٌ
Laminate	صَفَحَ/ رَقَقَ	Landing	هُبُوط
Lap	طَوَي/ لَفَّ	Latrine	مرحَاضَ
Lauch	إطلاقٌ	Laundry	حُجْرَةٌ الغسيل
Layout	تَخْطِيطٌ	League	رابطَةٌ
Leak	سَرَبَ/ رَشَحَ	Lean	نَحيفٌ/ نَحيلٌ
Lease	أجَرَّ/ إيجَارَ	Legacy	تُراثٌ
Legation	مَفوِّضيَّةٌ	Legend	اسطُورَة
Legitimate	شَرَعِيٌّ	Leisure	فَرَاغٌ

Leman	خدنٌ	Lend	أقْرَضَ/ دَانَ
Length	طُوف	Lesson	دَرْسٌ
Let	أذنَ	Lethargy	كَسَلَ
Letter	خَطٌّ/ رِسَالَة	Levy	فَرَضَ
Liberate	حَرَّرَ/ أَطْلَقَ	License	رُخْصَةٌ
Lie	كَذَبَ	Lift	مرفاع/ مصعد
Light	ضَوءٌ/ نورٌ	Like	مِثْلٌ
Like	أحَبَّ	Limit	حَدَّ
Limitation	تَحْديدٌ/ قصرٌ	Line	سَطَّرَ
Liquidate	صَفَّى/ سَيْلٌ	Listen	إسْتَمَعَ/ إنْتَبَهَ
Local call	مُكَالَمَة مَحَلِّيَة	Locate	أقامَ/ وَضَعَ
Locker	صُوَانٌ	Lodgement	إيواءٌ/ إيداع
Logic	عِلْمُ الْمَنْطِق	Loop	ربقَة/ عرْوَةٌ
Lose	أضاع/ خَسَرَ	Lubricate	زَلَقَ/ زَيَّتَ
Lurch	تَمَايل/ تَرَنَّجٌ	Lure	أغوَى/ أَغْرَى

M

Macerate	نَقَعَ/ دَافَ	Maintain	صَانَ/ دَاوَمَ
Make	جَعَلَ/ صَنَعَ	Manage	اَدَارَ/ قَادَ/ سَاسَ
Management	أدارةٌ/ سَياسَةٌ	Manager	مُديرٌ
Managing Director	مُديرمَسؤول	Mandate	توكيلٌ/ إنتدابٌ
Malformation	تَشَوَّهَ	Mania	مَسٌّ/ جُنُونٌ
Manifest	أظْهَرَ/ أوْضَحَ	Manifestation	مَظْهَرٌ/ إسْتِعْراضٌ
Manual	يَدَوِيٌّ	Manure	سَمَادٌ
Manuscript	مَخطُوطَةٌ	Map	حَافَةٌ/ هَامِشٌ
Marine surveying	مَسْحٌ بَحْرِيٌّ	Marketing	تَسْوِيقٌ
Martial	عَسْكَرِي/ حَرَبِي	Marvel	عَجِيبَةٌ/ مُعجزَةٌ

Mash	هَرِيسٌ/ نَفِيعُ الملْت	Mask	قنَاعٌ/ ستَار
Mason	بَنَّاء	Masticate	مَضَغَ
Match	بَارَى/ جَارَى	Mate	زَوْجٌ/ رَفِيْقٌ
Mature	نَضجَ	Maul	دَقَّ/ فَلَقَ/ نَهَشَ
Meal	وَجْبَةٌ/ طَعَامٌ	Measure	قَاسَ/ كَالَ
Mediate	تَوَسَّطَ	Mend	أصلَحَ
Merge	دَمَجَ	Mess	وَسَخَ/ أفسَدَ
Migration	هجْرَة/ إرتحال/ نُزُوح	Milky way	المَجَرَّة
Mimic	قَلَّدَ/ حَاكَى	Mind	تَبَصَّرَ/ إنْتَبَهَ
Mineralize	حَوَّلَ إلَى مَعْدَن	Mingle	مَزَجَ/ خَلَطَ
Mizzle	رَذَاذ/ مَطَرٌ خَفِيفٌ	Mock	خدعَ/ قَلَّدَ
Moderate	هَدَّأَ/ خَفَّفَ	Modify	تَغْيِيرٌ/ تَنْغِيمٌ
Moister	رَطَبَ/ خَضَلَ	Molar	طَاحنَةٌ
Monetary	نَقْدِي	Monitor	أحْتَكَرَ
Monotonous	رَتِيبٌ/ مملٌ	Mop	مَسَحَ
Morphology	علمُ التَّشكل	Mortgage	رَهْنٌ
Motivate	حَثَّ/ حَرَّضَ	Muffle	لَفَّ
Muff	لَبقَ	Multiply	ضَاعَفَ

N

Nab	خَطَفَ	Nail	سَمَّرَ
Napkin	فُوطَةٌ/ مِنْدِيلٌ	Narcotics	مُخَدَّرَاتٌ
Narrow	ضَيق	Nationalize	أمَّمَ
Nature	طَبيعَة	Navigation	مَلاَّحَةٌ
Near	قَرِيبٌ	Necessary	ضَرُورَةٌ
Neck	عُنُقٌ	Need	حَاجَةٌ
Neighbour	جَارٌ	Neglect	أهمَلَ/ تَغَافَلَ

Negotiate	فَاوَضَ	News	أخبارٌ
Nominate	رَشَّحَ	Notification	إشْعَارٌ/ إنْذَارٌ
Nutrition	تَغذِيَةٌ		

O

Obey	أطاعَ	Obligatory	مُلْزَمٌ/ إجْبَارِي
Oblique	مَائِلٌ	Obliterate	طَمَسَ/ مَحَا
Obscure	أظلَمَ/ عَتَمَ/ أبْهَمَ	Observe	لاحَظَ/ رَاعَى/ رَصَدَ
Obsolete	مَهْجُور/ عَتيق/ قَديم	Obstacle	عقبَةٌ/ حَاجزٌ/ عَائِقٌ
Obstruct	عرقَلَ/ سَدَّ/ زَحَمَ/ عَاقَ	Obtain	أحْرَزَ/ نَالَ
Obviate	تَحَاشَى/ تَدَارَكَ	Occlude	سَدَّ/ حَبَسَ/ إمْتَص
Occult	سَتَرَ/ كَسَفَ	Occupy	شَغَلَ/ إحْتَلَّ
Occur	حَدَثَ/ جَرَى	Oculist	طَبِيبُ عُيُون
Offend	أسَاءَ إلَى/ جَرَحَ إحْسَاس	Offer	عَرَضَ/ قدَّمَ
Official	رَسْمِي/ قَانُونِي	Offspring	نَسْلَ/ نَتَاجٌ
Omit	حَذَفَ/ أسقَطَ/ أهْمَلَ	Onlooker	مُشَاهِدٌ/ مُتَفَرِّجٌ
Operate	أدَارَ/ شَغَّلَ	Ophthalmology	طِبُّ العُيُون
Opponent	خَصْمٌ/ مُعَارِضٌ	Opportunity	فُرْصَةٌ/ مُنَاسَبَةٌ
Oppose	عَارَضَ/ قَاوَمَ/ ضَادَّ	Optimum	أفْضَلَ/ أمْثَلُ/ أحْسَنُ
Option	إخْتِيَار	Originate	نَشَأ/ بَدَأ
Oscillate	ذَبْذَبَ/ تَرَدَّدَ/ تَرَجَّعَ	Osculate	لَثَمَ/ مَسَّ/ قَبَّلَ
Out do	بَذَّ	Outlay	أنفَقَ/ صَرَّفَ
Out let	مَخرَجٌ/ مَنْفَذٌ	Output	نَتَاجٌ/ صَبِيبٌ
Oven	فُرْنٌ/ تَنُّور	Oven gas	غازَ الافران
Overall	كُلِّي/ إجمالي	Overbid	زايد
Overcome	غَلَبَ عَلَى	Overdo	بَالغ/ أفرطَ
Overflow	فَاضَ/ طَفَحَ/ غَمَرَ/ طَغَى	Overlap	تراكبَ/ تَدَاخَلَ/ تَشَابَكَ

Overlay	غَشَّى/ غطَّى/ طَلَّى	Override	دَاسَ/ أبْطَلَ
Overtake	تَجاوَزَ/ سَبَقَ	Overthrow	قَلَبَ/ أسْقَطَ

P

Pacify	هَدَّأ/ سَكَّنَ	Pack	حزمَةٌ/ حُزَّةٌ
Paddle	عَدَّفَ/ جَذَّفَ	Paint	دَهَنَ/ صَوَّرَ
Palpate	جَسَّ	Palpitate	وَجَبَ/ إرْتَجَفَ/ خَفَقَ
Parachute	مَظَلَّةٌ/ مهْبَطَةٌ	Parade	عَرضٌ/ إستعراضٌ موكَبٌ
Parallel	وَزَى/ شَابَهَ	Paralyze	شَلَّ/ عَطَّلَ
Parry	تَفادَى/ تَجَنَّبَ	Part	فَرَّقَ/ فَصَّلَ
Partake	إشْتَرَكَ	Partial	جُزْئي
Particularize	خَصَّصَ	Paste	اَلْصَقَ
Pathology	عِلْمُ الأمراض	Patrol	خَفَرَ/ عَسَّ/ طَافَ
Pave	وَصَفَ/ بَلّطَ	Pay	دَفَعَ/ أدَّى
Payment	دُفْعَةٌ/ عُقُوبَةٌ	Peculate	إخْتَلسَ
Penalize	عَاقَبَ	Penetrate	اخترق
Perform	أدَّى/ أنْجَزَ	Peripheral	مُحِيطِيٌّ/ سَطْحِيٌّ/ خَارجِيٌّ
Permute	أبْدَلَ	Perplex	حَيَّرَ/ أرْبَكَ
Perserve	ثَابرَ/ وَاظَبَ	Perspire	عرَقَ
Persuade	أقْنَعَ	Pervade	إنْتَشَرَ/ عَمَّ
Petrify	جَمَّدَ/ حَجَّرَ	Phonetics	علمُ الصَّوت
Photosynthesis	التَّمْثيل الضَّوئي	Phycology	علم الطحالب
Physical education	التَّربية البدنية	Physiology	علم الوظائف (فيسيولجيا)
Phytology	علم النباتيات	Pich	قرص/ ضَغطَ
Ping	أزَّ/ فرقَعَ	Playcard	لَوحَةٌ إعلان
Place	وَضَعَ/ وَظَّفَ	Pluck	إقْتَلعَ
Plumber	سَمْكَري/ سَبَّاك	Plunge	غطَّسَ/ غَمَرَ

Poison	سُمٌّ/ نَحَس	Polish	صَقَّلَ/ لَمَّعَ
Portray	وَصَفَ/ مَثَّلَ	Possess	إمْتَلكَ/ إقْتَنَى
Postpone	أرجَأ/ أجَّلَ	Postulate	إفرتَرَ/ سَلَّمَ
Potentiality	إمكانيّة/ إحْتِمَاليَّةٌ	Poultry	طُيور داجنةٌ
Pour	صبَّ/ سَكَبَ	Precaution	حَذَر/ حيطة/ إحتراس
Precede	سَبَقَ/ تَقدَّمَ	Precipitate	رَسَبَ/ تَهَوَّرَ
Predict	تنَبَّأ/ تَوَقَّعَ	Prefer	فَضَّلَ
Preliminary	تَمْهيديٌّ/ تَحْضيريٌّ	Preparation	إعداد/ تحضيرٌ
Prescribe	وصف/ حدَّد	Preserve	حفظ/ صان/ وقَى
Press	ضغط/ كَبَسَ	Pressure cooker	قدْرٌ ضَغْطيَّةٌ
Presume	إفترض	Pretend	تَظاهَرَ/ إدَّعَى
Prevail	ساد/ عمَّ	Price list	قائمة الأسعار
Prick	وخزَ/ نخز/ ثقب	Print	طبعَ
Probale	مُحتَملٌ	Procedure	طريقةٌ/ أسلوبٌ/ إجزاءٌ
Proceedings	إجراءات/ مُداولاتٌ	Procure	حصل علَى/ نَالَ
Produce	أنتجَ/ أغل	Profession	مهنةٌ/ حرفة/ وظيفة
Proficient	بارعٌ/ حاذق	Profit	ربحٌ
Progress	تقدُّم/ رقيٌّ	Progress report	تقريرٌ عن تَقدُّم العمل
Promote	رَقَى/ عزّزَ	Prop	دعمَ/ سندَ
Propagate	نَشَرَ/ بَثّ/ أذاعَ	Propel	دَفَعَ/ سَيَّرَ/ دَسَرَ
Proportion	نسبةٌ/ تَناسُبٌ	Proposal	إقتراحٌ/ عَرْضٌ
Prospect	نَجَحَ/ ازدَهَرَ	Protection	وقاية/ حمَايَة
Protract	مَدَّدَ/ أطَالَ	Protrude	أنتجَ/ أبرزَ/ أخْرَجَ
Prove	بَرْهَنَ/ أثْبَتَ	Provide	زَوَّدَ/ جهَّزَ/ مَوَّنَ
Province	مُقَاطعَةٌ/ إقليم	Provision	مُؤونَة/ إعدادٌ
Provisional	مؤقّتٌ/ إحْتياطي	Provoke	حَرَّضَ/ استفَزَّ
Prowl	جال/ طافَ/ جَاسَ	Prudence	حَصَافَةٌ/ حكمَةٌ/ تَدبرٌ

Prune	قلَّمَ/ شذَّبَ	Puberty	بُلُوغ/ حُلْمٌ
Publish	نَشَرَ/ طَبَعَ/ أعْلَنَ	Pucker	غَضَّنَ/ جَعَّدَ
Puddle	وَحْلٌ	Puff	نَفَثَ/ نَفَخَ
Pug	طينٌ/ ملَطَ	Pull	جَرَّ/ سَحَبَ
Pulsate	نَبَضَ/ خَفَقَ/ تَذَبْذَبَ	Pulverize	سَحَقَ/ سَحَنَ
Pump	خَرَمَ/ ثَقَبَ	Punched card	بطاقَة مُخْرَمَة
Puncture	خَرَقَ/ ثَقَبَ	Purchase	إشترَى/ إبتاعَ
Purge	طَهَّرَ/ نَظَّفَ	Purify	صفَّى/ نَقَى
Pursue	تَابَعَ/ لاحَقَ	Purvey	مَوّنَ/ زَوَّدَ
Push	ضَغَطَ/ رَوَّجَ	Put	وَضَعَ

Q

Quake	إرتَجَفَ/ إهتزَّ/ إرتَعَدَ	Qualification	أهليّة/ كَفاءة
Quality	نَوعٌ/ جَودَة	Quantity	كَميَّة
Quarrel	شَاجَرَ	Quell	هَدَّأ/ أخْمَدَ
Quench	أطفَأ/ أخْمَدَ/ كَبَحَ	Question	سألَ/ إستفهَمَ/ إسْتَجْوَبَ
Queue	صَفَّ	Quit	تَرَكَ/ هَجَرَ

R

Rabbet	فَرَزَ	Rabble	رَعاعٌ/ السُّوقَة
Rack	رَفَ/ دَمَارٌ	Racket	ضَجَّ
Radiance	الإشاعيَّة	Radiate	تألقَ/ شَعْشَعَ/ سَطَعَ
Radical	جُذري/ أصلي	Range	صَفَّ/ رَتَّبَ
Raid	أغَارَ	Rain	أمْطَرَ
Rain coat	مِطَرٌ/ معطَف المطر	Rain proof	صامد للمَطَر
Rake	مَالَ	Rally	حَشَدَ
Ram	دَكَّ/ طَرَقَ/ تَضَاغَطَ	Ramble	هَامَ/ جَالَ
Ramify	تَفَرَّعَ	Random	عَشْوَائي/ عَرَضي

Random sample	عَيِّنَة عَشْوائِيَّة	Range	مَدَى/ مَجال
Rank	رَتَّبَ/ صَفَّ	Ransack	نَهَبَ/ سَلَبَ
Ransom	إفتَدَى	Rap	نَقَرَ/ دَقَّ/ هَزْهَزَ
Rapport	علاقَة/ صِلَةٌ	Rarfy	خَلْخَلَ
Rase	هَدَّمَ/ مَحَقَ/ دَمَّرَ	Rasp	بَرَدَ/ قَشَطَ
Rate	قدَّرَ/ ثَمَّنَ	Ration	حَصَّةٌ/ جَرَايَة
Rationalism	إنطاق/ المذهَبُ العَقْلِي	Rattle	خشخَشَ
Ravage	خَرَّبَ/ أتلَفَ	Raze	هَدّمَ/ دَمَّرَ
React	تَفَاعَلَ	Real estate	عَقَارٌ
Realize	حَقَقَ/ أدركَ	Ream	سحَلَ/ قَوَّرَ/ رُزْمَةٌ
Reap	حصد/ جنى	Rear	شَيَّدَ/ رَبِّي
Rebate	إفترزَ/ خفض	Rebuff	رَدَّ/ صَدَّ
Recall	إستدْعَى/ ألغَى	Recapitulate	لَخَّصَ
Recapture	إستَرَدَّ	Recede	تَراجَعَ/ إنحَسَرَ/ إنْسَحَبَ
Receive	تَسَلَّمَ/ إسْتَقْبَلَ	Reception	إستقْبَال
Reciprocal	عكسي	Recite	تلا/ رَوَى/ سَرَدَ
Reckon	عَدَّ/ حَسَبَ/ قدَّرَ	Reclaim	إستَرَدَّ
Reclamation	إسترداد	Recognition	تَعَرَّفَ/ تَمَيَّزَ
Recoil	إرْتَدَّ	Recommend	إمْتَدَحَ/ زَكَّى/ أوْصَى
Recommendation	تَوصيَة/ تَزكية	Recondition	أصلح/ جَدَّدَ
Record	سَجَّلَ/دَوَّنَ	Recover	إستَعَادَ/ أعَادَ
Recreation	إستجمامٌ	Recruit	جَنَّدَ/ ضَمَّ
Rectify	صحَّحَ/ عَدَّلَ	Recur	عَاوَدَ/ تكَرَّرَ
Redirect	أعَادَ التَّوْجيه	Reduce	قَلَّلَ/ خَفَّفَ
Reeve	أسلَكَ	Reference	اسنادَ/ مَرْجَعٌ
Refine	نَقَى/ كَرَّرَ/ صَفَّى	Reflexion	إنعكاس
Reform	أصلحَ/ قوَّمَ	Refrain	أحْجَمَ عَنْ/ إمتَنَعَ عَنْ

Refuse	رَفَضَ	Refute	دَحَضَ/ فَنَّدَ
Regency	وصاية	Regulate	نظَّمَ/ ضَبَّطَ
Reject	طَرَحَ/ نَبَذَ	Relay	رَحَّلَ/ تَابَعَ
Release	أطلَقَ/ حَرَّرَ	Relevant	مُناسِبٌ
Relief	إسعافٌ	Relieve	خَلَّصَ
Rely	إعتمد/ عَوَّلَ	Remain	بَقِيَ/ ظَلَّ
Remark	لاَحَظَ	Remedy	عَالَجَ/ دَاوَى
Remit	أحال/ أعادَ	Rend	مَزَّقَ/ فَلَقَ
Repair	رمَّمَ/ أصلَحَ	Repeat	كَرَّرَ/ أعَادَ
Repel	رَدَّ/ صَدَّ	Repose	سكَنَ/ إستَقَرَّ
Represent	مَثَّلَ	Repress	كَتَبَ/ كَظَمَ
Request	طَلَبَ/ إلْتَمَسَ	Requisition	مُصَادَرَةٌ
Rescue	أنقَذَ/ خَلَّصَ	Reserve	حَجَزَ
Reside	أقامَ/ سَكَنَ	Resist	قَاوَمَ
Resolve	صَمَّمَ/ عَزَمَ	Resonate	رَنَّ/ رَجَّعَ
Respire	تَنَفَّسَ	Respond	أجَابَ/ استجابَ
Responsibility	مَسؤولِيَّة	Restrain	كَبَحَ/ كَظَمَ
Restrict	قَيَّدَ/ حَدَّ	Resume	إستَأنَفَ
Retreat	تَرَاجَعَ/ تَقَهْقَرَ/ إنْحَسَبَ	Revamp	جَدَّدَ/ أصْلَحَ
Revoke	ألْغَى/ أبْطَلَ	Revolt	ثَارَ/ تَمَرَّدَ
Revolver	مُسَدَّسٌ	Reward	جَازَى/ كَافَأَ
Ring	دَقَّ/ رَنَّ	Rise	إرْتَفَعَ/ عَلاَ
Rival	مُنَافِسٌ/ مُزَاحِمٌ/ نِدٌّ	Rive	مَزَّقَ/ شَقَّ
Roar	هَدَرَ/ قَصَفَ/ زَأرَ	Roast	حَمَّصَ/ شَوَى
Rob	سَرَقَ/ سَلَبَ	Roll	لَفَّ/ دَحْرَجَ
Rot	تَعَفَّنَ/ فَسَدَ	Roughen	خَشَنٌ
Rub	فَرَكَ/ دَلَكَ	Ruffle	غَضَّنَ/ جَعَّدَ

Ruin	خَرَّبَ/ دَمَّرَ	Rupture	مَزَّقَ/ فتنَ
Rust	صَدأَ		

S

Sacrifice	ضحَّى	Sag	ارتَخَى/ تَدَلَّى
Sail	أبْحرَ/ أقْلَعَ	Sanction	أقَرَ/ صَدَّقَ عَلَى
Satisfy	أرْضَى/ أقْنَعَ	Scab	جُلْبَةٌ/ جَرَبَ/ فرقةٌ جُرْح
Scan	تَصَفَّحَ/ تَفَحَّصَ	Scar	نَدْبَةٌ/ أَثَرٌ
Scarlet	قرمزي	Scatter	نَثَرَ/ بَعْثَرَ
Schedule	قَائمَةٌ/ جَدْوَلٌ	Scheme	خُطَّةٌ/ مَشْرُوعٌ/ مَنْهَجٌ
Scissor	مقَصٌّ	Scope	مَجَالٌ/ مَدَى
Scrap	كَسَّرَ/ تَشَاجَرَ	Scratch	خَدَشَ/ هَرَشَ
Screech	صَاحَ/ ضَجَّ	Scroll	دَرْجٌ
Scurb	حَكَّ	Scruple	إرتَابَ/ شَكَّ
Scrutinize	تَفَحَّصَ/ تَحَرَّى/ دَقَّقَ	Search	بَحَثَ/ فَتَّشَ
Sectionalize	جَزَّأَ	Sector	قطَاعٌ/ قسمٌ
Secret	خَفِيٌّ/ سرٌّ	Select	انتَقَى/ اخْتَارَ/ انْتَخَبَ
Send	أرْسَلَ/ بَعَثَ/ أوْفَدَ	Sensivity	حَسَّاسيَّة
Separate	فصَلَ/ فرَّقَ	Serial	مُتَسَلْسَل
Series	سلسلة/ تَتَابُع/ توَال	Serious	خَطيْرٌ/ جدِّي
Service	خدْمَةٌ/ وَظيْفَةٌ	Session	جلسَة/ دَوْرَةٌ
Settle	سَوَّى/ حَسَمَ/ قَرَّرَ	Setup	تَرْكيبٌ/ تَرْتيبٌ
Shackle	شَكَّلَ/ رَبَطَ/ قَيَّدَ	Shade	ظلٌّ/ طَيْفٌ
Shake	هَزَّ/ رَجَفَ	Shape	شَكَّلَ/ كَيَّفَ/ صَاغَ
Shave	كَشَطَ/ قَشَرَ/ شَحج	Shear	جَزَّ/ جَلَّمَ
Sheathe	أغمَدَ/ غَلَفَ/ دَرَعَ	Shed	لَمَعَ/ بَرَقَ
Shift	نَقَلَ/ أزَاحَ	Shorten	قَصَّرَ/ أوْجَزَ

Show	أظْهَرَ/ أبْدَى/ عَرَضَ	Shower	إنْهَمَرَ/ رَش
Shrink	تَقَلَّصَ/ ضَاقَ	Shroud	غَطَّى/ غَشيَ
Shuffle	خَلَطَ/ راوَغَ	Shut	أغْلَقَ/ أقْفَلَ
Shutter	مصراعٌ	Siege	حِصَارٌ
Signal	إشارَةٌ/ رَمْزٌ	Similarity	تَشَابُهٌ/ تَمَاثُل
Simplify	بَسَطَ/ سَهَّلَ	Simulate	تَصَنَّعَ/ حَاكَى
Sincere	مُخْلِصٌ/ صَادقٌ	Sing	أنشَدَ/ غَنَّى/ شَدَا
Single	اختَصَّ	Sink	غَطَّسَ/ غَاصَ/ غرَقَ
Siren	صَفَّارَةٌ	Situation	مَوْقِعٌ/ حَالَةٌ
Sizzle	أزَّ/ نَشَّ	Skate	تزَلَّجَ/ تزَلَّقَ
Skelton	نَحيفٌ/ نَحيلٌ	Skim	قَشَدَ
Skimp	قَتَرَ عَلى	Skip	قَفَزَ/ تخَطَّى
Slack	أرخَى	Slake	أضْعَفَ/ خَفَّفَ
Slap	لطَمَ/ صَفَحَ/ سَفَعَ	Slash	شَقَّ/ قَطَعَ/ جَلَّدَ
Sleek	مَلَّسَ/ صَقَلَ	Slice	شَرِيحَةٌ/ قِطْعَةٌ
Slide	زَلَقَ/ زَلَجَ	Slim	هَزِيلٌ/ نَحيفٌ/ ضَئِيْلٌ
Slip	زَلَقَ/ زَلَجَ	Slump	هَبَّطَ/ إنْهَارَ
Slush	طَيَّنَ/ مَلَّطَ	Smart	نَشيطٌ/ حاذق/ رَشيقٌ/ أنيقٌ
Smash	حَطَّمَ/ سَحقَ/ هَشَمَ	Smear	لطَّخَ/ لَوَّثَ
Smell	شَمَّ	Smelt	صَهَرَ/ نَقَى
Smoke	دَخنَ	Smudge	لَطَّخَ
Smuggle	هَرَّبَ	Snap	كَسَرَ/ قَصَمَ
Snare	فَخٌّ/ شَرَكٌ	Snatch	اختطفَ/ انتزَعَ/ اخْتَلَسَ
Sneak	تَسَلَّلَ/ نَسَلَ	Sniff	نَشقَ/ تَشَمَّمَ
Snip	قَصَّ/ قَرَضَ	Snub	صَدَّ/ رَبَطَ
Soak	نَقَعَ/ بَلَّلَ	Soar	حَلَقَ/ حَامَ/ سَمَا
Society	مُجْتَمَعٌ/ جَمْعِيَّةٌ	Solar	شَمْسِي

Solution	حَلٌّ	Solve	حَلَّ
Soot	سَنَّجَ/ لَوَّثَ	Soothe	هَدَّأَ/ سَكَنَ/ خَفَّفَ
Sorb	إمْتَصَّ/ إمْتَزَّ	Sort	فَرَزَ/ صَنَّفَ
Sow	بَذَرَ/ نَثَرَ	Space	وَسَّعَ/ بَاعَدَ
Spade	حَرَفَ/ عَزَقَ	Sparge	نَضَّحَ/ رَشَّ/ بَلَّلَ
Spatter	رَشَّشَ/ تَرَشْرَشَ	Specify	عَيَّنَ/ حَدَّدَ
Specimen	عَيْنَةٌ/ نَمُوذَجٌ	Speculate	تأمَّلَ/ ضَارَبَ
Speed	أسْرَعَ/ عَجَّلَ	Spell	نَوْبَةٌ/ فَتْرَةٌ
Spill	أراقَ/ أهْرَقَ	Spin	دَوَّمَ/ دَارَ
Splay	فَلْطَحَ/ حَدَرَ	Split	شَقَّ/ فَلَقَ
Spoil	أفْسَدَ/ أتْلَفَ	Sponsor	كَفَلَ/ رَعَى/ ضَمَنَ
Spontaneous	عَفْوِيٌّ/ تلقَائي	Spore	بُوَيْغَةٌ
Sport	عَبَثٌ/ مزاجٌ/ لَهْوٌ	Spray	رَشَّ/ رَذَّ/ نَضّحَ
Spread	نَشَرَ/ بَسَطَ	Sprinkle	نَضّحَ/ نَثَرَ
Spur	استحثَّ/ هَمَزَ/ نَخَسَ	Spy	تَجَسَّسَ
Squash	هَرَسَ/ سَحَقَ	Squeak	صَرَّ/ صَرَفَ/ صَوَّتَ
Squeeze	عَصَرَ/ كَبَسَ/ ضَغَطَ	Squib	إنبجاسٌ/إفمجازٌ/ تَدَفُّق
Stab	طَعَنَ/ أفْحَمَ	Stabilize	مَتَنَ/ أَقَرَّ/ رَسَخَ/ ثَبَّتَ
Stabilizer	مُقِرٌّ/ مُوَازِنٌ	Stack	رُكَامٌ/ كُدْسٌ/ كُوَم
Stadium	مَلْعَبٌ/ مُدَرَّج	Stage	مَرْحَلَةٌ/ طَوْرٌ/ مَسْرَح
Stain	صَبَغَ/ لَوَّنَ/ بَقَعَ	Stamina	شِدَّةٌ/ مَتَانَةٌ
Stamp	خَتَمَ/ دَمَغَ/ وَسَمَ	Standard	قياسٌ/ معيار
Standard time	تَوْقِيتٌ قَيَاسي	Stapler	دَبَاسَة
Start	بَدَأَ/ بَاشَرَ/ إستَهَلَ	Starve	جَاعَ/ حِرْمَانٌ
Starting point	نُقطَةُ الإنطلاق/نُقطَةُ الْبَدْء	State	عَيَّنَ/ عَرَضَ/ بَسَطَ/ قَرَّرَ
Statement	تَصْرِيحٌ/ عَرَضٌ/ بَسْطٌ	Station	مَحَطَّةٌ/ مَرْكَزٌ
Stationary	ثابتٌ/ مُسْتَقِرّ	Stationery	قرطاسية/ وِرَاقَةٌ

Statistics	عِلمُ الإحْصَاء/ إحصَائيات	Statue	تمثَال/ نُصُب
Stave	ثَقَبَ/ حَطَّمَ	Stay	دَعَمَ/ سَنَدَ/ شَدَّ
Steam	بُخَار	Steel	الصُّلْب/ فُولاد
Steep	نَقعَ	Steer	وَجَّهَ / قَادَ
Stencil	رَوْسَمَ	Step	خُطْوَةٌ
Sterility	جَدْبٌ/ عُقْمٌ	Sterilize	طَهَّرَ/ عَقَمَ
Stick	أَلْزَقَ/ أَلْصَقَ	Stifle	خَنَقَ/ أخْمَدَ
Still	هَدا/ يَسكن	Stimulate	نَبَّهَ/ أَثَارَ/ خَفَنَ
Stipulate	تَعَاقَدَ عَلَى/ إشْتَرَط	Stir	قَلَّبَ/ حَرَّكَ
Stitch	خَاطَ/ دَرَزَ	Stoke	أذْكَى/ أوقَدَ
Stomach	مَعْدَةٌ	Stoop	أنحْنَى
Stop	سَدَّ/ أوْقَفَ	Store	ادّخَرَ/ خَزَفَ
Storm	عَاصفَةٌ/ زَوْبَعَةٌ	Slow	مَلأَ/ عَبَا
Straddle	فَجَّ	Strafe	قَذَفَ/ قصَفَ
Straggle	ضَلَّ/ شَرَدَ	Straighten	عَدَلَ/ سَوَّى
Strangle	ضَيَّقَ/ خَنَقَ	Strap	حَزَمَ/ رَبَط
Stratify	تطَبَّق/ نَضَّد	Stray	شَرَّدَ/ ضَلَّ
Stress	شدَّدَ عَلَى/ ضَغَطَ عَلَى	Stretch	مَدَّ/ بَسَطَ
Stride	خَطَا	Strike	ضربَ/ سَكَّ/ طَرَقَ
Strip	عَرَّى/ جَرَّدَ	Stripe	خَطَّطَ/ قَلَّمَ
Strive	جَدَّ/ كَدَحَ	Structure	إنْشَاء/ بنيَة
Struggle	كافَحَ/ صَارَعَ/ نَاضَلَ	Strut	دعمَ
Study	دَرَسَ/ بَحَثَ/ تَأمَّلَ	Stumale	عَثَرَ/ زَلَّ
Stun	دوَّخَ/ أذهَلَ/ صَعَقَ	Stupefy	خدَّرَ/ خَبَلَ
Subdue	أخْضَعَ/ كَبَتَ	Sublime	صَعَدَ
Submerge	غَمَرَ/ غَطَّسَ	Submit	خَضَعَ/ أضعَنَ/ إستَسْلَمَ
Subscribe	إشتَرَكَ/ إكْتَتَبَ/ تَبَرَّعَ	Subsidiary	إضافي/ فَرْعي
Subsist	عَاشَ/ بَقِيَ	Substantiate	أثبتَ/ بَرهَنَ

Substitue	أبْدَلَ/ بَدَّل	Substend	قَابَلَ/ إكْتَنَفَ
Succeed	نَجحَ/ أفْلَحَ/ فَازَ	Suck	إمْتَصَّ/ مَصَّ
Sue	إلتَمَسَ/ تَوَسَّلَ	Suffer	إحتَمَلَ/ تَحَمَّلَ
Suffuse	غمَرَ/ خَضَّبَ	Suit	نَاسَبَ/ لائَمَ/ صَلَحَ
Summit	قمَّة/ ذروة	Summon	دَعَا/ إستدْعَى
Super imposition	تراكب	Superiority	تَفوُّق/ أفْضَلِيَّة/ إستعلاء
Superiority complex	مُركَّب الإستعلاء	Supersede	نسخَ/ أبطلَ
Supersonic	فوقَ السَّمْعي	Supervise	رَاقَب/ نَاظَرَ/ أشْرَفَ عَلَى
Supple	لَيِّنَ/ طَرَّى	Supplement	مَلْحَق/ تَكْمِلَة/ إضافة
Supply	أمَدَّ/ زَوَّدَ/ جَهَّزَ	Support	دَعمَ/ سَنَدَ/ سَاعَدَ
Suppose	افترضَ	Suppress	كَتَبَ/ كَتَمَ
Surgery	جَراحَة	Surpass	جَاوَزَ/فَاقَ
Surprise	بَاغَتَ/ أدهَشَ/ أدهَلَ	Surrender	سَلَّمَ
Survey	مَسَحَ/ تَقَصَّى	Suspect	إرْتَابَ/ شَكَّ
Suspend	غَلَّقَ/ دَلَّى/ أَرْجَأ	Sustain	إحتَمَلَ/ تحَمَّلَ/ مَثَّل
Swab	مَسَحَ/ نَظَّفَ	Swash	لَطَمَ/ عَجَّ
Sway	تَمَايَلَ/ ترنَّجَ	Sweat	عَرِقَ/ رَشَحَ
Sweep	كَنَسَ/ جَرَفَ/ كَسَحَ	Swell	انتفخَ/ تورَّمَ
Swerve	إنحَرَفَ	Swing	رَجَّحَ/ خَطَرَب
Swirl	دَوَّمَ/ لَفَّ	Swish	هَفَّ/ حَفَّ
Swivel	دار/ لفّ	Syllabus	منْهَاج/ مَنْهَجٌ
Symbolize	رَمَزَ	Sympathize	تَعَاطَفَ
Synthesis	تَرْكِيبٌ/ توليفٌ	Systematize	رَتَّبَ

T

Table	جَدْوَلٌ/ قائمة/ منضَدَةٌ	Tablet	قُرْصٌ/ لَوحٌ
Tackle	عَالَجَ	Taint	لَوَّثَ/ أَفْسَدَ
Take	أخَذَ/ تَناوَلَ	Talk	تَكلَّمَ/ تَحدَّثَ/ نَطقَ

Tally	سَجَّلَ/ حَسَبَ/ وَافَقَ/ طَابَقَ	Tame	دَجَّنَ/ روَّضَ
Tamp	سَدَّ/ حَشا/ رَصَّ	Tan	دَبَغَ/ سَفَعَ
Tangle	شَبَّكَ/ عَقَدَ	Tanker	صِهْرِيجِيَّةٌ
Tap	صُنْبُورٌ/ نَفْرَةٌ/ دَقَّةٌ	Tape	شَرِيطٌ
Target	هَدَفٌ/ دَرِيئَةٌ/ مَرْمَى	Tarrif	تَعْرِفَة
Tarry	أبطَأَ/ تَلَكَّأَ/ مَكَثَ	Taste	ذَاقَ/ تَذَوَّقَ
Taw	دَبَغَ	Tax	ضَرِيبَةٌ/ رَسْمٌ
Teach	عَلَّمَ/ دَرَّسَ/ لَقَنَ	Tear	مَزَّقَ/ شَقَّ/ نَهَشَ
Teem	سَكَبَ/ صَبَّ	Telegram/Telegraph	أبْرَقَ
Tell	أخبَرَ/ رَوَى/ قَالَ	Temper	لَيَّنَ/ لَطَّفَ
Tend	رَعَى/ خدمَ	Tender	رقَقَ/ أوْهَنَ
Tension	تَوَتُّرَ/ جُهدٌ	Terminate	أنْهَى/ إنْتَهَى
Test	إخْتَبَرَ/ فَحصَ	Thaw	ذابَ
Thesis	مَبْحَثٌ/ أطرُوحَةٌ	Threaten	هَدَّدَ/ أنْذَرَ
Thrive	نَجَحَ/ إزْدَهَرَ	Throw	رَمَى/ قَذَفَ/ طَرَحَ
Thrust	دَفَعَ/ أَقْحَمَ/ غرزَ	Thunder	رَعَدَ/ قَصَفَ/ دَوِّيَ
Thwart	عَاقَ/ عَارَضَ	Tickle	نَغَزَ/ دَغْدَغَ
Till	حَرَثَ/ أصْلَحَ	Ting	رَنَّ/ طَنَّ/ صَلَ
Tire	تَعبَ/ كَلَّ	Title	لَقَبٌ/ عُنْوَانٌ
Tonic	مُقَوٍّ/ مُنَشِّط	Toss	قَذَفَ/ رَمَى/ هَزَّى
Totalize	أجْمَلَ	Tote	حَمَلَ/ نَقَلَ
Totter	تَرَنَّحَ/ تَمَايَلَ	Touch	لَمَسَ/مَسَّ
Toughen	مَتَّنَ/ صَلَّبَ	Tourism	السِّيَاحَة
Tow	جَرَّ/ سَحَبَ	Trade	تَاجَرَ/ بَادَلَ
Train	دَرَّبَ/ مَرن	Transactions	مُدَاوَلاتٌ
Transfer	نَقَلَ/ حَوَّلَ	Transgress	تَعَدَّى/ تَجَاوَزَ
Transparency	شَفَافِيَّةٌ	Trap	صَادَ/ صَدَّ

Travel	سَافَرَ/ ارتَحَلَ/ جَالَ	Tread	وَطِئَ/ خطأ
Treat	عَامَلَ/ عَالَجَ	Tremble	إرْتَجَفَ/ إرْتَعَدَ/ إرْتَعَشَ
Trench	خَنْدَقٌ	Trend	اتَّجَهَ/ نَحا
Trespass	تَعدَّى/ تَجَاوَزَ	Triangulate	ثَلَّثَ
Trick	خُدْعَةٌ/ حيلَةٌ	Trickle	نَدَّ/ قَطَرَ
Trigger	زَنَدَ/ قَدَحَ/ فَجَّرَ	Trim	هَذَّبَ/ شَذَّبَ/ زَيَّنَ
Trip	زَلَّ/تَعَشَّرَ	Triumph	نَصْرٌ/ نَجَاحٌ
Trouble	أَقْلَقَ/ أزْعَجَ/ اتعَبَ	Truss	سَنَّمَ
Trust	وَثِقَ/ صدَّقَ	Try	جَرَّبَ/ إخْتَبَرَ/ قَاسَ
Tuck	ثَنَى/ شَمَّرَ	Tug	جَرَّ/ سَحَبَ/ شَدَّ
Tumble	سَقَطَ/ هَوَى/ تَدَهَوَّرَ	Tune	لَحَّنَ/ رَنَّمَ/ نَغمٌ
Twinkle	وَمَضَ/ تَلألأ	Twirl	دَارَ بَرَمَ/ فَتَلَ
Twist	فَتَلَ/ لَوَى	Typify	مَثَّلَ

U

Ugly	قَبِيحٌ/ رَمِيْمٌ/ بَشعٌ	Ulcer	قَرحَةٌ
Ultimate	نِهَائِيٌّ	Ultimation	إنْذَارٌ
Umpire	حَكَمٌ/ فَيْصَلٌ	Unanimity	إجْمَاعٌ
Uncoil	حَلَّ/ فَكَّ	Undergo	تَحمَّلَ/ غَانِيَ
Undermine	قَوَّضَ/ هَدَّمَ	Undertake	تَعَهَّدَ/ فَكَّ/ أبْطَلَ
Undo	حَلَّ/ فَكَّ/ أبْطَلَ	Undulate	مَاجَ/ تَموَّجَ
Unfold	بَسَطَ/ نَشَرَ	Uniformity	إنتظامٌ/ إتساقٌ/ تَجَانُسٌ
Unify	وَحَّدَ	Union	إتحادٌ/نَقَابَةٌ
Unique	فَرِيدٌ	Unit	وَحْدَةٌ
Unite	وَحَّدَ/ ضَمَّ	Unleash	حَرَّرَ/ أطْلَقَ
Unlink	فَصَّلَ/ فَكَّ	Unload	أفْرَغَ/ فَرَغَ
Unroll	بسط/ نَشَرَ	Uphold	دَعَمَ/ سَنَدَ

Uplift	رَفَعَ	Uproot	إجتثَّ
Upset	قَلَّبَ/ عكَسَ	Up to date	حَدِيْثٌ/ جَدِيْدٌ/ عَصْرِيٌّ
Upturn	عَطَفَ	Upward	صاَعَدَ
Urban	مدنيٌّ	Urge	إستَحَثَّ/ حَفَزَ
Urgent	مُلحٌّ/ عَاجلٌ/ مَاسٌ	Usage	إستعمالٌ
Useful	نَافعٌ/ مُفيد	Usual	عَادي/ مُعْتادٌ
Utility	مَنْفَعَةٌ/ فَائدَةٌ	Utilyze	إستَخْدَمَ/ إسْتَعْمَلَ

V

Vacancy	خُلُوٌّ/ فراغٌ/ شُغورٌ	Vaction	عُطْلَةٌ/ إخلاءٌ/ إفراغٌ
Vaccinate	لَقَحَ/ طَعَّمَ	Vague	غَامِضٌ/ مُبْهَمٌ
Value	قيمة	Valve	صمام
Vanish	تلاشي/ زال/ إضمحل	Vapour	بُخَارٌ
Vaporize	بَخَّرَ	Variability	تَغيرِيَّةٌ/ تَقَلّبيَّةٌ
Variable	مُتَغَيِّرٌ/ مُتَبَدِّلٌ	Variance	تَبايُن/ تَفَاوُت/ فَرق
Variation	تَبدَّل/ تَغَيَّرَ	Varnish	بَرْنَق/ طَلَبَ
Veer	إنْحَرَفَ/ غَيَّرَ	Vegetative	نَبَاتي/ خُضَري
Vehicle	مَرْكَبَةٌ/ عَرَبَةٌ	Veil	حَجَبَ/ سَتَرَ
Vein	وَرِيدٌ/ عَرْقٌ	Velocity	سُرْعَةٌ
Vend	بَاعَ	Vender	بَائعٌ
Vent	فُتْحَةٌ/ ثَقْبٌ/ مَنْفَسٌ	Ventilate	هَوَّى
Ventilation	تَهْوِيَةٌ	Venture	غَامَرَ/ جَازَفَ/ خَاطَرَ
Verdict	حُكْمٌ	Verge	شَفيرٌ/ حافةٌ
Verify	أثْبَتَ/ حَقَقَ	Vest	خَوَّلَ/ عَهدَ إلَى
Veto	رَفَضَ/ عَارَضَ	Vex	أغاظَ/ أثارَ/ حَيَّرَ
Vibrate	إهْتَزَّ/ إرْتَجَّ/ تَذَبْذَبَ	Vie	تَنَافَسَ/ تَبَارَى
View	شَاهَدَ/ عَايَنَ	Violate	إنْتَهَكَ/ نَكَثَ

Virgin	بِكْرٌ/ عَذْرَاء	Visa	تأشيرة/ فيزَا
Visit	زَارَ/ عَادَ	Visual aids	مُعينات بَصَرِيَّةٌ
Visualise	تَخَيَّلَ/ تَصوَّرَ	Vital	حَيَوي
Vitality	حَيَوِيَّةٌ/ نَشَاطٌ	Vitiate	لَوَّثَ/ أفْسَدَ/ أتْلَفَ
Voice	صَوتٌ	Volatilize	طَيَّرَ/ صَعَّدَ
Volcanize	عَرَّضَ	Voltage	فُلْطِيَّةٌ
Volume	حَجْمٌ/ مُجَلَّدٌ	Volunteer	مُتَطَوِّعٌ
Vomit	تَقَيَّا/ قَاءَ	Vote	اقْتَرَعَ/ صوَّتَ
Voucher	مُسْتَنَدٌ/ إيصالٌ/ قَسيمَةٌ	Vouchsafe	أجَازَ/ مَنَحَ
Voyage	رحلةٌ/ سَفْرَةٌ		

W

Wad	حَشَا/ لَفَّ/ سَدَّ	Wade	خَاضَ
Waft	دَفَعَ	Wager	رَاهنٌ
Wagon	عَرَبَةٌ/ مَرْكَبَةٌ	Wait	إنتظَرَ
Waiting list	قائمةُ الإنتظار	Waive	تَرَكَ/ تَجَنَّبَ
Wake	صَحَا/ إسْتَيْقَظَ/ نَبَّهَ	Walk out	إضرابٌ
Wander	جَالَ/ طَافَ	Wane	تَضَائَلَ/ تَنَاقَصَ
Ward	حَرَاسَةٌ/ حَمَايَةٌ/ وَصَايَةٌ	Warden	حَارِسٌ/ قَيِّمٌ/ مُرَاقِبٌ
Warm	دَفأ/ سَخَّنَ	Warn	حَذَّرَ/ أنْذَرَ/ أخْطَرَ
Warp	فَتَلَ/ لَوَى	Wash	غَسَلَ/ جَرَفَ
Waste	بَدَّدَ/ ضَيَّعَ/ أنْهَكَ	Watch	رَاقَبَ/ رَصَدَ
Waterfall	شَلاَلٌ	Water proof	صَامِدٌ للماء
Water pump	مضخَّةُ ماء	Wave	مَوَّجَ/ لَوَّحَ/ خَفَقَ
Way	طريق/ سبيلٌ/ مَجْرَى	Weak	ضَعيفٌ/ وَاهِنٌ
Wealth	ثَرْوَةٌ/ وَفْرَةٌ	Weapon	سلاَحٌ
Wear	لَبسَ/ إرتَدَى	Weary	أتْعَبَ/ أرْهَقَ

Weave	نَسَجَ/ حَاكَ/ حَبَكَ	Weed	عُشبٌ
Weap	بَكَى/ ذرَفَ/ قَطَّرَ الدَّمْعَ	Weigh	وَزَنَ
Weigh bridge	جِسْرُ قَبَان	Weld	لَحمَ
Well	بِئرٌ/ نَبْعٌ/ حَوْضٌ	Wet	بَلَّلَ/ خَضَّلَ/ نَدَى/ رَطَّبَ
Whet	شَحَذَ/ سَنَّ	Whip	سَوط/ مجلدةٌ
Whirl	دَوَّمَ/ كَفَّ/ دَارَ	Whistle	صَفَرَ
Whittle	بَرَى/ نَجرَ	Widow	أرمَلَة
Wiggle	ذَبْذَبَ/ رَجَّ	Wilt	ذَبَلَ/ ذَوَى
Wimble	ثَقَبَ/ حَفَرَ	Win	رَبحَ/ نَالَ/ فَازَ
Window	نَافِذَةٌ/ شُبَّاكٌ	Wing	جَنَاحٌ
Wipe	مَسَحَ/ نَظَّفَ	Wiper	ممسَحَةٌ/ مَسَّاحَةٌ
Wireless	لاَسلْكي	Withdraw	سَحَبَ/ استَرجَعَ
Wither	ذَبُلَ/ ذَوَى	Withhold	أمسكَ/ احتَبَسَ/ احْتَجَزَ
Witness	شَهِدَ/ شَاهَدَ	Wobble	تَمَايَلَ/ تَرَاوَحَ
Wonder	تَعَجَّبَ/ دَهَشَ	Work	عَمَلَ/ اشتَغَلَ/ صَنَعَ
Worry	أزْعَجَ/ أقْلَقَ	Wound	جُرْحٌ
Wrack	حَطَّمَ/ دَمَّرَ	Wrap	غَلَفَ/ لَفَّ
Wrapper	مُغَلَّفٌ/ غلاَفٌ	Wreck	حَطَّمَ
Wrench	لَوَى/ فَتَلَ	Wrin	عَصَرَ
Wrinkle	جَعَّدَ/ غَضَّنَ	Wrong	خَطَأ/ بَاطَلَ/ أذَى
Wry	الْتَوَى/ تَعَوَّجَ		

X

X-ray	شُعَاءُ سينيٌ	X-ray analysis	تَحْليل باشعة اكس
X-ray machine	مكْنَةُ الأشعَّة السِّينيَّة	X-ray screen	سَيَّارُ الأشعَّة السِّيْنيَّة
X-ray tube	أنْبُوبُ الأشعَّة اكس	X-ray waves	أمواجٌ سينيَّةٌ

Y

Yank	شَدَّ	Yaw	إنعَرَجَ/ إنْحرَفَ/ زَاغَ
Yeast	إخْتَمَرَ	Yield	أنتجَ/ أغلَّ/ خَضَعَ
Yoke	قَرَنَ/ ضَمَّ		

Z

Zeal	حَمَاسَة/ حَميَّة	Zealous	مُتَحَمِّسٌ
Zenith	سَمْتٌ/ أوْجٌ/ ذَرْوَةٌ	Zest	حَيَوِيَّةٌ/ لَذَّةٌ
Zig zag	تَعَرُّجَ	Zip	أزَّ
Zodiac	دَائِرَةُ الْبُرُوج	Zonal	نطَاقِي/ مَنْطَقي
Zoom	أَزَّ/ زَمَّ		